D1758138

FAMOUS FOR A REASON

The Story of The Famous Grouse

CHARLES MACLEAN

THIS EDITION FIRST PUBLISHED IN 2015 BY

BIRLINN LTD
WEST NEWINGTON HOUSE
10 NEWINGTON ROAD
EDINBURGH
EH9 1QS

WWW.BIRLINN.CO.UK

COPYRIGHT © CHARLES MACLEAN, 2015

ALL RIGHTS RESERVED.
NO PART OF THIS PUBLICATION MAY BE REPRODUCED, STORED OR TRANSMITTED
IN ANY FORM WITHOUT THE EXPRESS WRITTEN PERMISSION OF THE PUBLISHER.

ISBN 978 1 78027 252 8

BRITISH LIBRARY CATALOGUING-IN-PUBLICATION DATA
A CATALOGUE RECORD FOR THIS BOOK IS AVAILABLE FROM THE BRITISH LIBRARY.

TYPESET AND DESIGNED BY JULES AKEL

PRINTED IN LATVIA BY LIVONIA

CONTENTS

THE
MATTHEW GLOAG
FAMILY

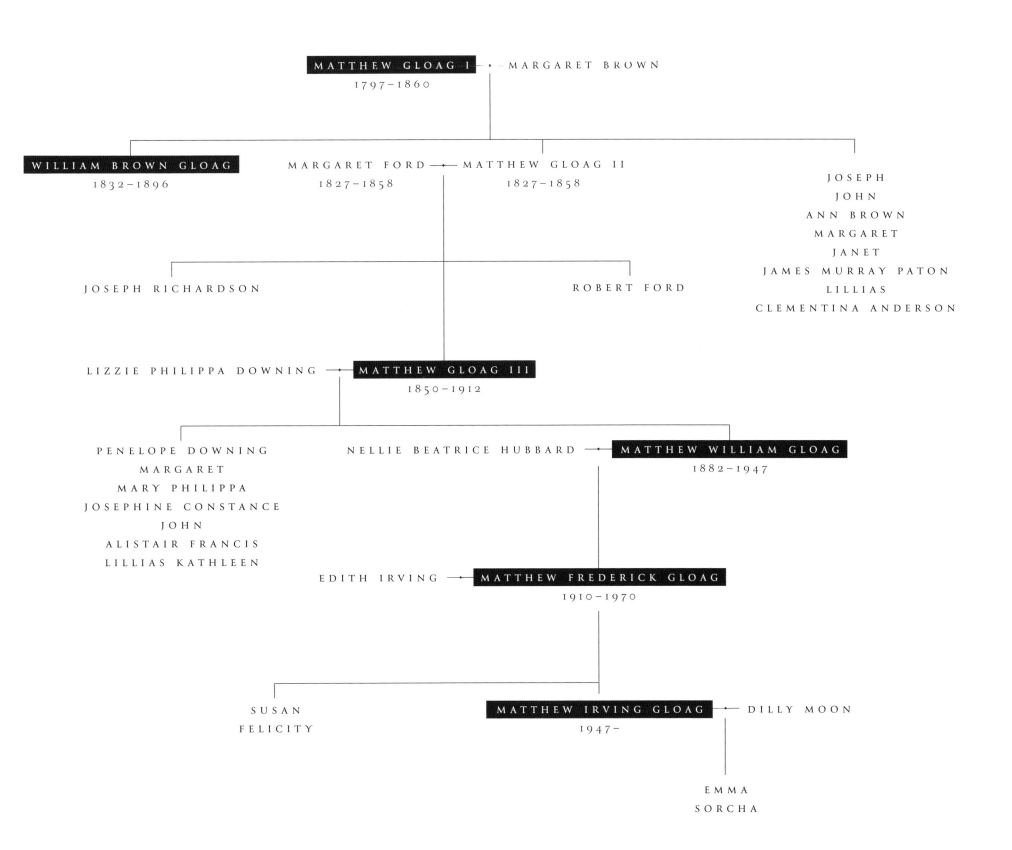

MATTHEW GLOAG I
1797–1860
MARGARET BROWN

WILLIAM BROWN GLOAG
1832–1896

MARGARET FORD
1827–1858
MATTHEW GLOAG II
1827–1858

JOSEPH
JOHN
ANN BROWN
MARGARET
JANET
JAMES MURRAY PATON
LILLIAS
CLEMENTINA ANDERSON

JOSEPH RICHARDSON

ROBERT FORD

LIZZIE PHILIPPA DOWNING
MATTHEW GLOAG III
1850–1912

PENELOPE DOWNING
MARGARET
MARY PHILIPPA
JOSEPHINE CONSTANCE
JOHN
ALISTAIR FRANCIS
LILLIAS KATHLEEN

NELLIE BEATRICE HUBBARD
MATTHEW WILLIAM GLOAG
1882–1947

EDITH IRVING
MATTHEW FREDERICK GLOAG
1910–1970

SUSAN
FELICITY

MATTHEW IRVING GLOAG
1947–
DILLY MOON

EMMA
SORCHA

FOREWORD

MATTHEW IRVING GLOAG

I AM DELIGHTED THAT THIS BOOK HAS BEEN COMPILED. It catalogues in its own way the birth and rise of The Famous Grouse, an iconic whisky brand that is now recognised throughout the world. I am also more than proud to be associated, both in name and personal input, with its original parent company, the Perth-based wine merchant, Matthew Gloag & Son.

I am the fifth Matthew Gloag and the sixth generation since the business was started in 1800, so I was really destined to become part of the company from the moment that the minister doused my head with water and called my name out to the assembled gathering. I joined the company in 1965 at the tender age of seventeen, starting my wine training by donning a boiler suit and being put to work in the Perth wine cellars, washing bottles and shifting about casks and crates of wine.

My grandfather had died a few months before I was born, so my father, Matthew Frederick Gloag, was now running the company. His heart was in wine (he had been wine adviser to the Australian New South Wales Government during the war when Germany had controlled the French, Italian and German wine trades), but it was also shared with a lifelong interest in his old regiment, The Black Watch, and in his passion for cars, even taking part in the Monte Carlo rally.

Two years later, I moved to London, a young man eager to throw off the burden of expectation and get out into the world. Nevertheless, like my father, I was becoming enthused by the wine industry and worked for eight months as a relief manager for Brown and Pank wine shops before crossing the channel to France to continue my training with Maison Calvet. The following year, I headed for Australia, working my passage on the Lyle Shipping Line, but my time there was cut short when I was called back to Scotland nine months later due to my mother suddenly becoming seriously ill.

It was at this point that what might hitherto have been seen as a silver-spooned existence was fatefully turned on its head. I returned home to find my family completely caught up with the care of my mother. On one particular day, having taken her nurse to Perth railway station, I came back to find that my father had suffered a fatal heart attack on the landing outside my mother's bedroom. He was lying at the bottom of the stairs. My mother then died two days later.

No tax provision had been made for such an unexpected occurrence. Death duties were crippling, and my two sisters and I found ourselves not only losing our parents and our security, but also, as it transpired, our family home and business. The trustees of the estate were left with no alternative but to put the Bonhard estate, home to our family for three generations, and the business on the market. Matthew Gloag & Son did not sell immediately but was bought eventually by the Glasgow-based Highland Distillers, in what was more or less a number-crunching exercise, the plan being to sell off the whisky stocks to brokers but retain the prized, elite brand name—The Famous Grouse.

The new working regime in which I found myself was both terrifying and alien. I was twenty-one years of age, still pretty green behind the ears and totally shell-shocked by my parents' untimely deaths. I was appointed a director of Matthew Gloag & Son, but had yet to complete my training in full, and now I was expected to sit at the boardroom table with my new, fellow directors, mostly corporate accountants, more interested in the whisky brand rather than our core vintner business. They seemed quite baffled by my authority to be sitting in the boardroom and even more so by my desire to continue to be involved in the business. When they realised that I was quite resolute in staying put, a phrase was soon coined within the murmurings of Highland's management, 'What do we do with the MIG factor?' Matthew Irving Gloag, my full name. And once a phrase is coined…

I suppose if one is treated with a certain degree of disdain, one kicks back in similar fashion. I had no real allies on the new board, and there was no one willing to give me much-needed fatherly guidance, so I probably did come over as rebellious and lacking in respect. It was therefore quite opportune for all concerned that I was then distanced from the main operation in Perth by being sent north for six months to learn about the whisky industry, working at Highland's distilleries in Speyside, first at Tamdhu, then Rothes, before moving back south to Glasgow to work at the Clyde Bond.

At the outset, I think that the Highland's staff were slightly nonplussed by me—I was young, long-haired, and I had 'the name'—but, as it transpired, I found myself working with down-to-earth people who took me at face value and definitely made no allowances for who I was. Many of them remain good friends of mine to this day.

It was not until 1975 that I eventually began to find my feet in the company. I got on well with Dienhard's, our distributors in England, and with Saatchi's who were handling our advertising. I got myself involved with an M.C.C. pre-season cricket tour to Germany, and a sponsored event at Jack Stewart's North Wales Shooting School, and thereafter if anything out of the ordinary came the way of the company, it more often than not ended up on my desk.

This coincided with The Famous Grouse selling strong on the home market, bucking the current trend at that time, so Highland increased the funding for The Famous Grouse, lifting all financial constraints on what we could do.

We went on to sponsor The Famous Grouse Carriage Driving Championships from 1984 to 1994, the Scottish Rugby team from 1993 to 2008, as well as being a main sponsor of the Rugby World Cup in 1991 and 1995. We were heavily involved with the Royal Show and The Game Fair, and even sponsored Parliamentarian of the Year at Westminster through our Orcadian malt whisky brand, Highland Park.

During this time, I served twice as Chairman of the Licensed Trade Association and, on a personal suggestion by HRH the Duke of Edinburgh to myself, I applied for a Royal Warrant as suppliers of whisky to Her Majesty the Queen. This was subsequently granted and I remain Grantee to this day.

All this made for high-profile exposure of The Famous Grouse whisky, and I still can't help but feel a clandestine burst of pride over what we achieved during those years and the position that we helped the brand secure in the global market.

I'm not sure what the past Matthew Gloags would have made of how their company has evolved. They would be sad, maybe grumble, that the wine business has gone, and that the family enterprise name, Matthew Gloag & Son, and its whisky brand, The Famous Grouse, has been absorbed into a larger entity, but there is no doubt that they would be tickled by the fact that the myths and legends that surround their family and the success of The Famous Grouse whisky continue to live on. There is no better proof of that than the publication of this book.

MATTHEW I. GLOAG
October 2015

INTRODUCTION

GLEN GRIBBON

THE ORIGINAL IDEA TO CREATE A BOOK that brought to life the history of The Famous Grouse brand and the Gloag family came after Bill Farrar, the Edrington Marketing Director, and Matthew Gloag had one of their regular catch-up meetings. Matthew is the last member of the Gloag family to be directly involved in the management of The Famous Grouse and despite being retired from full-time duties for thirteen years has retained all of the passion and enthusiasm that he had for the brand when working on it. I know this because he still likes to send me regular e-mails berating me about marketing activity that he disapproves of!

If there is one word that links the many people who contributed to the creation of the *Famous for a Reason* book it is the word "passion". There is something about Scotch whisky in general that gets under the skin of people. Spend a few hours at Glenturret Distillery in Crieff, the spiritual home of The Famous Grouse, on a crisp autumn sunny morning with the smell of whisky in the air and you will get a sense of the magic that is Scotch whisky. However there is something special about The Famous Grouse that seems to elevate this passion to a new level.

I think every chapter in this book helps explain why this brand is so special and why it has captured and retained such a strong group of advocates and supporters. I believe the Gloag family connection is tremendously important in this respect. The Gloag family have always been a part of the brand and Matthew's signature remains on the bottle for this very reason. However, when I speak to the many people who have helped build this brand over the years, they all talk about being part of a broader Family—A Famous Grouse Family.

I believe consistency has also played a part in creating a Family connection through the years. Ask anyone who has worked closely on The Famous Grouse what makes the brand special and I guarantee they will say "Quality". The Family know that The Famous Grouse make the best blended Scotch whisky that you can buy and they are very, very proud of this. This commitment to creating quality Scotch whisky if anything has been enhanced by the current owner, Edrington, who have a reputation within the Scotch industry for the highest production standards.

So you will find that the words Family, Passion and Quality run through this book. It has been a monumental task to research the archive, connect all the dates and interview all of the key people who helped shape the brand. There are very few people who know as much about Scotch whisky history, production and quality as Charlie MacLean, the author. Charlie has been able to combine his knowledge and his creativity, with what is a fascinating brand archive. However, he would not have been able to write the book without the support of Aleta Donaldson. Aleta is still a vital part of The Famous Grouse marketing team in Perth and she has worked on the brand for over twenty-eight years. She has been the driving force behind the book, not just through her organisational skills, but through her continued passion to tell a great brand story.

Aleta helped to set up many interviews and it is the great stories that came from these that I think make this book not just a wonderful archive, but also a wonderful read.

The list is long but there are a number of people that we have to thank for their support:

Matthew and Dilly Gloag

Jim Grierson

Iain Halliday MBE

Bill Farrar

Fraser Morrison

Ian Curle

Ken Grier

Gerry O'Donnell

Corrine Kidd (née Williamson)

Linda Hood.

Former employees who were interviewed:

Sir Ian Good CBE

John Goodwin MBE

John Ramsay, Master Blender Emeritus

Andrew Kettles

John Hughes

Roy Bignell and his daughter, Allyson

John McDermott

(the late) Jack Kidd BEM, and his daughter, Freda

Robin Butler

George Paterson

Gina Long MBE (née Harley)

Hazel Anderson.

We are also grateful to Dougie Taylor and John Corstorphine for their assistance with the archive, and Alex Hennessey and Louis Flood for their assistance with the imagery.

The Famous Grouse finds itself in very good health in the current day. The Blended Scotch whisky category is not growing globally as single malts and international whiskies become more popular. Yet it remains the largest whisky category in the world, selling 93 million cases (of 12 bottles) worldwide in 2014, and a short visit to any bar in some of the high-growth blended Scotch markets, such as Angola, Turkey or Hungary will soon convince you that blended Scotch whisky has a positive future. The Famous Grouse in 2014 was the fourth largest standard blended Scotch brand and remains the number one blend in the U.K. and of course the home market—Scotland. The brand is benefiting from a new communication campaign, Famous for a Reason, as well as new improved packaging. There is of course a new generation of the Family coming through, with all the passion and commitment to quality that the previous generation had. They will ensure the next chapter to be added to this book is just as inspiring as the current nine.

GLEN GRIBBON

DIRECTOR, THE FAMOUS GROUSE

October 2015

CHAPTER I

MATTHEW

GLOAG I

(1797–1860)

AMONG ALL THE PROVINCES OF SCOTLAND, IF AN INTELLIGENT STRANGER WERE ASKED TO DESCRIBE THE MOST VARIED AND THE MOST BEAUTIFUL, IT IS PROBABLE HE WOULD NAME THE COUNTY OF PERTH.

Thus does Sir Walter Scott begin *The Fair Maid of Perth*, published in 1828, four years after Margaret Gloag opened her grocery shop in the city Sir Walter was contemplating, and seven years before she was joined in the business by her husband, Matthew.

The city and county of Perth were changing. Although the town itself retained many features from its long and distinguished past, its population was steadily increasing—more than doubling (to 20,000) between 1775 and 1831—and had long outgrown the boundaries of the medieval burgh. Elegant Georgian suburbs now fringed the public parkland north and south of the burgh, known as the Inches, and within the burgh itself many old buildings had been demolished to make way for broader streets, capable of coping with the increased traffic. Several important public buildings date from this period, including the County Court and Perth Prison.

Perth has a long and distinguished history. Since Kenneth MacAlpin united the kingdoms of the Picts and the Scots in 843, Scottish monarchs were crowned at Scone, two miles outside the burgh, and until 1482, when King James III transferred the seat of the monarchy to Edinburgh, Perth was considered the capital of Scotland.

It had been a trading centre for over a thousand years: its situation on the edge of the Highlands, surrounded by fertile farmland and within easy reach of Lowland markets all contributed to this. But the key factor in the town's early commercial success was the River Tay, which facilitated the flow of goods in and out of Perth long before the coming of the railway and metalled roads in the mid-nineteenth century.

By the beginning of the thirteenth century Perth was a flourishing port, conducting brisk trade with France, the Baltic ports and the Low Countries; importing wines, pottery and silks, and exporting hides, linen, bleached cloth, beef and salmon. It had been granted the status of Royal Burgh by King

Previous page:
Perth from Boatland *by David Octavius Hill, 1826*
Opposite: Loch Tay, Perthshire.

William the Lion in the twelfth century, and in 1213 Alexander Necham, Abbot of Cirencester, wrote:

Great Tay, through Perth, through towns,
through country flies,
Perth the whole kingdom with her wealth supplies.

During the eighteenth century the city's principal manufacture was linen, and Perth merchants dealt directly with the Continent. In 1797 there were no fewer than forty-six watermills within four miles of the city, all engaged in bleaching and printing linen and cotton. Then came a slump, which lasted into the 1820s.

As the Country Town of Perthshire, Perth was also the seat of local government, a major cattle market, a centre of education (Perth Academy, founded in 1760, had a national reputation) and the only place outside Edinburgh and Glasgow where there was an established printing and publishing industry. It was also a resort of the country gentry from the hinterland, who came into town for meetings, dinners, the theatre, balls and dances. The highpoints of the year's sporting calendar for all classes were the Perth Races and the cricket match between Perthshire and Forfarshire, both held on the North Inch.

The countryside around the city was fertile and prosperous. It was divided up into estates—some of them very large—and farms, managed according to the principles of husbandry established by the 'improvers' of the eighteenth century in the period we now call the 'Agricultural Revolution'—a revolution which for the first time allowed the country gentry to enjoy material standards which had previously been the privilege of peers and great landowners.

As Professor Smout writes in *A History of the Scottish People 1560–1830*:

The life of a Scottish gentleman at the beginning of the eighteenth century seemed almost unbearably uncouth in the recollection of his successors at the end… We need only cast a casual glance around the Lowland countryside today to see that many of the houses built by the Scottish gentry at the turn of the eighteen and nineteenth centuries would have been the envy of the peerage a hundred years before.

Map of Perth, John Tallis, 1851.

story continued on page 8

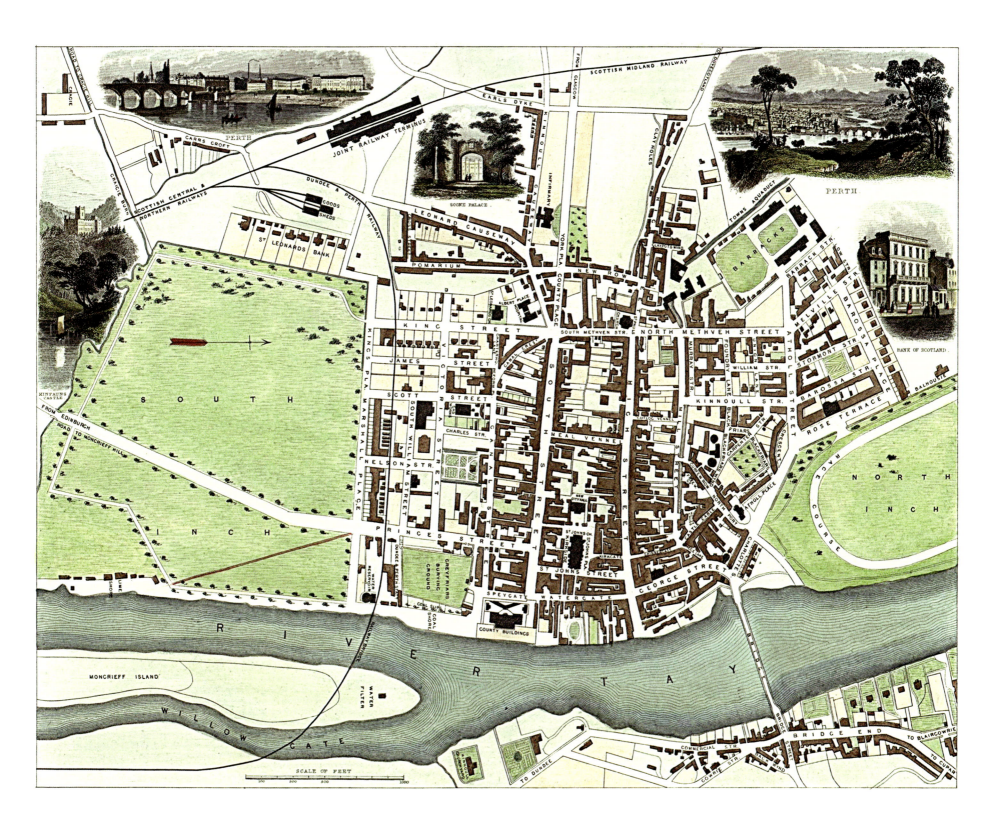

PERTH

CARRS CROFT

SCOTTISH MIDLAND RAILWAY

FROM GLASGOW

EARLS DYKE

CLAY HOLES

JOINT RAILWAY TERMINUS

SCONE PALACE.

PERTH

SCOTTISH CENTRAL & NORTHERN RAILWAYS

CRAIGIE BURN

DUNDEE & PERTH RAILWAY

GOODS SHEDS

LEONARD CAUSEWAY

KINNOULL CAUSEWAY

YORK PLA

INFIRMARY

TOWNS AQUADUCT

BARRACKS

BANK OF SCOTLAND.

KINFAUNS CASTLE

ST LEONARDS BANK

POMARIUM

NEW ROW

COUNTY PLACE

ALBERT PLACE

BARRACK STR.

MELVILLE STR.

BAROSSA STR.

BAROSSA PLACE

BALHOUSIE

KING STREET

SOUTH METHVEN STR.

NORTH METHVEN STREET

MURRAY STR.

FOUNDRY LANE

WILLIAM STR.

STORMONT STR.

BAROSSA STR.

ROSE TERRACE

KINGS PLA

MARSHALL PLACE

JAMES STREET

VICTORIA STR.

ATHOLL STREET

SOUTH WILLIAM STREET

CANAL STREET

MILL STREET

SKINNERGATE

HIGH STREET

KINNOULL STR.

BLACK FRIARS

BLACKFRIARS

STORMONT STR.

RACE COURSE

SCOTT STREET

CHARLES STR.

MEAL VENNE

KIRK VENNE

CHARLOTTE STR.

NORTH INCH

SOUTH

INCH

NELSON STREET

PRINCES STREET

DUNDEE ROAD

GREYFRIARS BURYING GROUND

SOUTH STREET

ST JOHNS CH.

ST JOHNS PL.

KIRKGATE

GEORGE STREET

CHARLOTTE STR.

FROM EDINBURGH ROAD TO MONCRIEFF HILL

LIME SHORE

WATER RESERVOIR

COAL SHORE

ST JOHNS STREET

SPEYGATE

WATERGATE

CITY HALL

COUNTY BUILDINGS

BRIDGE

MONCRIEFF ISLAND

WATER FILTER

RAILWAY BRIDGE

R I V E R   T A Y

WILLOW GATE

COMMERCIAL STR.

BRIDGE END

TO BLAIRGOWRIE

TO DUNDEE

TO CUPAR

SCALE OF FEET

100   200   500   1000

Left: A painting of
The Old Town Council House, Perth,
in the eighteenth century
by Alexander McLauchlan.

Right:
A street scene of Perth
in the 1830s.

This new-found prosperity brought demand for goods and services, particularly for luxuries like cheeses from the Low Countries, oranges and lemons from the Mediterranean, wines and spirits from France and Germany.

The leading high-class grocers in Perth at the turn of the eighteenth century—known generically as 'Italian Warehousemen' because they stocked such foreign delicacies—were John Bisset and John Brodie, both of whom had connections with George Sandeman, himself a native of Perth, who had established his port business in London and Oporto in 1790.

Thomas Sandeman was also a kinsman of George. He opened a shop in the Kirkgate, on the south side of the ancient Church of St John, in 1825, dealing in wines (including his Uncle George's port), whisky, beer and tea. He died in 1837 and was succeeded by his clerk, James Roy, who employed Arthur Bell as his traveller, with the job of riding about Perthshire taking orders from licensed premises and private customers, and collecting money owed to the business. In 1838 the firm's turnover was £5,458.

In 1851, aged twenty-six, Arthur Bell became a partner and employed his nephew, T.R. Sandeman (son of the firm's founder) as traveller. On James Roy's retirement in 1862 Sandeman joined Bell as a partner—but only for three years, after which Bell continued alone. At this time the firm employed a clerk, a cellarman and a boy; its capital was now £2,656, and annual profit less than £2,000.

Most of their goods arrived by sea, but such merchants depended upon the steadily improving road network to distribute groceries to customers in the countryside. Rather than keep their own horses and carts, they preferred to use local carriers, including Joseph Gloag, who had set up his business in the 1770s.

During 1797 Joseph Gloag had a son, named Matthew after his grandfather.

Tradition has it that Matthew began his career as an apprentice or assistant to the butler at Scone Palace, the magnificent seat of the Earl of Mansfield, two miles to the north of Perth. The description 'butler' derives from 'bottler'; a key task in the days when most wine and spirits arrived by the cask or large ceramic jar was bottling up their contents, as well as managing the cellar and looking after the household silver. Along with the housekeeper, the butler was the senior member of staff in a large household—a position of considerable trust—and acted as the 'liaison officer' between the laird and the male members of staff—as readers familiar with *Downton Abbey* will be aware! Matthew's boss at Scone was George Jameson.

By April 1816 Matthew was managing the household of James Murray Patton, Sheriff Clerk of Perthshire and owner of Glenalmond Lodge and Estate, some fifteen miles to the west of Perth. Patton was the son of Lord Glenalmond, Lord Justice Clerk of Scotland between 1867 and 1869. Previously he had been MP for Bridgwater in Somerset, and it was said that he secured his elevation to the bench to avoid being investigated for bribery in connection with his election to Parliament. He committed suicide in September 1869.

The sheriff clerk is the senior court officer in Scotland's sheriff courts, an important position with administrative responsibility for every matter over which the sheriff has jurisdiction. He organises the work of the court, assists the sheriff and keeps the court records; he is responsible for having summary warrants presented to the sheriff for signature and for notifying parties involved about any matters arising thereafter—for example, appeals that may require to be heard before the sheriff.

It is apparent from surviving correspondence that relations between master and servant were cordial; many years later Matthew would name one of his sons 'James Murray Patton Gloag'.

He was responsible for looking after Patton's townhouse in Perth, Marshall Cottage. In truth this was no mere 'cottage'. It was situated on the east bank of the Tay, overlooking both river and town, and has been described as 'one of the finest dwellings on the east bank ... a large L-shaped house with woods and extensive gardens to the south' by Jeremy Duncan in *Lost Perth*.

Photographs of the house support this: an attractive, homely place with a fountain in the garden, in the 'arts & crafts' style long before this was invented. Its gardens included a large number of 'exotic' trees, some of which were introduced by David Douglas. Clearly James Patton followed the example of his neighbours, the Duke of Atholl and the Earl of Mansfield, in planting such trees.

From surviving correspondence, it would seem that many of Matthew's duties were associated with what was happening at Glenalmond Lodge. There are instructions to purchase fruit and vegetables, powder and shot for use on the estate, and to

SCONE PALACE

Scone is two miles to the north east of Perth and was the principal royal centre of the Kingdom of Alba from at least the reign of Kenneth I mac Alpín (843–58), who moved the Stone of Destiny there. The kings of Dalriada and subsequent monarchs up to the present day were crowned upon it. The present palace was remodelled from a sixteenth-century castle between 1808 and 1812, designed by the well-known English architect, William Atkinson, in the Georgian Gothic style fashionable at the time. Atkinson went on to design Abbotsford for Sir Walter Scott and Chequers, the country retreat of Britain's prime ministers since 1917.

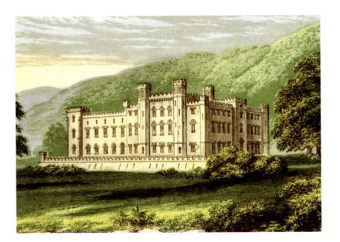

dispatch grouse shot on Glenalmond to Mr Patton's friends in Edinburgh:

Matthew,
The bearer will deliver a box containing 11 brace of Muirfowl killed yesterday, which you will dispose of as follows:

    2 brace to be sent to William Burn, Esq.,
    Architect, Edinburgh
    3 brace to Dr McWhirter, 24 York Place, Edinburgh
    2 brace to Dr Wood
    with Mr Thomas Patton's compliments
    2 brace to Dr Malcolm   do
    1 brace to Mrs Dunbar   do
    2 brace to I.M. Patton

It seems quite common to send Birds by coaches to Edinburgh tied by the feet with a Label stating the person to whom they are sent without any Box, creel, or other cover… You will however inquire as to this and either forward the Birds to Edinburgh in this way, or not as you may be advised…
Yours faithfully,
James Patton

On another occasion, the request begins:

MARSHALL COTTAGE

*Marshall Cottage was sold in March 1866.
The* Perthshire Courier *of 6th March described it as:
'beautifully situated on the banks of the
Tay, in the immediate vicinity of Perth, with
GARDEN AND GROUNDS extending to five Acres
or thereby. The House … contains four Public
Rooms, seven Bedrooms, three Drawing-Rooms,
Bathroom, Butler's Pantry, Scullery, Servant's
and other Apartments. There is also a Laundry
and Washing-House, a Porter's Lodge, with a
Coach-House, Stable and Cowhouse, Etc.'
It was purchased by the Hon. John Rollo
(who changed its name to Rodney
Lodge) and was demolished in 1898 to
make way for the railway bridge.*

*The Chaise takes down [to Perth] eight brace of
Muirfowl and a small bird …*

And concludes:

… one bird and a very small one to yourselves.

A postscript to this letter reads:

*P.S. You may send up some grapes by Capt Maitland's
gig, and some Pease by Pae's cart, as the pease here
are not ready – Do not send so many grapes by Capt
Maitland as may incommode him – and you will not
send any other fruit with him.
P.P.S. A can is also sent down for Oil to be sent up first
oppertinity [sic].
If you cannot get the Muirfowl packed tonight,
perhaps you might get them sent off by the 8 o'clock
coach tomorrow.*

In other letters to his former boss at Scone
Palace, George Jameson, he requests 'plate powder'
for polishing silver and a recipe for ginger wine. Such
were the diverse duties of a house manager, as well
as his principal job of attending to the cellar.

Within months of moving back to Perth, Matthew met and fell in love with Margaret Brown, whose family home was a tenement flat at 22 Athole Street (Atholl Street), in a block built in 1807 by her father, John (who was a mason to trade), as part of the expansion of Perth to the north. On the ground floor beneath the flat was a grocer's shop run by one Peter McRorie, who had reputedly started his business elsewhere in the town in 1801.

John Brown had previously owned the building and an adjoining block containing two more shops, but had been forced to mortgage them in 1814 for £1,300. Although he had hoped to pay off the advance quickly, this proved impossible, and he was obliged to sell the property the following year. It is likely that he remained as a tenant in one of the flats.

Perhaps on account of this misfortune, John Brown was obliged to send his daughter Margaret into service as a lady's maid to Lady Seton at Invermay House, eight miles from Perth.

Her letters to Matthew reveal that to begin with she was happy in her employment, although she admits to missing him: 'The people is all very kind but I must say I am very werrst [*i.e. low*] on Sunday evening'. But in only a couple of months, when the Seton family visited friends in East Lothian and Berwickshire, and she was away from home for five months, she was homesick and miserable:

Dear Matthew I have got a very bad cold and am not at all happy. DM [i.e. Dear Matthew] *my mistress is just a Devel if ever there was one. If I had been at Envermay* [i.e. Invermay] *I would have left her. She was kind enough to me when I was nere my friends but she nows how she has used me since I have left them.*

From Spott House she writes:

D Matthew I daresay you will be thinking I have forgot you but I am always in a bussell. We cam to Spott eight days past yesterday and I do not know how long we are going to stope … Be sure when you write and send me a long letter and all the news and what you are all doing and if my father is going about yet [he had been ill] *and if ever he has got himself drunk yet …*

From Murrayfield in Edinburgh:

You tell me that my Father bids me try and find another lady [i.e. change her mistress] *but I have sought all*

Nickelsons street and I asked all the porters and shore men and there is no person can find her out.

Although we have only one side of the correspondence with George Jameson and between the two young lovers, Matthew comes across as a serious and conscientious young man, mature beyond his years. He clearly has the full confidence of his former boss, whom he helps where he can. In April 1817 he buys a bible for £3 (and has it bound) and pays £2 to his father, when his entire savings are £13/2s/6d.

By the same score Margaret comes across as a straightforward, guileless soul, very much in love with her 'Dear Matthew', close to her family, sensible and blushingly discreet. Between 4th April and 4th June 'Margaret Brown' becomes 'MB' then 'Your Maggy'. Then in October she writes, again from Murrayfield:

Dear M you tell me you have told Mr James about your going to be married but My Dear since he has not sad eny thing about it do not say eny more about it till I see you and we will settle every thing. That will not be long now.

It would seem that Margaret left Lady Seton's employ and married Matthew in late November. Lady Seton writes on 8th December 1817:

Dear Brown,
So I hear that you was married the very day that you left me which I had no idea of. I am afraid you put yourself to great inconvenience by being so obliging as to remain with me to assist in making up my [illegible]. I must now wish you and your husband all happiness and that everything that is good attend you …
I shall send the money or pay you when I see you.
Seton

Their first child, named Joseph after his paternal grandfather, was born within a year. Mother and baby moved into Athole Street (Atholl Street), perhaps to her father's previous flat at number 22; Matthew continued as James Patton's manager and divided his time between here and Marshall Cottage, across the Tay.

Over the following twenty years, baby Joseph would be joined by nine siblings: John (b. 1820), Ann Brown (b. 1822), Margaret (b. 1824), Matthew (b. 1827), Janet (b. 1828), James Murray Patton (b. 1831), William Brown (b. 1832), Lillias

(b. 1835) and Clementina Anderson (b. 1839).

In spite of her previous 'reservations' about her former employer, it is clear from correspondence in 1824 that Margaret remained on very good terms with Lady Seton. Although the tone of the letters is clearly that of mistress to servant—Lady Seton continues to address Margaret as 'Brown', in spite of addressing the correspondence to 'Mrs Gloag'—she is unusually candid in the news and gossip she reports. In January she beseeches Margaret to find her a new lady's maid, the current one proving unsuitable:

In the first place she is very vulgar and so very [unclear] *that I cannot bear the idea of taking her with me to any place, and she is usually so very wanting in her own person and in everything that I can no longer put up with it. She is very un-neat in her work and cannot make a gown or even alter one. In short she does not understand housemaid work.*

In another letter she asks Margaret to buy her three pounds of tea, sending her a guinea, and deliver it to her father's house, from where she will have it collected. On 2nd September, Lady Seton writes movingly of her sister's sudden death, describing it as 'an insuperable loss … an affliction I can hardly sustain'. She goes on to say that she is 'building a little cottage near to Murrayfield [*Edinburgh*]', and asks Margaret to look out for a maid 'to come to be under my own maid'. She continues:

I intend keeping my own maid, and just one maidservant under her, who I should wish to be a tolerable cook, that is to say to be able to buy meat and to do my little dinner comfortably, to understand Housemaid work and to be a good washer and draper and to be able to attend at table … Wages are much lower, but you can give me a hint of what wages I should offer her.

In December she is writing from 25 India Street, Edinburgh:

My own cottage will not be ready until February or March, therefore I have been under the necessity of taking another house. After a great deal of trouble I have got a very small house indeed for a few months. Its consists only of a small dining room and bed closet for myself, and a kitchen and bed closet for the servants.

After this, the correspondence ceases.

In her letter of 2nd September 1824, Lady Seton wrote: 'I understand you have now taken up a shop. I hope you find it succeeds with you and I shall be glad to hear'. This was the premises on the ground floor of 22 Athole Street (Atholl Street), which had been operating as a grocer's since the property was built in 1807.

Although he remained in the service of James Patton until the mid-1830s, Matthew was soon describing himself as 'grocer' and ordering goods from his wife for use at Glenalmond Lodge, and presumably at Marshall Cottage as well:

You will be so good as to send 2 or 3lb of soda and a lb of sugar to [Glenalmond Lodge]. *I am wearied to be with you and* [away] *from here your loving husband.*

With the help of his boss, he was also advancing his career and social standing, being appointed Depute Librarian to the Society of Procurators Before the Courts of Law in Perth, Keeper of the County Buildings and Captain in the Volunteer Constabulary.

It was not until 1831 that Margaret applied for, and obtained, a licence to sell wines and spirits (and snuff); prior to this the trade was in general groceries, beer and ale (for which no licence was required). In 1835 Matthew joined her full time, and the shop's name was changed to 'Matthew Gloag'. Alas, Margaret died suddenly five years later from an acute attack of asthma.

Quoting from Parliamentary Papers (1854), in his important book *Drink & the Victorians*, Dr Brian Harrison reminds us that to be a licensed victualler—as shopkeeper, publican or 'drinkseller'—was a highly desirable and respectable position in society. 'Many were retired soldiers or domestic servants … Indeed, [*domestic*] service was "the nursery" for both trades [*licensed victualler and beer-seller*]'.

Professor Oram remarks: 'The obtaining of a licence may indicate the growth in business confidence as the domestic economy began to expand, but may also be linked to the general increase in the availability of whisky as licensed distilleries began to proliferate in the 1820s'.

The reason for the 'proliferation' was the Excise Act of 1823, which encouraged distillers to take out licences, and effectively laid the foundations of the modern Scotch whisky industry.

To understand the significance of this measure,

we must take a brief look at the history of Scotch whisky during the eighteenth century. Central to the story is tax avoidance.

Excise duty was first levied on Scottish spirits in 1644 as a temporary measure to raise money for the army of the Covenant during the Civil War. Although universally resented, it has been with us ever since. It was only imposed upon spirits offered for sale, originally at around three pence per gallon; no duty was payable upon spirits made 'privately' by a community or landowner, from home-grown grains, so long as they were not offered for sale. The quantity of whisky made by any community depended upon the surplus grain available in any season; barley was the favoured crop, but in lowland areas wheat and oats were used as well. Not surprisingly, few distilleries registered with the excise authorities.

The agricultural improvements during the eighteenth century led to a massive increase in surplus grains, while the movement of people into towns—a corollary of the Agricultural Revolution, which, by creating larger farms, reduced the number of small tenants—meant there was a ready market for whisky. Many more small and medium-sized distilleries registered to supply this demand—

between 1735 and 1737 alone the output of taxable whisky trebled.

Crop failure in 1757 led to a ban on distilling throughout Britain which continued until 1760, and forced most of the licensed distilleries out of business. Home stills were unaffected by the ban and began to meet the demand for whisky. These were the beginnings of the 'smuggling' era: one excise officer in Edinburgh estimated that during the 1760s private distillers were producing over ten times the amount of whisky produced by licensed distillers, around 500,000 gallons (1,300,000 litres) a year.

To counter the rise in the illicit trade many registered distilleries resorted to fraud in their excise declarations. The government passed a series of increasingly draconian measures in the attempt to prevent this, forbidding distilling in small stills, such as were used by domestic distillers, and ordering that the heads of stills should be padlocked and sealed, to prevent them being used without the authorities' knowledge.

This further discouraged producers from taking out licences. Hugo Arnot estimated in his *History of Edinburgh* (1779) that there were 400 illicit stills in the city in 1777 and only eight licensed. Led by the

Haig and Stein families, by now the major producers of legal whisky, the registered distillers formed a monopoly to flood the Lowland market with raw and fiery—but cheap—grain spirit. The unpleasant flavour of most of the whisky produced at this time was made palatable, certainly amongst the gentry and in many public houses, by mixing it with other ingredients such as lemons and spices, or with warm water and sugar, and serving it as 'punch' or 'toddy'. The majority of spirits went to England, to be rectified into gin.

In 1781 private distilling was banned altogether, and the following year no fewer than 1,940 small stills were seized, over half of them in the Highlands.

William Pitt's Wash Act of 1784 cut duty, but allied it to still capacity and to the amount of wash that could be distilled off each day. It also introduced the Highland Line, making different provisions for distilleries located above and below the Line. Highland distillers were favoured with lower tax and were allowed to use smaller stills, which they charged with weak washes and worked off slowly, producing flavoursome whisky. However, the Act insisted that they use only locally grown grain and forbade them to export their product outside the region.

The Lowland distillers responded to the Act by using stronger, thicker washes and developing a new kind of still—shallow and wide-bodied, with a large base and tall head—which could be worked off in a matter of minutes. Since there is less fractionation in rapid distilling, the quality of Lowland whisky was further impaired. Highland whisky was infinitely preferable but it was not available legally in the Lowlands.

By the 1790s the situation was impossible. Lowland distillers survived by making rotgut, and Highland distillers were not legally permitted to sell their better product below the Highland Line. In order to raise money for the war with France, the government imposed excise duties on everything they could think of—including bricks, candles, calico, paper, salt, soap, hides and leather—and when they could no longer be increased in number, they were raised in rate.

Meanwhile the smugglers became bolder, often condoned by the landowners, from whose ranks Justices of the Peace were appointed, and who themselves benefited from the illicit trade by being able to increase rents with some hope of obtaining payment. An official report in 1790 describes

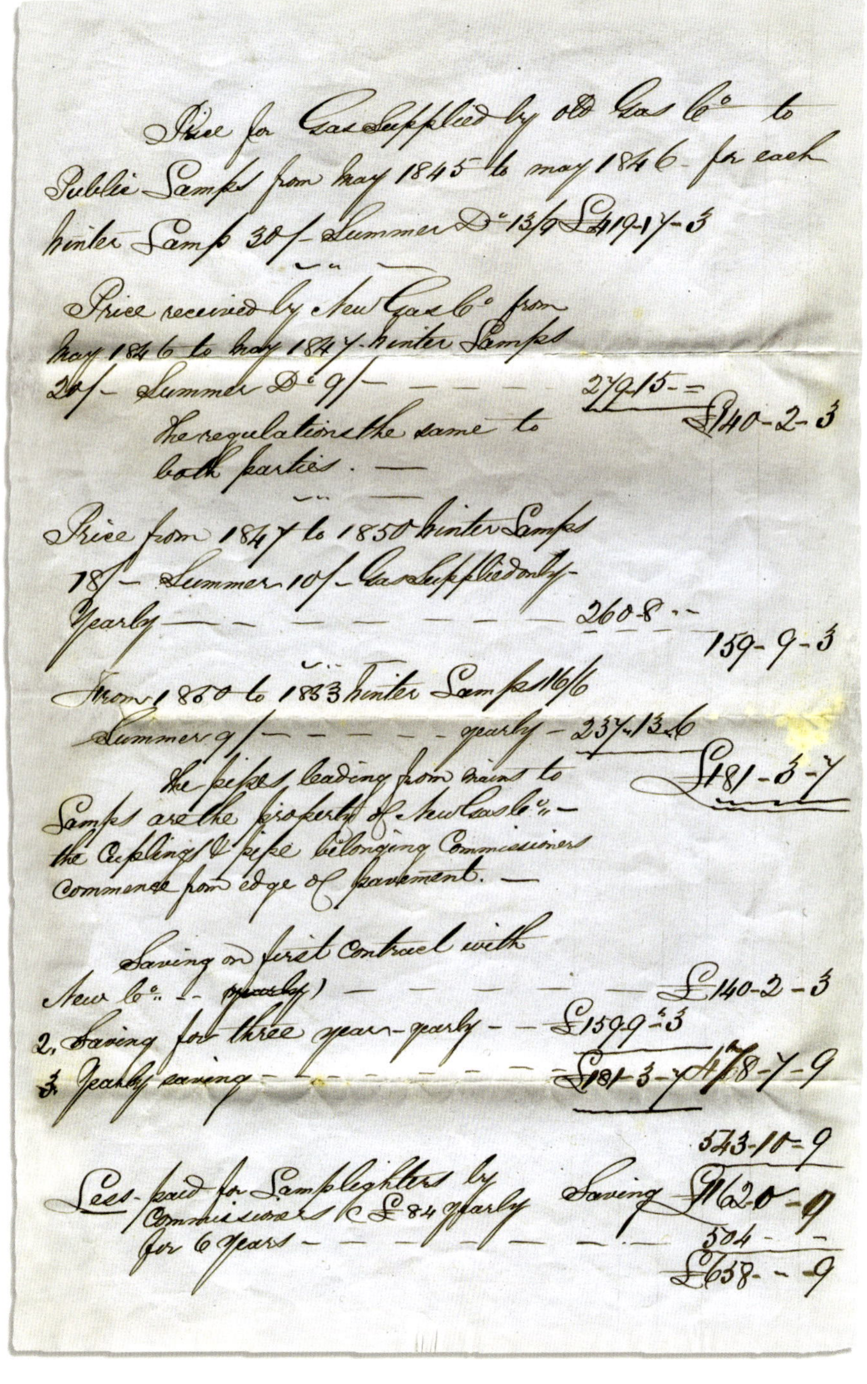

smugglers as 'travelling in bands of 50, 80, or 100 or 150 horses remarkably stout and fleet and having the audacity to go in this formidable manner in the open day upon the public high roads and through the streets of such towns and villages as they have occasion to pass'.

The government was bereft of ideas about how to cope with the situation. Duty was trebled in 1793, doubled again in 1795 and yet again in 1800. Further increases took place in 1804 and 1811, while the Excise Act of 1814 fixed the minimum still capacity in the Highlands at 500 gallons (1,300 litres). Legal distilling above the Highland Line all but ceased: by 1816 there were only twelve registered distilleries here, and the smugglers had a heyday.

Under pressure from the Scottish Excise Board, the Small Stills Act of 1816 abolished the Highland Line and permitted the use throughout Scotland of stills of not less than forty gallons (118 litres)

Receipt from New Gas Co. for supply to Atholl Street from the 1840s to the 1860s.

capacity. An Amending Act two years later also allowed weaker washes (which improved the quality of the spirit) and reduced duty by about a third. As a result, the number of legal distilleries increased from twelve to fifty-seven in the Highlands by 1819, and from twenty-four to sixty-eight in the Lowlands.

The years following Waterloo were marked by political and social unrest. Thousands of demobilised soldiers and sailors were without jobs; wages fell while prices rose. There was a marked increase in crime, and although Perth escaped the worst excesses, sheriff court reports abound with cases of muggings, rape, drunkenness, brawling, burglary and theft in the city, and highway robbery and murder on the roads outside.

There was growing concern among landowners in the Highlands about the growth of violent crime, mostly associated with food shortages, evictions and land clearances for sheep parks, but much of it blamed on the lawless smugglers. Also, improved communications with the Lowlands encouraged a number of lairds to establish their own legal distilleries—which, of course, competed with those of the smugglers.

The 4th Duke of Gordon, one of the most

powerful landowners in the north east, addressed the House of Lords on the subject in 1820, urging a further reduction of duty and a more moderate attitude towards legal distillers, in return for which he pledged that the landowners would cooperate with the excise officers in putting down smuggling.

A Commission of Inquiry into the Revenue was set up, under the chairmanship of Lord Wallace, and based on its findings the Excise Act of 1823 more than halved duty on spirits to 2s/5d per gallon and set the licence fee at £10 per annum. The Act sanctioned thin washes, introduced duty-free warehousing for export spirits, and opened the export trade to all. These changes laid the foundations of the modern whisky industry.

No longer was it necessary to design and operate stills primarily to avoid paying tax; no longer need there be a difference in quality between legally produced whisky and illicit whisky and no longer was it so desirable to work outside the law. Distillers could now choose their own method of working; what strength of wash to use and what size and design of still would produce the best whisky.

Between 1823 and 1825 the number of licensed distilleries in Scotland rose from 125 to 329; a hundred of these would not last beyond ten years. Many of the newly entered distillers were former smugglers and new distilleries were often built on sites of former illicit stills, on account of the water supply and because of established connections with local farms for the supply of grain and the disposal of draff, the husks and spent grains left after distilling which are a nutritious cattle-feed. Similarly distilleries were often built near drovers' inns, which had long been a source of custom before the days of licensed distilling. Smuggling convictions fell from 14,000 in 1823 to eighty-five in 1832.

However, the sharp increase in production from almost three million gallons (7,785,000 million litres) in 1823 to ten million gallons (25,950,000 million litres) in 1828 was nowhere near matched by demand, made worse by a general trade depression in 1829 and compounded by the invention of the continuous still by Robert Stein of Kilbagie Distillery, Alloa, in 1828 and perfected by Aeneas Coffey, former Inspector General of Excise in Dublin, in 1830.

Although expensive to install, such stills were cheap to run and produced strong (94% to 96% ABV), pure and comparatively bland spirit at a furious rate, since they did not have to be cleaned and recharged

Certificate for Dealers in Spirits, and Grocers and Provision Dealers, trading in Spirits.
(LICENCE FOR SPIRITS, &c.)

AT a General Meeting for granting Publicans' Certificates held by Her Majesty's Justices of the Peace acting in and for the County of Perth, holden at Perth, within the said County, on the *first* day of *May* in the Year One thousand eight hundred and *fifty five* for the purpose of authorizing persons to keep Common Inns, Alehouses, and Victualling Houses, Her Majesty's Justices of the Peace acting in and for the said County, assembled at the said Meeting, did authorize and empower *Matthew Gloag*

now dwelling at *Athole Street*

in the Parish of *Perth* and County aforesaid, to keep Premises for the Sale therein, but not elsewhere, of Spirits, Wine, or other exciseable Liquors, other than Porter, Ale, Beer, Cyder, or Perry, provided the said *Matthew Gloag* shall be licensed and empowered to sell such Liquors under the authority and permission of any Excise Licence to *him* on that behalf granted, on the terms and conditions following; that is to say, That the said *Matthew Gloag him* do not fraudulently adulterate the Liquors sold by *him* or sell the same knowing them to have been fraudulently adulterated; and do not use in selling the same any Weights or Measures which are not of the legal Imperial Standards; and do not knowingly permit any Breach of the Peace, or riotous or disorderly conduct within the said Premises; and do not supply Liquor to persons who are in a State of Intoxication; and do not sell any Spirits, Wine, or other exciseable Liquors, to be drunk or consumed on the said Premises, and do not sell or give out therefrom any Liquors, before Six of the clock in the morning or after Eleven of the clock at night of any day; and do not open *his* Premises for the sale of any Liquors, or sell or give out the same on Sunday; and, lastly, do maintain good Order and Rule within *his* Premises. This Certificate to continue in force upon the Terms and Conditions aforesaid, for One Year from the *fifteenth* day of *May* One thousand eight hundred and *fifty five*

The above Certificate is made out according to the Deliverance in the Book or Register appointed to be kept in Terms of the Act of Parliament.

Sutherland Clerk.

Certificate for Dealers in Spirits, and Grocers and Provision Dealers, trading in Spirits.
(LICENCE FOR PORTER, &c.)

AT a General Meeting for granting Publicans' Certificates, held by Her Majesty's Justices of the Peace acting in and for the County of Perth, holden at Perth, within the said County, on the *first* day of *May* in the Year One thousand eight hundred and *fifty five* for the purpose of authorizing persons to keep Common Inns, Alehouses, and Victualling Houses, Her Majesty's Justices of the Peace acting in and for the said County, assembled at the said Meeting, did authorize and empower *Matthew Gloag*

now dwelling at *Athole Street*

in the Parish of *Perth* and County aforesaid, to keep Premises for the Sale therein, but not elsewhere, of Porter, Ale, Beer, Cyder, or Perry, provided the said *Matthew Gloag* shall be licensed and empowered to sell such Liquors under the authority and permission of any Excise Licence to *him* on that behalf granted, on the terms and conditions following; that is to say, That the said *Matthew Gloag* do not fraudulently adulterate the Liquors sold by *him* or sell the same knowing them to have been fraudulently adulterated; and do not use in selling the same any Weights or Measures which are not of the legal Imperial Standards; and do not knowingly permit any Breach of the Peace, or riotous or disorderly conduct within the said Premises; and do not supply Liquor to persons who are in a State of Intoxication; and do not sell any Porter, Ale, Beer, Cyder or Perry, to be drunk or consumed on the said Premises, and do not sell or give out therefrom any Liquors, before Six of the clock in the morning, or after Eleven of the clock at night, of any day; and do not open *his* Premises for the sale of any Liquors, or sell or give out the same on Sunday; and, lastly, do maintain good Order and Rule within *his* Premises. This Certificate to continue in force upon the Terms and Conditions aforesaid, for One Year from the *fifteenth* day of *May* One thousand eight hundred and *fifty five*

The above Certificate is made out according to the Deliverance in the Book or Register appointed to be kept in Terms of the Act of Parliament.

Sutherland Clerk.

after each batch. In time, such stills were widely adopted by grain whisky distillers; malt distillers stuck to traditional pot stills.

Distillers large and small sold their products in bulk, by the cask. Patent-still grain whisky had a market among poorer people in the Central Lowlands, but the majority of it went to England for rectification into gin. Some malt distillers appointed agents; most sold direct to wine and spirits merchants, who sold the whisky to their customers in stoneware flagons holding eight and ten gallons (26 litres) or, increasingly after 1845, in glass bottles. Prior to this, glass was prohibitively expensive but in that year the duty on it was abolished.

As mentioned earlier, Margaret Gloag obtained a licence to sell alcoholic drinks in 1831, no doubt advised by her husband. After he joined the business full-time in 1835, Matthew used his extensive knowledge of wines and spirits, gained from over thirty years of managing James Patton's cellar, to

Opposite: Licences for Matthew Gloag to sell spirits, issued on 15th May 1855.

develop the firm's reputation for brandy, whisky, gin, claret, port, sherry, madeira and soft drinks. In regard to the latter, he secured an agency for distributing seltzer water, lemonade, soda water, 'sparkling beer' and ginger beer made by Schweppes & Co. of London.

By 1850 Matthew could number among his customers: the Duke of Atholl (Blair Castle, Blair Atholl), the Earl of Mansfield (Scone Palace), the Countess of Bedford, Viscount Dupplin (heir to the Earl of Kinnoull), Lord Rollo of Duncrub Castle (Perthshire), Lord Charles Ker (son of the Marquis of Lothian), Sir Robert Menzies of Ross House, Pitlochry, Sir John Mackenzie, Sir William Stewart and Sir Thomas Moncrieff (Moncrieff House, Bridge of Earn).

His youngest son, William Brown Gloag, and his three daughters, Margaret, Lillias and Clementina, helped him in the increasingly busy shop. Of the other three sons, the oldest, Joseph, had emigrated to Australia, and James Murray Patton Gloag went to work in London for a relative.

The third Gloag son, Matthew Junior, became a successful ironmonger in Perth, taking over the business of David Nathaneal in Kinnoull Street. Like his father, he was much used by the local gentry—for example, an entry in the butler of Fingask Castle's daybook for 18th May 1854 reads: 'Mr Gloag from Perth here to see about a new grate for the kitchen'.

He died without warning four years later, leaving property worth slightly over £1,800 [nearly £80,000 in today's money]. The inventory of his estate shows that he had no interest in his father's firm.

Matthew was followed to the grave within nine months by his wife, Margaret, and his brother William was left to sell off the ironmongery business to its foreman, a Mr Taylor, and his partner, a Mr Finlayson.

Taylor & Finlayson then issued a circular letter, informing customers that they had 'the Stock-in-Trade and Goodwill' of the business, with 'N.B. The present Stock-in-Trade Selling off at greatly Reduced Prices'. A note from William comments:

I don't know from whom they bought the goodwill. When I spoke of £20 or £30 for it I got a grunt as much as to say it had none. I think they may do very well as they both seem largely endowed with greed.

Professor Oram remarks that the settlement of Margaret Gloag's estate provides details of some of the major elements of furnishings etc. of the house of a burgh trader in the mid-Victorian period. 'These goods would probably be paralleled in Matthew's [*i.e. his father's*] flat in Athole Street.'

A letter to William from Margaret's lawyer in June 1858 lists articles which were 'specially bequeathed' under the terms of her will:

Your brother's gold watch and chest of drawers to Matthew the eldest son.
Mahogany wardrobe and silver snuff box to R… Gloag.
Four-posted mahogany bed head, bed, hair mattress, straw mattress, the pillows, bolster, 3 pairs of blankets and her gold watch to Joseph R. Gloag.
Family Bible to Matthew Gloag.
Silver spoons and tongs to Robert and Joseph equally.
Body clothes to her mother to be …?
Bed and table linen to be preserved for the children.

Matthew Gloag I died on the afternoon of 21st July 1860, leaving £3,700 (£160,000 in today's money). An inventory of his stock in trade, drawn up on 15th August, provides an interesting snapshot of the range of goods the Gloags were selling at the time (in order of value):

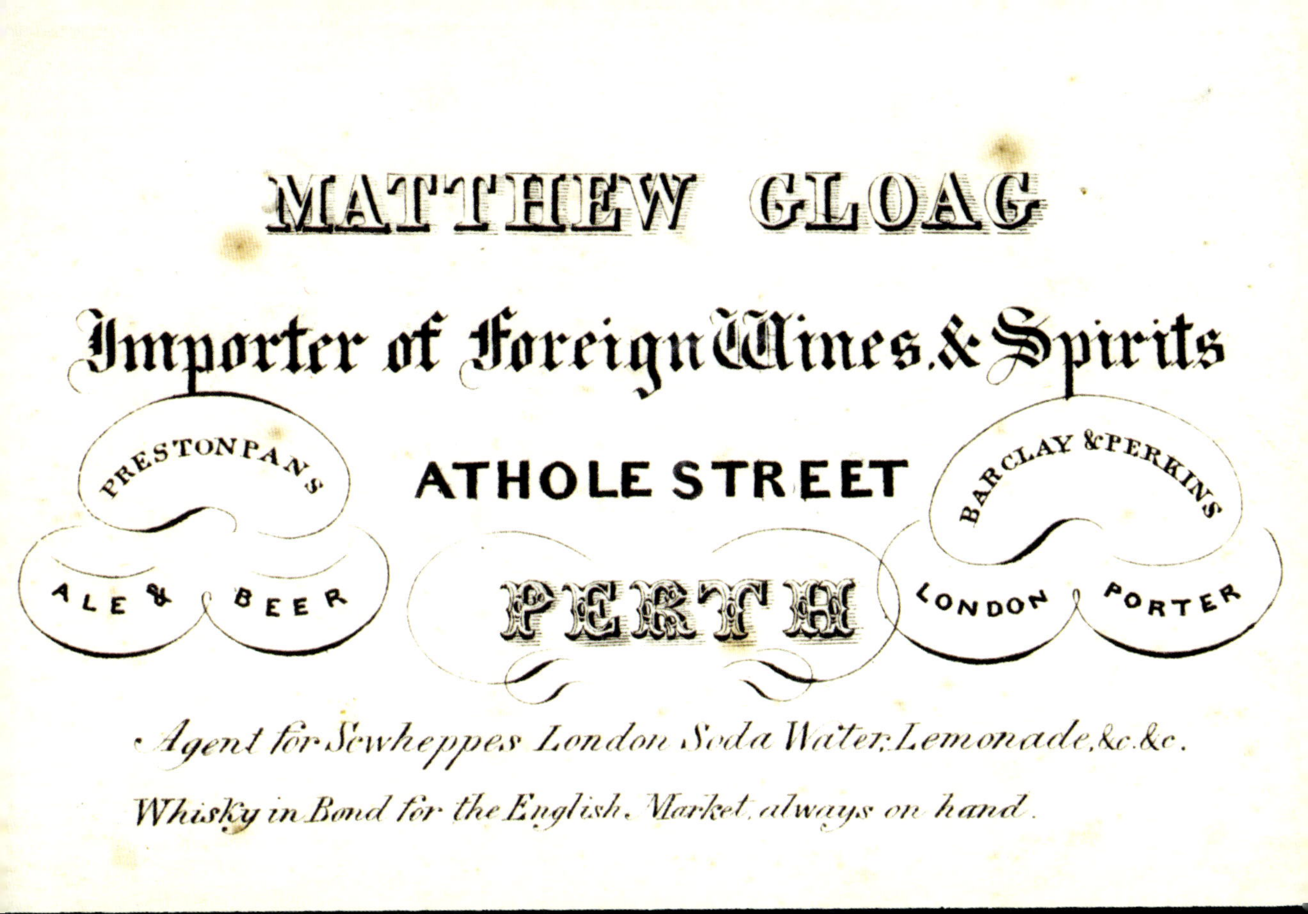

MATTHEW GLOAG

Importer of Foreign Wines & Spirits

PRESTONPANS ALE & BEER

ATHOLE STREET

PERTH

BARCLAY & PERKINS LONDON PORTER

Agent for Schweppes London Soda Water, Lemonade, &c. &c.

Whisky in Bond for the English Market, always on hand.

MATTHEW GLOAG'S BUSINESS CARD

The fact that Matthew I proudly states that he stocks 'Whisky in Bond for the English Market' supports the contention that he was blending malt and grain whiskies, at least by the late 1850s, while the stress laid upon having the agency for Schweppes soda water is a reminder that most blended whisky (and brandy) was drunk with soda at this time

Brandy, Whisky, British Brandy, Hock, Claret, Ginger Wine, Rum, Champagne, Port, Sherry, Hollands [gin], Cherry Brandy, Muscatel, Spirits of Wine, Curacao, Noyau; Porter, Ale, Beer, Seltzer Water; Tea [228 lbs], Cheese, Soft Sugar, Hard Sugar, Coffee Beans, Vinegar, Mixed Pickles, Lucca Oil, Biscuits, Maccaroni & Vermicelli, Rice, Mustard, Mushroom Catsup, Sauces, Preserved Ginger, Lozenges; Blacking, Candles, Ink, Soap, Starch, Brushes, Paper, Matches.

The inventory also contains a note at the end: 'Whiskey in Bond at Burntisland; 269 gallons', valued at £438/5s/3d (around £18,800 today) which is substantially more than the entire stock of the shop.

The absence of malt whisky stock in the cellar upon Matthew's death, combined with this large stock of grain whisky at Burntisland, suggests that

Left: Matthew Gloag's Abstract of Accounts for the years 1850 to 1855.
Opposite: A fanciful illustration of Burntisland Distillery, where Matthew had a large amount of whisky in bond.

PRICES OF WINES, &c.

Wines.

		Per Doz
PORT, newly bottled,		30s
	According to Age in bottle.	36s
		40s
		44s
		48s
		60s
SHERRY,		28s
		32s
	According to Quality, Pale or Brown.	36s
		42s
		48s
		60s
CLARET,		32s
		54s
	1st Growth (Lafitte)	78s
MADEIRA,		60s
CHAMPAGNE, Sparkling,		50s
	Fine, do. do.	54s
	Finest Pale, creaming,	72s
	Pints,	40s
HOCK,		54s
	Rhudesheimer,	60s
MOSELLE,		50s
	Sparkling,	60s
MUSCATEL, Quarts,		60s
	Pints,	30s
MARSALA,		26s
		28s

Wines in Wood at corresponding Prices.

Liqueurs.

		Per Bot
CURACOA, Quarts,		11s
	Pints,	6s
MARASCHINO, Quarts,		12s
	Pints,	6s 6d
NOYEAU, White,		10s
	Red,	10s
CHERRY BRANDY, Quarts,		4s
	Pints,	2s

And other Liqueurs.

PRICES OF WINES, &c.

Cordials.

	Per Doz
GINGER CORDIAL,	14s
GINGER and other British Wines,	16s
RASPBERRY VINEGAR,	18s

Spirits.

		Per Gal
BRANDY (Cognac), Pale, 1848,		36s
	Very Old Pale,	42s
	British, (for Culinary Purposes),	20s
HOLLANDS,		15s & 18s
RUM, Old Jamaica,		18s
	Very Old,	21s
WHISKY, Highland,		15s
	Burntisland,	17s
	Mixed,	17s
	Glenlivet,	18s
SPIRITS OF WINE,		24s

Malt Liquors.

		Per Doz
LONDON PORTER, Brown Stout,		4s
	Double Brown Stout,	5s
	Imperial,	6s
ALE,		5s
		6s
	Prestonpans,	7s
	do.	10s
	Bass's and Allsop's East India Pale	5s
	do., Burton,	6s
TABLE BEER,	Blackford,	2s
	Prestonpans,	2s 6d

Schweppe's Seltzer and Soda Water, Lemonade, &c.
Struve's Royal German Spa—Brighton Seltzer.
Groceries, Pickles, Sauces, &c.

PERTH, *September* 1860.

Matthew Gloag, Wine Merchant, 22 Athole Street, Perth, 1860 price list.

it was grain whisky his customers favoured. This is supported by a cryptic remark in [unpublished MS, 1929] *The History of the House of Dewar*, by J.L. Anderson, the company secretary, which reads: 'grain whisky was the mainstay in these days, and Highland malts were in limited demand in Perthshire'.

Not long before he died, however, Matthew Gloag issued a printed price list. Of particular interest is his listing of five different whiskies: 'Highland' at 15/- per dozen bottles, 'Burntisland' [*grain whisky*] at 17/-, 'Mixed' also at 17/- and 'Glenlivet' at 18/-.

It is not surprising that 'Glenlivet'—the term applied to the district we know as Speyside, not necessarily to the Glenlivet Distillery—was the most expensive, since the malt whisky from this region had a high reputation. It was still three shillings cheaper than 'Very Old Rum' and half the price of 'pale 1848 Cognac' (the only item on the list to be identified by age).

Professor Michael Moss observes that 'it is probable that the cheaper Highland whisky was a blend of new make Highland malts, while the Mixed whisky was a blend of well matured malt and grain whiskies'. The significance of this will become clear in the next chapter.

The notice of Matthew Gloag's death.

Inventory of the Stock in Trade of the late

Mr Matthew Gloag, Atholl Street, Perth

and bought by Wm Brown Gloag
from the Trustees
15th August 1860
Shop

Port	Yellow	2 bottles			
Do	Black	1 Dozen			
Sherry	Red	1 do & 5 bot			
Do	Black	2 do & 6 bot			
		5 Doz & 1 bottle a 28/	7	2	4
Brandy 18 Gals in Wood & 5 1/2 Doz a 34/ ℔ Doz			113	1	..
British Brandy 9 bottles a 20/ ℔ Doz			..	11	8
Whisky 48 Gals - In transit from Distr 120.55 = 168 1/2 a 13/3			111	12	8
Hollands 5 Doz a 23/ ℔ Doz			5	15	..
Ginger Wine 21 Doz a 11/ ℔ doz			11	11	..
Rum 10 Gals in Wood & 2 Doz a 15/9 ℔ Gal			11	..	6
Champagne 5 1/2 Doz a 39/ ℔ Doz			10	14	6
Hock 15 Doz a 32/ ℔ Doz			24	..	..
Claret 1/2 Doz a 15/6 ℔ Doz			..	7	9
Sherry Brandy 3 1/2 Doz			4	18	..
Muscatel 2 1/2 Doz a 24/ ℔ Doz			3	..	..
Spirits of Wine 8 bottles a 30/ ℔ Doz			1	..	..
Porter Red 11 Doz Green 2 Doz Yellow 3 Doz = 16 Doz 4/			3	4	..

Forward

Wine Cellars
No 1

Inventory and valuation of the stock bought by William Brown Gloag, August 1860.

No of Bins	Description of Wine		Doz	Bot	Price
1	Port	Green	18	6	
2	Do	Do	10	1	
3	Do	Yellow	2½	–	
4	Do	Do	2½	7	
5	Empties				
6	Do				
7	Do				
8	Port	Yellow	3	4	
9	Do	Do	24	11	
10	French Port Brown		4	10	
11	Muscatel Red		3	3	
12	Port	Yellow	26	9	
13	Do	Do	25	1	
14	Do	Do	26	5	
15	Spanish Port Black		–	10	
16	Port	Yellow	5	2	
17	Do	Do	2	4	
18	Do E.s Pints Green / Do Yellow		3 / 28	2½ / 4	
19	Do	Do	2½	11	
20	Claret	Red	3	10	

2″1 10 @28//day **380 11 4**

No 2   Forward

In Perth, the Queen and Prince Consort were met with 'the acclamations of countless thousands, among whom there evidently prevailed but one unalloyed feeling of loyalty and delight'.

QUEEN VICTORIA'S

VISIT TO PERTH

1842

AROUND SIX O'CLOCK ON 31ST AUGUST 1842, H.M.S. *ROYAL GEORGE*, A MAN-OF-WAR CONVERTED TO ROYAL YACHT, ENTERED SCOTTISH WATERS OFF ST ABBS HEAD. IT BORE QUEEN VICTORIA AND PRINCE ALBERT ON THEIR FIRST VISIT TO THEIR NORTHERN KINGDOM. Like so many of her subjects, the royal couple were inspired by the novels of Sir Walter Scott, who had arranged the visit of Victoria's uncle, King George IV, twenty years earlier. But that visit was to Edinburgh and its neighbourhood alone; the Queen had in mind something more ambitious—a 'Royal Progress' which would take her from Edinburgh to Perth, then on into the Highlands via Dunkeld and Aberfeldy, where she and Prince Albert would be guests of the Marquis of Breadalbane at Taymouth Castle.

Soon after 8 a.m. on 1st September, the royal party stepped onto Scottish soil at Granton Pier, to be welcomed by the Duke of Buccleuch, who was both her host in Edinburgh and Captain General of the Royal Company of Archers, the Sovereign's Bodyguard in Scotland. Escorted by the Archers and a squadron of dragoons, the royal company made its way from Leith to Edinburgh.

They arrived at the city boundary two hours earlier than expected, and in spite of the elaborate system of signals which had been devised to alert the magistrates, the Lord Provost and Council were not there to meet her as planned. The citizens greeted her enthusiastically, however—'though the crowd and crush were such that one was really continually in fear of accidents', Victoria wrote in her diary. Indeed, the Earl of Errol was nearly run over by the Queen's carriage and her bodyguard mistook the city's Honour Guard for a gang of assassins, leading to a near-fatal brawl!

The Queen kept well away from the Palace of Holyroodhouse, which was in poor repair and surrounded by stagnant pools of raw sewage, and proceeded to Dalkeith Palace, seat of the Duke of Buccleuch outside Edinburgh. From here she was due to travel to Perth, where she would stay at Scone Palace as a guest of the Earl of Mansfield, then to Dunkeld for luncheon, and finally to her destination at Taymouth Castle.

Upon arriving at Perth, the Queen was met by the Lord Provost, with the Magistrates and Council, escorted by four 'divisions' of High Constables. She was handed the keys of the city, and then accompanied through Perth on her road to Scone Palace 'amid the acclamations of countless thousands, among whom there evidently prevailed but one unalloyed feeling of loyalty and delight', according to a contemporary account.

'Nearly 500 denizens of the city, with a number of respectable gentlemen from the country' then sat down to a 'sumptuous banquet' in the City Hall of Perth to mark the occasion.

Matthew Gloag was invited to supply the food and wines. This was a considerable honour, given the number of wine merchants in Perth at this time, and a clear indication of Matthew's standing in the city. A detailed account of the event is provided in *Perth: Its Annals and Archives*:

The delicacies were provided by Mr Gloag, wine-

Queen Victoria's carriage enters Perth.

Queen Victoria's carriage leaves Perth.

merchant, Athole Street—Law-Librarian and Keeper of the County Buildings—and altogether the fruits, confections, Etc. were such as to do him general credit in the selection, and no cost seemed to have been spared to render the entertainment worthy of the occasion.

The royal party did not attend the civic banquet but proceeded direct to Scone Palace for an equally lavish dinner, and next day proceeded to Dunkeld for lunch in a large tent. Here she was met by:

...the Athole Clans, in full uniform, led by their respective chiefs and commanded by Lord Glenlyon, [who] made a very imposing and martial appearance. The Hon. Captain Murray, his Lordship's brother, led a Grenadier company sixty strong—the men composing which were six feet, and upwards, in height—clad in Athole tartan, with white belts, and having the word Athole inscribed on their knapsacks, and carrying battle-axes. Captains Drummond and McDuff followed with a hundred men similarly dressed, armed with swords and targets. The Duke of Leeds (Viscount Dunblane) followed with his clan, clothed in Dunblane tartan. Next came McInroy

of Lude's men, who wore the Athole tartan with black jackets and belts. The Kindrogan, Dirnanean, Faskally, Balnakeilly, Middlehaugh, Urrard and Tullymet clans followed, in their respective tartans, led by their chiefs and officers. After the clans came the tenantry, in the Highland costume. Together they formed a body upwards of eight hundred strong.

Such a vivid and romantic gathering, combined with their week at Taymouth Castle—which *The Times* described as being 'on a scale of magnificence beyond anything that the most florid imagination could conceive'—made a huge impression upon the Queen and Prince Albert. The Prince wrote to his stepmother, the Duchess Marie of Saxe-Coburg and Gotha:

The country is full of beauty, of a severe and grand character; perfect for the sport of kings [i.e. deer stalking], and the air remarkably pure and light; in comparison with what we have here [in London]. The people are more natural, and are marked by that honesty and sympathy which always distinguish the inhabitants of mountainous countries, who live far away from towns.

Queen Victoria and Prince Albert watch a Highland Reel from a balcony of the castle.
The royal party stayed at the castle for three days.

Opposite: Taymouth Castle.

Two years later they returned to Perthshire, as guests of Lord and Lady Glenlyon at Blair Castle for three weeks, and in April 1852 they purchased the Balmoral Estate on Deeside in Aberdeenshire. The royal passion for the Highlands, its people and field sports, made Scotland and 'things Scottish' highly fashionable among the English upper and middle classes—a fact which Matthew Gloag and his descendants cannily exploited.

CHAPTER II

WILLIAM BROWN

GLOAG

(1832–1896)

22 Athole Street, Perth,

September 1860.

William B. Gloag begs most respectfully to intimate that he has succeeded to the Business so long and so successfully carried on by his late Father, Mr Matthew Gloag. The Stock of Wines and Foreign Spirits were carefully selected and imported from the oldest Houses in the Trade.

W. B. G. has fully resolved to give his Friends and the Public the full advantage of the recent reduction on the duties on Wines and Foreign Spirits. He encloses a Card of the present Prices, which (age and quality considered) he believes will give satisfaction.

W. B. G. trusts that, by close application to Business, and a strict adherence to the principles adopted by his late Father, he may have continued to him the same liberal patronage.

*** *Orders promptly attended to, and carefully packed.*

W.B. Gloag's notice to existing customers that he had succeeded to the family business.

In SETTLING HIS ESTATE, Matthew Gloag's stock in trade was valued independently, and the inventory shows how the business had grown during its first thirty-six years of trading—a trading network which had expanded considerably beyond its Perth roots but which was still firmly based on sales across the counter of the shop in Athole Street.

Matthew's cellars held large quantities of port and sherry, eighteen gallons of brandy, seven bottles of British brandy (made by mixing small quantities of brandy with neutral spirit), forty-eight gallons of whisky, ten gallons of rum, fifteen dozen bottles of hock, half a dozen bottles of claret, three and a half dozen bottles of cherry brandy, two and a half dozen bottles of muscatel, large quantities of beer and porter and twenty-one bottles of ginger wine.

None of the wine, sherry, port or brandy was distinguished by its make, vintage or shipper; the whisky was described as having been distilled at the Grange Distillery, Burntisland, Fife, and the beer and porter brewed at either Inchture (between Perth and Dundee) or Prestonpans (East Lothian).

As we have seen, his grocery and general stock provides an insight into the kind of goods carried by a general store in the mid-nineteenth century. The sales ledgers reveal that he had accounts as far away as Edinburgh, Liverpool and London: 'Mr Cutbush' of Highgate Nursery in London, 'Mr Dipple' and 'Mr Charlton', a chandler there, the famous architect, David Bryce in Edinburgh.

The rapid expansion in such distant trade during the 1840s and 1850s is in direct correlation to the expansion of the railway network. The Dundee and Perth Railway was opened in 1847, terminating at Barnhill, on the east bank of the Tay, outside the city until the first railway bridge was built two years later—a flimsy wooden structure with a swing span to allow ships to pass beneath it. In 1848 the Edinburgh and Northern Railway reached Perth, carrying passengers and goods from the capital via the ferry at Burntisland, as did the Scottish Central Railway. The latter had been formed to connect the Scottish Midland Junction Railway, running from Perth to Aberdeen, with the mighty Caledonian Railway, which gave direct access to the English railway network via Glasgow. By 1850 Perth was one of Scotland's major railway hubs.

With Joseph Gloag, Matthew's oldest surviving son, in Australia and James Murray Patton Gloag now established as a paper merchant and stationer

in London, it was natural that William Brown Gloag should take over his father's business. Since the death of his sister Lilias in 1859 and the marriage of his other two sisters—Margaret to Edwin Grasley and Clementina to John Galletly—he was his father's only remaining assistant in the shop.

Within a month of Matthew's death his offer of £3,000 for the 'heritable properties in Athole Street (£400), his household furniture (£177/10/-), his shop furniture (£22/10/-), his stock in trade (£1,500), book debts due to him (£900)' had been accepted by the trustees.

It would seem that he wanted to buy another house on Athole Street in 1865/66. There is a letter in the archive to William's solicitors, Messrs Spottiswoode & Pinkerton, from an estate agent which provides an interesting, if incomplete description of a relatively substantial property, which may give an idea of what the Gloag house at 22 Athole Street was like:

Perth 29 December 1865
Gentlemen,
I am [obscure] your letter of this date relative to the house in Atholl Street advertised by me for sale.

Including two of the attics only with inside stair it is let for £19.18/- the remaining three attics can be let for at least £3.12/- per annum.
Although a former owner let them lower and I have intimated the rent would be raised. £23.10/-
A part of these premises is let for possession beyond Whitsunday next. There is an obligation to [obscure] in repair of the stair and staircase and the price asked for the whole including the gas and water fittings and other fixtures is £320 – 13/4d feu duty which doubles every 19th year. I remain gentlemen,
Yours truly,
David Hepburn

The letter is accompanied by one from James Spottiswoode, saying: 'I suspect in the face of it you will hardly make an offer, but you can let me know'.

There could have been no better time to enter the wine and spirits business. At the beginning of the year a commercial treaty had been signed with France, and a month later William Ewart Gladstone, Chancellor of the Exchequer, after a prolonged campaign, reformed duties on wines and spirits imported from the Continent: duty on brandy was halved and that on wine cut from 5/- to 3/- (25p to 15p) per gallon.

An inventory of 1859.

Then, on 28th August 1860, Gladstone steered a Spirits Act through Parliament, which in the long-term would prove to be a key measure in the development of the whisky industry.

For the first time, the Act permitted the blending of malt and grain whiskies under bond, before duty had to be paid. It also allowed the storage of blended Scotch in vats and the filling of casks under bond.

Together, these provisions made it possible for blenders to make and hold large quantities of blended whisky. As Michael Moss writes: 'This confirmed blending as an established technique and made it far more commercially attractive'.

The passing of the Spirits Act in 1860, which permitted the blending of malt and grain whiskies before duty had to be paid, gave a big boost to blended Scotch.

In a printed letter dated 'September 1860', informing customers of his purchase of the business, William B. Gloag wrote that he was 'fully resolved to give his Friends and the Public the full advantage of the recent reduction in the duties on Wines and Foreign Spirits'. He enclosed his father's printed price list of stock (see page 30), with only slight adjustments.

The random mixing of whiskies from various different distilleries had long been practised—even the mixing of whisky with other spirits or herbs—but this was invariably in the interest of producing a cheaper drink, of debatable quality. Nevertheless, it is safe to suppose that some spirits merchants and licensed grocers experimented with mixing whiskies for the more discriminating end of the market, and this was facilitated by the Forbes Mackenzie Act 1853, which allowed the vatting of malts before duty had to be paid. The Act also prohibited the consumption of wines and spirits in grocers' shops, which was thought to encourage 'tippling' among women, the spirits they bought being entered as 'potatoes' or 'oatmeal' on the weekly grocery list.

The same year, Andrew Usher & Company, the Edinburgh-based agent for Smith's Glenlivet, put the first true 'brand' of Scotch whisky on the market. It was called Usher's Old Vatted Glenlivet, a mix of malt whiskies of different ages, and (possibly) from different distilleries which soon became one of the most popular whiskies of the day.

After the Spirits Act of 1860, Ushers O.V.G. (as it came to be called) became a blend of malt and grain whiskies, and many other wine and spirits merchants and Italian warehousemen, including W.B. Gloag, either began, or stepped up, their production of blended Scotch.

Sir Robert Usher, Andrew Usher II's son, wrote in 1908: 'Before 1860 very little Scotch whisky was sent for sale in England [*i.e. as such and not for rectification into gin*], but after that the trade increased in leaps and bounds'. Sir Winston Churchill, a keen whisky drinker, supported this view in 1945: 'My father would never have drunk whisky except when shooting on a moor or in some very dull, chilly place. He lived in the age of brandy and soda.'

Because blended whisky brings together the varied and variable products of several distilleries, it is possible to create drinks with far broader appeal than the strongly flavoured, generally smoky malts or thin and fiery grain whiskies of the day, and it is possible to achieve consistency of flavour, batch to batch. And since customers could now rely on their favourite blend tasting the same, time and again, it was possible to brand it: without consistency—in any product—you cannot create a 'brand'.

No doubt William Gloag was aware of all this. He was also acutely aware of the importance of quality, in relation to age and wood maturation. This was

William Alexander Robertson (1831–1897) went into partnership with John W. Baxter in Glasgow in 1861, and by the 1870s they were considered to be the very 'hub' of the whisky industry, acting as brokers and blenders. Several men who would become whisky legends served their apprenticeships at Robertson & Baxter, including Sir Alexander Walker and Lord Dewar.

unusual at this time, when most whisky continued to be sold young, and without an age statement. Letters and promotional flyers in the archive demonstrate this. As early as 1868 he was writing:

The improvement that takes place with age in whisky is not alone due to the disappearance of certain undesirable qualities but also in a high degree due to the development of the flavours and aromatic ethers that come over from malt and grain in the process of distillation.

It is thus of paramount importance that only the very best materials that can be procured should be used in the manufacture of whisky. When these only are used and when the whisky has been sufficiently matured in sherry casks (which are of un-purchasable benefit to it) there can be no more wholesome spirit and in purity fragrance and easiness of digestion it is superior to the finest French brandy.

As a beverage when sufficiently diluted with water it is invaluable in repairing the exhausted forces of nature and its exhilarating properties are due far more to its valuable ethers so subtle and fleeting as almost to elude chemical analysis than to the mere alcohol which holds them in solution.

This is a significant statement, but it is in keeping with the general opinion of the day. In *British and Foreign Spirits* (1864) Charles Tovey wrote:

The prevalent notion among whisky drinkers, especially in Scotland, is that several varieties of whisky blended is superior to that of any one kind; and it is not an uncommon circumstance to find in a gentleman's cellar, a hogshead or half a hogshead of whisky nearly always full, although the cask is continually being drawn from. The custom is to get the cask filled with four or five different qualities of the best whisky. When about eight to ten gallons is [sic] consumed, the cask is filled up again with any Whisky that is particularly approved, and thus the spirit becomes well matured and the blend perfect. And speaking of being well matured brings us to a very important consideration.

In England, especially in the south, whisky has not had fair play; it is generally offered for sale and brought into consumption quite new from the still, and in this state is not fit for drinking: it is heating and intoxicating, and soon disorders the system. The effects of a debauch after drinking is a punishment long remembered. Spirit merchants and dealers should allow whisky the same privilege awarded to Brandy or Rum, that of age

story continued on page 56

William Sanderson (1839–1908) set up as a wine and spirit merchant in Leith in 1863. The first entry on his record book is for 'Mixture Whisky': '10 gallons Glenlivet, 10 gallons Pitlochry, 5 gallons Reduced mixed Aqua, 8 gallons grain, 4 gallons water, half gallon aqua shrub [i.e. spirits mixed with lemon juice], 8 gallons grain Aqua'. After this initial experiment, he turned his hand to making cordials until the creation of VAT 69 in 1882.

John Dewar (1805–1880) came to Perth from near Aberfeldy in 1828 to work as a cellar-man in his uncle's wine merchants. Nine years later he was made a partner in the firm, and in 1845 he opened his own wine and spirits shop on Perth's High Street. In 1860 he employed his first traveller and, according to A History of the House of Dewar, 'branched out by selling blended whisky in branded bottles under his own label as a guarantee of quality, rather than in kegs and jars'.

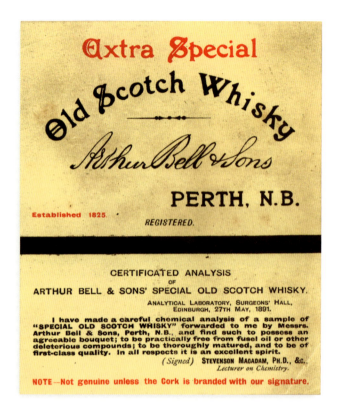

ARTHUR BELL (1825–1900) was mixing his own whiskies at Speygate, Perth, by 1862. This year he made an unsuccessful attempt to enter the London market with two blends, one selling at 5/2 per gallon, the other at 6/-, by appointing the first ever Scotch whisky agent in London (for any brand), a Mr Young, who reported: 'London people thought that Bell's whisky had too heavy a taste' and was not strong enough. To which Arthur replied rather petulantly: 'Your friends do not seem to be aware that the finer whiskies in Scotland are only made at 11 to 11.6 o.p. [i.e 'over proof'—i.e. 65.3% vol] and that, when kept for a couple of years, they fall in strength at least three per cent. We do not usually send out our whisky to customers who are particular as to quality until it is of that age, but if your friends value the strength more than the quality, we must just send them new whisky.' Mr Young was soon replaced, but subsequent agents did no better and Bell withdrew from the London market in 1871.

William Gloag, with top hat,
crosses the Tay at Caputh in 1887.

in Bond; and this may be easily done, with scarcely any additional cost, as we will show.

When the distilling season commences, about October or later, the merchant should collect all his fresh emptied sherry butts, hogsheads, or quarter casks, and if the market is favourable, send the casks to his distiller, whether in Ireland or Scotland; arrange for them to be filled and bonded, which the distiller will probably do free of any warehouse rent for several years, and he will pay duty and forward such casks as are required from time to time.

No spirit can pay better for bonding than Whisky, the first outlay, averaging from two shillings to three shillings per gallon, is very little, and the improvement by age is far superior to the trifling interest upon *the first cost. Nothing tends more to increase the reputation of a spirit merchant than supplying good and well matured spirit.*

It seems that William Gloag shared this opinion!

The practice of topping up a cask with several different makes, rather like a sherry solera, was once common in houses with large cellars during the latter decades of the nineteenth century, and may well have been followed by spirits merchants before 1860. Also, the custom of blenders sending their own casks to distillers for filling with new spirit is followed to this day.

Notwithstanding his interest in whisky, William continued to develop the firm's wine list and to fulfill his promise to customers to pass on to his customers 'the full advantage of the reduction in the duties on Wines and Foreign Spirits'. By the late 1860s he was listing six different clarets, including the first growth Château Margaux. He had also started to buy Burgundy, listing Chambertin at 48/- a dozen, and sparkling wine from the region at 54/-. He offered no less than seventeen different liqueurs, including Curaçao, Grande Chartreuse, Maraschino di Zara and Parfait Amour.

By the mid-1870s he had transformed the business by investing in substantial quantities of the great 1869, 1870 and 1874 vintages. His list now contained well-known clarets like Margaux, Haut Brion, Pichon-Longueville, Leoville Las Cases and Mouton d'Armailhacq. The legendary Château d'Yquem—then, as now, recognised as the very finest Sauternes—was on the list, as was 1868 Marcobrunn hock.

He was importing sherry through Glasgow from agents in Cadiz. Brandy, while mainly obtained through Bordeaux and shipped to Leith, was also imported from Danzig. Rum from Jamaica came via Greenock, and Dutch Geneva was bought through agents in Rotterdam. He was offering a range of sherries from Manzanilla to Oloroso, a number of ports, some for laying down and some matured, four Madeiras and several French brandies. In relation to the branding of the latter he makes the interesting observation:

It is a mistake to suppose that the shippers whose names are associated in the public mind with fine brandies are distillers. Most of the vineyard proprietors of the Charente themselves distil the grapes of their own growing and the shippers act as middlemen, much in

The blending and bottling operation in the basement of Matthew Gloag's shop in Athole Street.

the same way that the champagne merchants buy best wine from farmers in their districts and prepare it for consumption under their brand.

In regard to Brandy in cases and champagnes, the shippers—keenly alive to their own interests by keeping their names before the public and stimulating in every possible way the demand for goods bearing their names—have succeeded in investing Brands with more than intrinsic value and in securing for themselves princely rewards.

Brandy was the most popular spirit among the English middle classes at the time, usually mixed with soda water, but by the mid-1870s supplies had all but dried up, owing to the destruction of almost fifty per cent of French vineyards, including those around Cognac, by the aphid Phylloxera vastatrix, known as 'the devastator', which had arrived from America around 1858, and was first noted in the Languedoc region in 1863.

Unscrupulous spirit manufacturers on the Continent seized the opportunity to make 'brandy' from patent-still grain-spirit flavoured either with a dash of true brandy (wine distilled in pot stills) or with essences. Between 1881 and 1888, the making of legitimate brandy virtually ceased, and even once production was resumed in the 1890s, one trade journal remarked scathingly:

No one who understands his business does not know that a large quantity of the veriest rubbish reaches us from Cognac, or that the medium qualities from that centre contain an admixture of plain spirit before or after distillation.

Blended Scotch had now reached a level of quality and consistency to replace brandy, and this was a key contributor to what became known as 'the whisky boom' during the later decades of the nineteenth century. Responsible blenders like William Gloag were tailoring the flavour of their blends to southern and overseas palates.

'Smoothness' was perceived as a sign of quality, and the malts of Speyside bestowed such mellowness, leading to a spate of distillery building in that region in the 1890s, as we will see. Increasing emphasis was placed on the benefit of maturation in ex-sherry casks, to achieve the same goal. In 1960, the firm was proudly stating that its whiskies were 'all matured by us in either fresh Sherry Casks or Refill Sherry Casks', and it seems likely that the practice was introduced by William.

The larger whisky houses, often now, like Gloag's, being managed by the sons of their founders, established offices in London and elsewhere in England. The two leading Perth firms, John Dewar & Sons and Arthur Bell & Sons, are typical.

John Dewar made his oldest son, John Alexander, a partner in 1879, and J.A. brought in his younger brother, Tommy, five years later and sent him to London. J.A. was twenty-three when he joined the firm; Tommy was twenty. Arthur Bell's oldest son, Arthur Kinmont, was apprenticed to a wholesale spirits merchant in Edinburgh in 1886, aged sixteen, and became a partner in 1895, while his younger brother, Robin, was sent by their father to Australia to prospect business in 1892.

William Gloag remained in Perth, although there is a suggestion in his surviving correspondence with his extended family and old schoolfriends in England, Australia, India and Ceylon that they might have helped expand the business. As Richard Oram writes:

Perhaps most significant is the evidence for a network of 'Perthians' of William's generation established in India by 1859, many of whom were either former school mates, brothers or cousins of the same, or relatives of someone he had known. The closeness of this Perth 'Mafia' was mirrored by the tight-knit Scottish mercantile community and it is possible that such a circle was exploited by Gloag's to kick-start the colonial trade which is certainly evident by the close of the century.

The 'home trade' remained the key market, but it was now much expanded from Matthew I's day.

By 1872 the majority of the railway network in Britain had been constructed. This made it possible for provincial business centres like Perth to reach distant markets and compete, on a relatively even basis, with those in the major population centres of the Midlands and South East. The railways also guaranteed speedy links with provincial ports, especially those for the Atlantic and Imperial trade routes, like Liverpool and Glasgow.

What's more, the railways stimulated tourist traffic, and from the middle of the century onwards this made a considerable contribution to the revenue of Perthshire and the Highlands. Queen Victoria's passion for the Highlands made the region highly fashionable among the English middle and upper classes. Small towns like Pitlochry, Crieff and Blairgowrie in Perthshire, and Ballater, Braemar and Grantown on Spey in Aberdeenshire, and Moray prospered from seasonal holidaymakers, while the aristocracy and upper classes rented shooting, fishing and stalking lodges during the season, leasing the sporting activities that went with them. The very wealthy bought estates and built substantial country houses and castles on them.

Wisely, William Gloag, following the example of his father, focused on such customers, not only supplying local estates like Innerhadden (Earl of Mexborough) and Fingask (Sir Peter Murray Threipland), but making contact with sporting tenants through estate owners.

Unfortunately, records of what whiskies went into William's blends have been lost, but he was sufficiently involved in the wider whisky trade to buy fifty £10 shares in the new North British [grain whisky] Distillery, Edinburgh, in 1887. This project was floated by a group of Edinburgh blenders, led by Andrew Usher II, who resented attempts by the Distillers Company (an amalgamation of the seven leading grain distilleries, controlling seventy-five per cent of grain whisky production) to fix prices.

From 1864 William had been assisted in the business by his nephew, Matthew William Gloag, son of his brother Matthew, the ironmonger in Perth.

Young Matthew was fourteen when he began to work for his uncle, but even as a teenager he made several visits to Bordeaux to buy wines. Here he became friendly with Octave Calvet, the principal of the well-known firm of negotiants, Messrs J. Calvet et Cie. M. Calvet was so impressed by his knowledge of wine that, in 1873, he offered him a job in Bordeaux.

The same year, his uncle had offered him a share of the business in Perth if he returned home. He was in a quandary, as a letter to M. Calvet dated September 1874 shows:

Dear Sir,
I am very sorry to say that I have just received from my uncle a letter in which he insists that I decide between remaining in Bordeaux and going back to Perth. He says: 'I am sorry to inform you that I have had again to part with my assistant and am so sick of these constant changes that I must ask you to make up your mind if you mean to accept the offer I made you last year of an interest in my business; this kind of thing cannot go

story continued on page 64

The South Street Port (Perth)
by John D. Stewart
1883.

on &c., &c. I trust this might not inconvenience Mr Calvet very much. You could do everything in your power to accommodate him and might be of use to his House in this country'.

It has seemed to me the best and most straightforward was to write you of this at once at the risk of annoying you during your well-earned holiday and in the meantime I have only acknowledged receipt of the letter without replying one way or the other.

I do not know if I told you that the 'interest' in question is one third of his business with a prospect of succession and it has come down on me so suddenly that I do not know what to do.

It seems to me however much I might prefer the activity and push of your House to Perth as a place of business it is neither in your interest nor mine that I should hastily refuse what is really a very liberal offer. So I shall await with anxiety to hear what you advise. Of course there will be no immediate hurry.

I am, Dear Sir, yours very respectfully,

M. Gloag

Matthew worked with Maison Calvet for four years, then returned to England in 1878, to work for Arnold, Perrett & Company, of Bideford, Devon, wine and spirits merchants, and owners of the Wickwar Brewery, Gloucestershire. In 1892 he was appointed managing director of the company's wine and spirits department, based in their new London branch at Lower Belgrave Street.

In 1895 Matthew and his wife, Lizzie (they had married at Georgham, North Devon, in 1880) moved back to Perth to take over the family business from his uncle, who was ailing. He paid £2,600 (now around £147,500) for the stock, and began business on his own account in November 1895.

William Gloag died, childless, in August the following year, leaving £24,000 (now *c.* £1.37 million). Shortly before he died he published a catalogue of his wine and spirits stock. This includes:

Eight Bordeaux wines, priced between 12/- and 48/- the dozen, with 'Choice old Vintage Wines' (including Chateaux Brane-Cantenac, Leoville Las-Cases, Gruaud-Larose, Haut-Brion, Margeaux, Lafite, etc.) from 54/- to 108/- the dozen, 'clarets in wood from £10/10s per Hhd. of 46 gallons duty paid' and White Graves, Barsac and Sauternes from 18/- to 96/- the dozen.

Seven Burgundies, priced between 18/- and 48/- the dozen, including 'Chambertin, Musigny,

Vougeot, Romanée, Côte Rôti, etc. 50/- to 84/-'.

Three 'White Wines'—Chablis, Meursault and Montrachet (24/- to 72/-), 'all well-known Champagnes at lowest current rates' including Perrier-Jouët, Moët & Chandon, Pommery, Heidsieck and Pol Roger, six Hocks, three Moselles, six French Brandies, two gins, one rum, Madeira, Marsala, Australian, Californian and Italian wines.

His list of whiskies is generic rather than by brand or distillery (apart from Ben Nevis, one of the largest distilleries in the Highlands at the time, and the two Irish whiskeys, Jameson's and Power's). All are malts, most with age statements, except for the two oldest and most expensive whiskies, Choice Liqueur and Special Reserve, which we can assume to be blends.

Of special interest is the stress he places on his experience as a whisky trader, 'throughout the United Kingdom':

MR GLOAG has had many years' experience of the distribution of Scotch Whisky throughout the United Kingdom, and his special attention is devoted to supplying the types of Whisky, soft delicate and mellow, now recognized as the best and most wholesome.

ATHOLL STREET,
PERTH, July, 1896.

SIR,

I HAVE TO ANNOUNCE WITH DEEP REGRET THE DEATH OF MY UNCLE, MR WILLIAM B. GLOAG.

HIS BUSINESS OF WINE-MERCHANT, WITH WHICH I WAS CONNECTED FROM 1864 TO 1878, WITH THE EXCEPTION OF AN INTERVAL SPENT IN BORDEAUX AND OTHER CENTRES OF WINE INDUSTRY, WAS TRANSFERRED TO ME SOME MONTHS SINCE, AND WILL IN FUTURE BE CARRIED ON IN MY OWN NAME.

I BEG, THEREFORE, RESPECTFULLY TO SOLICIT A CONTINUANCE OF THE PATRONAGE ENJOYED FOR NEARLY A CENTURY BY THE LATE MR GLOAG, HIS FATHER, AND PREDECESSORS, AND TO OFFER THE ASSURANCE OF CAREFUL PERSONAL ATTENTION TO ALL ORDERS ENTRUSTED TO ME.

I AM,

SIR,

YOUR MOST OBEDIENT SERVANT,

MATTHEW GLOAG.

CHAPTER III

MATTHEW

GLOAG III

(1850–1912)

SCOTSMEN THE WORLD OVER USE IT NEAT TO
WARM THEM WHEN COLD, DILUTED TO REFRESH
THEM WHEN WARM, REVIVE THEM WHEN EXHAUST-
ED, AN AID TO DIGESTION, A MEDICINE IN SICK-
NESS, A SEDATIVE FOR SLEEPLESSNESS AND UNIVER-
SALLY TO CELEBRATE THE MEETING WITH, OR THE
PARTING WITH FRIENDS, CONFIDENT THAT USED
IN MODERATION IT WILL SUIT THE SITUATION AS
NOTHING ELSE WILL DO, AND WITH NOTHING BUT
GOOD EFFECT. MILLIONS OF MEN IN EVERY CLIME
HAVE FOUND THAT THESE SCOTSMEN ARE RIGHT.

MATTHEW GLOAG, 1896

ESTABLISHED IN THE YEAR 1800.

MATTHEW GLOAG, Wine Merchant
(FOR FIVE YEARS WITH THE FOREMOST GROWERS AND SHIPPERS OF BORDEAUX AND BURGUNDY),
INVITES ATTENTION TO HIS
PURE AND DELICATE CLARETS, FROM 12/- PER DOZ.
RICH AND NOURISHING BURGUNDIES, FROM 18/- PER DOZ.
THE SPECIAL INVALID'S PORT, STRENGTHENING and SUSTAINING, 36/- PER DOZ.
AND TO HIS
OLD GLENLIVET WHISKIES,
Which are the Finest Offered to the Public, and Moderate in Price.

Full Price-List on Application. *Immediate and Careful Personal Attention to all Orders, Small as well as Large.*

MATTHEW GLOAG, Wine Merchant, Atholl Street, Perth.

EVEN BEFORE HIS UNCLE'S DEATH IN 1896, Matthew Gloag had begun to expand the family business: his extensive knowledge of the English wine and spirit trade and his connections in France allowed him to identify new openings. Now trading as 'Matthew Gloag & Son', his first move was to secure the Calvet agency, taking six hogsheads of 1893 Cantenac claret as his first consignment in June.

Then he immediately turned his attention to expanding the firm's Scotch whisky trade, inspired by the ever-increasing interest in Scotch, and by the success of his neighbours, John Dewar & Sons and Arthur Bell & Sons.

He registered his first branded blended Scotch, Brig o' Perth, in 1896, describing it in his sales brochure as 'Clean and delicate of flavour and of genuine age. In every way of very great excellence'. It sold for 37/- (£1.85) the case of a dozen bottles,

story continued on page 76

viii

ESTABLISHED
IN THE
YEAR 1800.

MATTHEW GLOAG, 1817.
WILLIAM B. GLOAG, 1860.
MATTHEW GLOAG, 1896.

MATTHEW GLOAG'S

FAMED

PERTH WHISKIES

IN HIGH REPUTE FOR NEARLY A CENTURY.

'BRIG O' PERTH' BLEND

Is the finest quality offered to the public at **36/-** per dozen,
net cash, carriage paid.

SOUND OLD SCOTCH

For Keepers, Ghillies, &c., **30/-** per dozen.

FULL PRICE LIST ON APPLICATION.

MATTHEW GLOAG,

Wine Merchant,

ATHOLL STREET, PERTH, N.B.

Bordeaux, 1872-1878. Bideford, 1878-1892.
7a Lower Belgrave Street, London, S.W., 1892-1896.

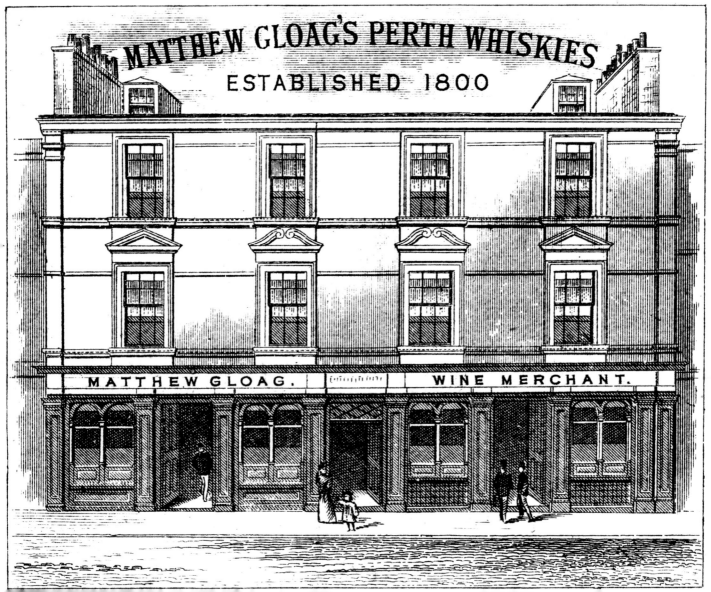

The eponymous JOHN DEWAR had died in 1880, leaving £35,000 (around £2 million in today's money). The year before he died he brought his son, John Alexander, into the business, and six years later J.A. sent his younger brother, Thomas Robert, to prospect the London market. In this he was astonishingly successful. By 1891 the name 'Dewar' had assumed such significance in the whisky trade, that it was felt prudent to register it as a trademark. Indeed, a later commentator would write that 'Tommy Dewar was probably more responsible than any other single individual for the success of Scotch whisky in London'. In six years he had increased sales of the brand by 250 per cent. In 1893 J.A. Dewar was elected Lord Provost of Perth, a position he held for six years, and he went on to become Member of Parliament for Inverness. Tommy also dabbled in politics, being appointed High Sheriff of the City of London in 1897, and later elected Member of Parliament for Tower Hamlets. In 1901 he was knighted.

333

We, John, Earl of Kimberley,
Baron Wodehouse, a Peer of the United Kingdom
of Great Britain and Ireland, and a Baronet, a
Member of Her Britannic Majesty's Most Honourable
Privy Council, a Knight of the Most Noble Order of
the Garter, Her Majesty's Principal Secretary of State
for Foreign Affairs, &c. &c. &c.

Request and require in the Name of
Her Majesty, all those whom it may concern to allow

Mr Matthew Gloag (British Subject) travelling

on the Continent

to pass freely without let or hindrance, and to afford him every
assistance and protection of which he may stand in need.

Given at the Foreign Office, London, the 3 day of April 1894

Kimberley

Signature of the Bearer.

Matthew Gloag

ESTABLISHED IN THE YEAR 1800.

MATTHEW GLOAG'S
FINEST CHAMPAGNE CIDER

IS UNDOUBTEDLY THE VERY NICEST AND MOST REFRESHING BEVERAGE, OF A BLAMELESS CHARACTER, FOR THE SUMMER WEATHER, AND FOR ALL SPORTS.

IT IS NOT STRONGLY ALCOHOLIC OR PRO-VOCATIVE OF THIRST, BUT IT IS SATISFYING, EXHILARATING, AND UNQUESTIONABLY MOST WHOLESOME.

TO BE HAD ONLY OF

MATTHEW GLOAG,
WINE MERCHANT,
ATHOLL STREET,
PERTH.

Advertising his 'most wholesome' Champagne cider.

Opposite: Matthew Gloag's passport.

and joined the firm's Old Highland Whisky Matured (a blend of malts), Finest Old Glenlivet (G. & J.G. Smith's) 'over seven years old' single malt and Sir John Power's Old Dublin Whisky on his stock list.

By the following year, this list also included a testimonial from the medical journal, *The Lancet*, dated 3rd July 1897:

The flavour of Whisky is entirely a matter depending upon the skill in blending, while its wholesomeness may be measured by the time the spirit has been allowed to mature. The above Whisky [Brig o' Perth]*, though of full alcoholic strength, possesses a delicate and soft flavour, and is free from any excess of colouring matter and extractives.*
It is clearly a wholesome and well-blended Spirit, possessing age, and is desirably smooth and mellow to the taste.

At the time it was a common practice to assert the quality of whiskies by affixing testimonials from eminent chemists or county analysts to the bottle or including them in sales cards. For example:

I have analysed Messrs A Crawford's Three Star Liqueur Extra Special Very Old Scotch Whisky and have proved it to be of old and well matured Spirits, blended with skill and having an agreeable bouquet and flavour. It is a whisky of the highest quality, and I can recommend it as of the highest class purity and in every way sound. W. Iveson MacAdam, F.R.S.E., F.I.C., F.C.S., &c.

This quotation also illustrates another common practice of the day—which Matthew Gloag avoided—that of emphasising the purity, age and wholesomeness of the whisky in the brand name, to reassure and add value. 'Extra Special', 'Fine Old', 'Finest Select Old', 'Specially Selected Old Highland', 'Very Old Rare Liqueur', etc. Such descriptions often had nothing whatsoever to do with the quality of the whisky!

As were his uncle and grandfather, Matthew Gloag was keen to attract the attention of the many sportsmen who came to Scotland for the shooting and fishing, and thus was born, in 1897, The Grouse Brand, described as 'Extra Quality, Choice Liqueur. Smooth, soft, delicious flavour and bouquet', at 49/- (£2.45) the twelve-bottle case.

His daughter, Phillippa, drew a picture of that quintessentially Scottish game bird, the Red Grouse, for the label—possibly based on a watercolour by

Estabd 1800

Matthew Gloag 1817
W.B. Gloag 1860
Matthew Gloag 1896

Matthew Gloags
Perth Whiskies

Purest, Oldest, Mellowest, Best.

The famous
"Grouse"
Brand

40/- per doz:

Sample bottle by post 3/6

(Export 21/- per case f.o.b.)

Brig o' Perth Brand 36/- per doz:
Sample bottle by post 3/2

(Export 18/- per case f.o.b.)

The Lancet of July 3rd 1897 says
" This Whisky is clearly a wholesome and
" well blended Spirit possessing age, and
" is desirably smooth and mellow to the
" taste.

Terms. Cash. one doz: and upwards
carriage paid to railway station.

To be had only of

Matthew Gloag

20-24 Atholl Street Perth N.B.
and Agents

ESTABLISHED
IN THE
YEAR 1800.

MATTHEW GLOAG 1817
W. B. GLOAG 1860.
MATTHEW GLOAG 1896·

Matthew Gloag's
PERTH WHISKIES.

PUREST.   OLDEST.   MELLOWEST.   BEST.

The Famous

Grouse

Brand.

40/- per doz.

NET.

Sample Bottle

by post 3/6.

(Export, 21/- per Case F.O.B.)

BRIG O' PERTH BRAND,

36/- per dozen net.   Sample Bottle by post 3/2.
(Export, 18/- per Case F.O.B.)

The *LANCET* of July 3rd, 1897, says :—"This Whisky is clearly a
wholesome and well blended spirit possessing age and is desirably
smooth and mellow to the taste."

TERMS, CASH. One dozen and upwards carriage paid to any
Railway Station in England or Scotland.

To be had only of

MATTHEW GLOAG,

20—24 ATHOLL STREET, PERTH, N.B.

AND AGENTS.

TELEGRAMS: "MATTHEW GLOAG, PERTH."

the well-known ornithological artist, Archibald Thorburn—and within a year, Matthew was advertising the brand as 'unique as an aid to digestion and preventative of acidity'.

At the same time he introduced The Famous Grouse Brand, described as 'Soft and mellow, guaranteed to be over eight years old, and recommended as a veritable Whisky de Luxe', and selling at 41/- (£2.05) the case (carriage paid as far as London; sample half bottles at 1/9). To my knowledge, this is the first time the term 'de Luxe' was applied to a whisky. Notwithstanding this, it is interesting to note that originally The Famous Grouse was initially priced below The Grouse Brand. By 1910 this had been reversed.

He also introduced Perth Royal ('As supplied to the Royal Perth Golfing Society and other Clubs') at 41/- the case—no doubt designed to attract golfers—and a 'champagne cider', aimed at teetotallers, guaranteed to be 'absolutely pure' and promoted as 'an agreeable non-intoxicating drink', good for rheumatism.

All the whiskies were sold under the generic heading: 'Gloag's Perth Whiskies', and for Christmas 1897 he offered three cases of wines and spirits,

Matthew Gloag outside his shop in Athole Street in 1899.

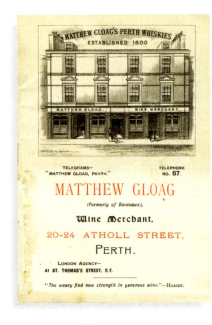
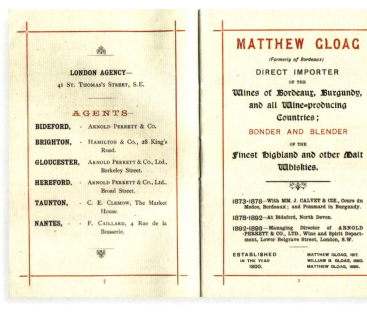

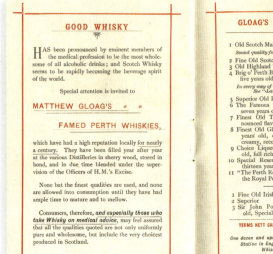
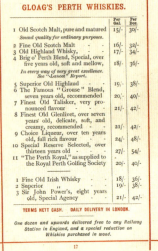
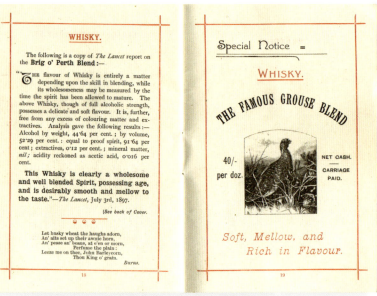

A few pages from Matthew Gloag's 1899 price list.

which all included either Brig o' Perth or The Famous Grouse Brand.

The fact that, during his first full year of trading, which ended on 31st January 1897, Matthew spent £1,449 on stocks of whisky, £964 on wine and £251 on beer indicates the vigour with which he approached the business. More than half these stocks were soon sold on to customers; the residue was laid down. Other outgoings include £141 on 'bottles, jars, casks, etc.', £231 on salaries and wages, and £164 on 'advertising, printing, stationery, postages, etc.'. His largest single expense was excise duty, totalling £1,558—a third of the firm's sales that year, which totalled £4,662.

William Brown Gloag had taken over the firm just as blended Scotch whisky was taking off. Unfortunately for his nephew, after forty years of almost continuous growth, the industry was about to go into severe decline.

Three factors contributed to this.

First was over-production. During the decade thirty-three new malt distilleries were commissioned. Annual production rose from nineteen million proof gallons (85 million litres) in 1889 to almost twice that ten years later, while stocks in bond were at a record level of just over 103 million proof gallons in 1899, and continuing to rise.

Second was a combination of the general downturn in the British economy after 1900, and a change in fashion. Scotch was no longer as popular among the middle classes as it had been: the new king, Edward VII, crowned in January 1901, preferred champagne …

Third was the sensational crash of one of the leading blending houses, Pattison & Co. Ltd of Leith.

In the late 1890s Pattison & Co. Ltd were as well known as Johnnie Walker, Dewar's or James Buchanan & Co.—known as 'The Big Three'.

Even in an age of extrovert entrepreneurs, the controlling directors, Walter and Robert Pattison, were reckoned to take conspicuous consumption too far. They had built opulent premises on Constitution Street and large bonded warehouses at Bonnington. 'During the past year', reported *The Scotsman* in 1898, 'they have, upon their own showing, paid nearly £20,000 on advertising all over the world, and this year the sum has been more then trebled'. The modern equivalent would be over £1,100,000.

One of the company's stunts was to supply public houses with 500 African grey parrots, trained

An interesting pitch to the 'ladies'!

to repeat 'Pattisons' is best'! Robert Pattison spent a fortune on his mansion near Peebles, some nineteen miles south of Edinburgh, and if he missed the last train home, it was said that he simply hired another!

To finance their operation the brothers sold stock and bought it back at inflated prices by obtaining Bills of Exchange which were later discounted. They also overvalued property and paid dividends from capital. By the time liquidation proceedings began in 1899, there was a shortfall of £500,000 (£28.5 million in today's money!); their assets were worth less than half this amount.

In July 1901 criminal proceedings were raised against the brothers for 'fraudulent flotation [*of Pattisons Ltd, in 1896*], other frauds and embezzlement'. Scotland's senior judge, the Lord Justice General, sentenced Robert Pattison to eighteen months' imprisonment, and his brother Walter to eight months.

The company's credit network within the whisky industry was massive, and when the crisis came it 'pulled under at least nine firms'. More significantly, it shattered confidence in the whisky industry, which had until then been regarded as 'blue chip' and a sound investment.

THE ROYAL COLLEGE OF ST PETER IN WESTMINSTER IN 1890— LITTLE DEAN'S YARD.

Better known simply as Westminster School and standing in the precincts of Westminster Abbey in London, St Peter's College was and remains one of Britain's leading independent schools. It has always had a high reputation for scholarship—today it can boast the largest Oxford and Cambridge acceptance rates of any secondary school or college in Britain. Founded in 1179, the school's notable alumni include seven prime ministers, Ben Jonson, John Dryden, Robert Hooke, Christopher Wren, John Locke, Jeremy Bentham and Edward Gibbon—and, more recently, A.A. Milne and Tony Benn. The fact that Willie Gloag was sent to such a distinguished private school is clear evidence of the family's social standing at this time.

Secure in its well-established, middle- and upper-class market base, and selling wine as well as whisky, Matthew Gloag & Son was relatively unscathed by these tumultuous happenings within the whisky industry.

By the turn of the century the firm's sales had risen to £9,514, owing largely to extensive advertising in both national and local English papers and quality magazines like *Country Life*, *The Field* and *Judy*. Indeed, the firm became well enough known for Gloag's to be linked to the mighty house of Dewar by a wag parodying Sir Harry Lauder's popular music-hall song 'Roaming In The Gloaming' with the appalling doggerel:

In the Gloaging
Oh my Dewarling
Think not whiskily of me.

Matthew had the good taste not to use this in his advertising!

By 1900 Matthew was being assisted by his eighteen-year-old son, Matthew William ('Willie') Gloag, who had recently left Westminster School, where he had been a boarder since his parents returned to Perth in 1895, and who had spent some months working in Bordeaux for the Calvet family.

He did not remain long with the family firm, however. In October 1900 he joined the army and was commissioned as a sub-lieutenant into the 4th (Perthshire) Volunteer Battalion, The Black Watch. This may have surprised his parents: in surviving letters home from school in 1893, Willie had announced: '[*I have decided*] to enter the police to get a pension then be a merchant that is what I would like to do. I think I would not like to be a soldier.' It may be that patriotic fervour associated with the early phases of the Boer War had encouraged him to sign up.

By February 1902, he volunteered to serve in the 31st Imperial Yeomanry (Fincastle's Horse), having been gazetted as a full lieutenant early in the year. He joined his regiment at Piershill Barracks, Edinburgh, for training, prior to being dispatched to South Africa in late April.

Willie's contingent departed on the Union Castle liner SS *Galeka* on 18th April 1902 and arrived in Cape Town on 12th May.

His letters home amply express his enthusiasm for army life. From Cape Town his battalion travelled

story continued on page 88

The High Street, Perth in the late 1890s. In the foreground is the meeting of North and South Methven Streets.

by train to Victoria West in Cape Colony, a journey of several days. A week after arriving there he wrote to his parents:

The place is sand desert, quite white, with only a few scrubby bushes growing about, beautiful blue sky by day but very cold it is at night, freezing hard. We got half our horses today and we are getting the remainder soon…

We are going on a trek in a day or two to take part in a great drive of Boers. There are over 700 collecting not 70 miles from here… Myself and my troop are to form part of the support by day and outposts by night, so I shan't get much sleep…

We have some great fun with our half-trained horses. A lot of the men in my troop have been kicked severely… Some of the ponys and horses buck like blazes… We are living under canvas and go out riding twice a day and do field firing and all sorts. I find I have hardly a minute to myself from 6.30 am to 8 or 9 pm, but the life is second to none.

On 25th May 1902 he wrote:

I should like to have a couple of cases of Grouse whisky here, and could you let me have the Cross and Blackwell's agent out here's name and we could get some things on the wholesale principle it would be much nicer than getting them from the store where you have to pay farcical prices…

We have now received all our horses. I have 33 under my care…

It is now 6 pm and I am writing by candle light in my 8' x 5' tent. I sleep on the hard ground which I am quite used to and sleep as soundly as at home… The dust has been something awful today, you couldn't see a thing when the wind blows the slightest and hundreds of horses and mules moving in 4 or 5" of dust on the treks. We are going to be inspected by a blooming General tomorrow…

P.S. Please excuse the rot I write.

The Peace of Vereeniging was signed on 31st May—to Willie's frustration. He received the news on 2nd June and wrote:

Peace has been declared in the Orange River Colony and the Transvaal, so orders came to 'stand by' but tonight we have word that we are to trek tomorrow at 7 am to Orange River Station on the boundary of the

Colony. I don't think there will be any more fighting if as we hear they've given the rebels the same terms as the Boers, which I think is absurd. We are very sick to think we may get no fighting.

In terms of the peace treaty, the two Boer republics—the Transvaal and Orange Free State—were absorbed into the British Empire, with the promise of self-government in the future. (The promise was fulfilled in 1910.) Willie's squadron were now employed on 'police duties', tracking down and arresting Boers who refused to acknowledge the peace—and spending a great deal of time shooting and hunting game. From Mynfontein on 29th June he wrote:

We came to this place a week today and are having a real good time… In the morning we do a certain amount of drill and in the afternoon unless we are an orderly officer etc. we are free and we go for a ride or buck-shooting, of which there are any amount here, but unless they are driven on to you, you can never get close to them, they are so very wild. I have had several shots at them but never close… I shouldn't mind remaining here for the rest of the year as you can get any amount of fun, and you are a happy little family of 5 officers…

The farmers hereabouts are Boers and are not half bad chaps. There is one I know very well, he is a thorough Dutchman but speaks very good English. I have been twice to his house…

He wrote again from Mynfontein on 14th July:

I do a great amount of riding each day. I keep my two ponies continually on the move. On Saturday I did over 30 miles. Yesterday, Sunday, about 20 and this morning before breakfast 18. It is very jolly riding about with a ripping little pony, beautiful sunshine all day long. I am very sorry not to have had a fight, because one feels such a goose when one comes home… The American Govt. is hiring a lot of our time expired men at £1 a day, officers 55/- [£2.75]. I wouldn't mind going there after I have finished here, because one feels such a chicken having no fighting. The worst of it is the climate I believe is not good, but I should like to see a bit of the world before I settle down to business.

Nothing came of this, and, regretfully, Willie was soon on the move again, to De Aar, Prieska, Diklipeport; patrolling, policing and hunting game. Nor did he forget the family business during his great

story continued on page 92

St Albans, Perth,

The Gloag family, 1904.

Standing, left to right: Josie, (family friend), Willie and Philippa.

Seated, left to right: Alistair, Penelope, Nellie,

baby Kath, Maggie and John.

adventure. In late July he reports meeting a brother officer, Lieutenant Hepburn, whose father was a shipping magnate and a director of the Savoy Hotel in London—'a very influential man' who 'likes a good glass of both [*port and sherry*] and old, old brandy and as he is very rich he isn't particular what he pays'. Willie persuaded his friend to write to his father about 'our Port and Sherry … I think the two bins of brown would suit him. If you do not hear from him, however, let me know and I will speak to Hepburn again.'

In the same letter he also writes:

My groom's name is Swan and one day when I was out for buck he mentioned to me that he intended to become a barman. He is just the sort of nice spoken respectable boy of 20 which father wants in his shop. He has been at the plough most of his days, but he would be a very handy person over at Athole Street.

On 21st August he writes:

Having now brought the affairs in the NE of Cape Colony to a successful issue ??? we have received orders to trek down to Victoria West where we shall be demobilized and I expect I shall embark for *home worse luck! About the first week in October.*

Willie Gloag's experiences in South Africa were seminal, and he recognised this:

I am really spending what I shall probably look back on as the happiest years of my life, no worries, no regrets and an education that neither books nor Oxford or Cambridge can give you.

After his return to Perth, he continued to serve part-time in the 4th Battalion, The Black Watch, and was commissioned captain on 7th January 1905. As a result of the Haldane Reforms of 1908, the Territorial Army was established and this unit became the 6th (Perthshire) Battalion, The Black Watch (Royal Highlanders). At this time he was the Officer Commanding the Perth Company.

Willie Gloag returned to Perth in the autumn of 1902, in time to help his father with the firm's 'Christmas Present De Luxe': two bottles of Club Dry Champagne, two bottles of The Grouse Brand Liqueur Scotch Whisky, one bottle of Margot et Fils Old Cognac, one bottle of Quinto Santa Martha Old Tawny Port.

THE FAMOUS
"GROUSE" Whisky,
Purest, Oldest, Mellowest, Best.
40s. per dozen cash, carriage paid (Export 21s. f.o.b.)
Sample Bottle, by post, 3s. 10d.
Sole Proprietor, MATTHEW GLOAG, PERTH, N.B.
ESTABLISHED 1800.

Although sales had dipped after the high point of 1900, by 1905 they had again topped £9,000, and Matthew's capital had more than doubled to £9,600. Although he continued to expand the whisky side of the business, he will have been glad that he was not one hundred per cent committed to this trade, for the next few years were difficult for the whisky industry.

We have seen that by 1900 production far outstripped demand. It became increasingly difficult to sell at a profit the large stocks of mature malt whisky accumulated during the 1890s. The malt distillers were nervous about their complete reliance upon the blending houses, and looked back wistfully to the days when they controlled the industry.

In an effort to regain some of that control they stepped up their demand—begun as early as 1893—that the term 'whisky' should be limited to malt whisky, and during 1903 orchestrated a campaign in the press promoting their case. Not surprisingly, the blenders supported the grain whisky producers.

The debate smouldered on through 1904 and 1905; then, in October that year, the London Borough of Islington raised a prosecution under the Food & Drugs Act 1875 against two wine and spirit merchants for retailing whisky 'not of the nature, substance and quality demanded'. Their blends contained only ten per cent malt to ninety per cent grain, although this

story continued on page 96

The High Street, Perth in the late 1890s.
On the corner is the Post Office
on the junction of Scott Street.

TO OUR READERS.

If you want a drop of genuine
GOOD SCOTCH WHISKY,
send 7s. 6d. to

Matthew Gloag,
PERTH, N.B.,

for two bottles of his Famous
"Grouse" Brand.

Or write for Price List.

The Editor of JUDY says:—"It is the best
of Whiskies."

Grain Whisky nationally, with the slogan 'Not a Headache in a Gallon'.

On 12th August 1905 The Famous Grouse name was registered.

There was much comment in the press, and confusion among wine and spirits merchants. Anticipating an opportunity to take advantage of this—or perhaps hedging his bets against a future decision which might restore the original judgment— Matthew Gloag sent a sample of The Grouse Brand to the Institute of Hygiene for testing.

Its report is displayed on the opposite page.

Armed with this, Matthew wrote to *The Daily Telegraph* to tell its readers to buy their blends only from reputable Scottish wine and spirit merchants, and if they wanted malt whisky, not to trust 'all malt advertisements, for the simple reason that many London distributors of honourable intention, and even eminence, do not themselves know whether their whiskies are "all malt or not"'.

A new marketing campaign for 'Gloag's Perth Whiskies' was launched soon afterwards in England and overseas. Every potential customer, whether an individual or a firm, was sent a price list and offered samples, and Matthew was now placing particular

proportion was not uncommon for cheaper blends, even those made by reputable companies.

In the initial hearing, the magistrate found in favour of the Crown and ruled that 'whisky', whether malt, grain or blended, must be made in a pot still. The case was immediately appealed, but in June 1906 the bench of lay magistrates announced that they were equally divided, so no decision could be reached.

On the day after this was announced, the Distillers Company Ltd (the principal grain distiller) cheekily advertised its Cambus Patent Still Scotch

INSTITUTE OF HYGIENE.

THE FAMOUS GROUSE BRAND.

Registered.

No.
1381.

Date of Issue
15th May, 1906.

This is to bear witness that

THE "GROUSE" BRAND SCOTCH WHISKY of Mr MATTHEW GLOAG of Perth, N.B., has been passed by the Examining Board of the Institute of Hygiene as fulfilling the Standard of Purity and Quality required by them. A Certificate has been granted in these terms, and the Executive Council have signed and affixed the Seal of the Institute thereon.

Issued this Fifteenth day of May, 1906.

(Signed) **J. GRANT RAMSAY,**
Director & Hon. Secretary.

W. G. M'DOWELL, L.R.C.P., &c.,
Medical Director & Registrar.

DEVONSHIRE STREET, HARLEY STREET, LONDON, W.

emphasis on Grouse, explaining that after blending the whisky was left to marry in barrels, sometimes as long as three years, prior to bottling—a practice which had been pioneered by Dewar's first master blender, Alexander Cameron, only a couple of years previously.

During 1906 Gloag's business prospered, and it became clear to Matthew that the old shop on Athole Street, which had served the firm well since 1824, was no longer large enough to cope. He bought a site on the corner of Kinnoull Street and Mill Street from J. Pullar & Sons, cleaners and dyers in Perth, for £1,200 and built a handsome new property, which he named 'Bordeaux House'. He also took his son William into full partnership.

In February 1908, on the petition of all parties (malt distillers, grain distillers and blenders), a Royal Commission was set up to investigate 'Whiskey and Other Potable Spirits', and the same month, a London doctor sang the praise of The Grouse Brand in the *Daily Mail*:

The product of none but the best materials, it is blended with great judgement and care. It possesses characteristics of the highest order, is mellow and soft on the palate, and is of good appearance in the glass. There are no admixtures whatever, according to the paragraph devoted to this blend in the Institute of Hygiene official handbook, the colour being solely derived from the sherry cask in which the whisky is matured. Speaking generally it is a whisky of age, genuine character and wholesomeness.

The acumen of the manufacturer in perceiving the value of the Institute of Hygiene's certificate of absolute purity has as one of its results the fact that any physician who wishes to prescribe a pure whisky for medical purposes now has one to hand, already thoroughly analysed and tested, and certified as pure without any further trouble on his part.

There could have been no better advertisement, and Matthew was quick to incorporate the letter in his promotional literature, mailed at once to all his customers. Encouraged by this ringing endorsement, he also sought to expand his overseas market: towards the end of 1908 he was sending samples and showcards for The Grouse Brand to P.H. Petry & Co., a firm of wine merchants on Broadway, New York City.

Notwithstanding any doubts Matthew might have entertained, the Royal Commission reported

in July 1909 that the term 'Scotch whiskey' [*whisky was spelled with an 'e' throughout the report*] embraced malt, grain and blended whisky, no matter how little malt was in the blend. Along with other blenders, Matthew will have heaved a sigh of relief.

The firm's high profile was rewarded with a sharp rise in sales during 1909; however in April that year the whisky industry had a far graver problem to face: David Lloyd George, Liberal Chancellor of the Exchequer and himself a teetotaller from a strict Temperance family, presented his 'People's Budget'.

Among other major reforms, this introduced old-age pensions, unemployment benefit and national insurance, and—partly to pay for these measures—increased duty on spirits by a third. One of the leading figures in the industry, Peter Mackie of White Horse Distillers, commented: 'The whole framing of the Budget is that of a faddist and a crank and not a statesman. But what can one expect of a Welsh country solicitor, without any commercial training, as Chancellor of the Exchequer in a large country like this?'

The Budget was thrown out by the House of Lords, but prime minister Herbert Asquith went to the country looking for a mandate to limit the power

Matthew Gloag's 1906 trade price list.

of the Upper House in relation to finance. He won the election with a majority of two, and the Budget was passed. One contemporary observer later noted: 'From that date the home trade [in whisky] began to sicken, and there has been a continual if irregular decline ever since'.

Matthew Gloag was appalled, writing to his customers and advising them to lay in stocks before the new rates of duty were introduced, in a letter dated 1st May 1909, the day after the new rates of duty were applied:

RISE IN DUTY ON SPIRITS OF 3/9 PER GALLON
Dear Sir,
Acting on the belief that the Spirit Duties might be raised by the Budget, we cleared large quantities of Whisky from bond, and although enough was not cleared to supply the needs of all our customers, we are prepared to accept orders for the Brands undernoted at the special prices quoted, during the present week only. Afterwards the increased price of 7/- per doz. Bottles on former quotations must be charged. The present high standard of excellence will be fully maintained. Awaiting the favour of an early reply if a supply should be required,

We are, Dear Sir,
Your most obedient Servants.
MATTHEW GLOAG & SON
Finest Old Highland Whisky, 'Brig o' Perth' Brand
40/- per doz
Liqueur Whisky, 'Grouse' Brand
44/- per doz
Finest Old Scotch Whisky, 'The Perth Royal'
44/- per doz
Finest Old Blended Glenlvet Whisky
46/- per doz
'Grouse' Brand, Extra Quality, Choice Liqueur
52/- per doz
Special Reserve Selected Old Scotch Whisky
58/- per doz
Rare Old Liqueur Whisky
63/- per doz

Perhaps remembering the advice given by Charles Tovey, and adopted by his uncle in the 1860s (see p.52), he also encouraged customers to buy a cask and allow the spirits to continue to mature, publishing a booklet, *How to Keep Whisky—The Advantages of a Cask*:

INCORPORATED
INSTITUTE of HYGIENE

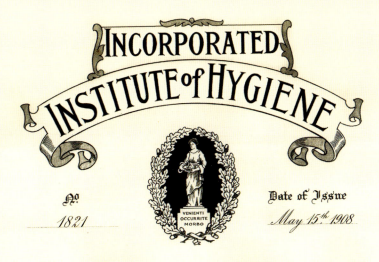

VENIENTI
OCCURRITE
MORBO

№
1821

Date of Issue
May 15th 1908

This is to Certify that

the "Grouse" Brand Scotch Whisky of

Mr Matthew Gloag of Perth, N.B. has

been passed by the

Examining Board of the Incorporated Institute of Hygiene

as fulfilling

the Standard of Purity & Quality required by them

in evidence of which the Council have affixed the Seal of the

Institute hereon.

This Certificate, awarded for the Third year, remains in force, subject
to the Rules and Regulations of the Institute, until the
14th day of May 1909
after which date a New Certificate may be applied for if the standard of quality or merit has been maintained

Issued this Fifteenth day of May 1908.
By order of the Council.

General Director & Secretary.

DEVONSHIRE St., HARLEY STREET, LONDON, W.

We recommend this way of keeping Whisky, as it is by far the most satisfactory and economical way if at all possible.

It does away with the trouble of bottles, drawing corks, and the accumulation of empties. The Whisky is always improving in quality in a cask, whereas it does not improve in bottle, and the prices are cheaper than in bottle when ordered in quantities of three gallons or more for filling up.

He went on to explain that the cask should be tapped halfway up and kept topped up.

Sales soared to record levels as customers sought to 'beat the Budget'.

When the new rates of duty took effect on 30th April 1909, Matthew wrote to a London customer, Peter Ralli of the well-known Indian trading house, Ralli Brothers:

We are sorry that Spirit duties have been increased to such a serious extent, because they tax still more heavily whisky and brandy which are almost necessities of life to some people, and also the chloroform of the Doctors and the household Eau de Cologne.

Despite an increase of 7/- (35p) a case on all the firm's spirits, Matthew and Willie Gloag were determined not to jeopardise the quality of their brands in an effort to keep down price. On 17th May 1909, Matthew wrote to D.R.W. Kemp, a customer in Comrie, Perthshire:

As we think the great increase in duty will stimulate demand for the cheaper sorts, we think that it will be greatly to the advantage of those who can afford it to maintain quality and give the public something good, more especially as the duty on fine whisky is no more than the common sorts.

Willie was dispatched on a sales tour in south east England, sending his father orders for wines and spirits, and the names of possible outlets. The firm's good name was reinforced by the steady promotion of The Famous Grouse, and the launch of two new whiskies which had not been matured in ex-sherry casks, Anti-Gout Whisky (42/- the case) and Anti-Diabetic Whisky (48/- the case), and which were 'free from sweet, colour and wine flavour'. A booklet entitled *Notes on Whisky* was published, listing 'Gloag's Perth Whiskies'—now ten blends (including

Anti-Gout and Diabetic), seven 'Unblended All-Malt Whiskies' and three 'Fine Old Irish Whiskies'.

The list of single malts—'Over seven years old and pure as distilled'—is especially interesting (prices are per dozen bottles):

1. *The Glenlivet*
(George & John Gordon Smith's): 43/-
2. *The Glenlivet*
(George & John Gordon Smith's), 1892: 60/-
3. *Glen Grant*
(J & J Grant): 43/-
4. *Long John's Ben Nevis: 43/-*
5. *Talisker*
(Island of Skye) 'The Talisker was goot': 43/-
6. *Laphroaig (Islay): 43/-*
7. *Lagavulin, over Ten Years Old: 45/-*

It is intriguing that the blends are described as being 'free from harshness and from excessive peaty or smoky flavour', given that the last three malts are famously smoky.

Notes on Whisky contains an interesting introduction from Matthew, stressing the health benefits of whisky, a matter which he clearly believed to be a key selling factor, and setting out his business philosophy:

It has been my constant aim and endeavour to produce and supply Whiskies which will be at once pure, light, delicate in flavour, easily digestible, and especially possessed of the valuable ethers which are known to sustain the action of the heart, and without which the usefulness of Whisky from a medical point of view is greatly lessened. These ethers are chiefly to be found in the costly Whiskies of the north and west of Scotland, Whiskies which are too expensive for general trade and for all but merchants having a high-class demand and customers able and willing to pay an adequate price, and it may be mentioned that all my brands contain their proportion of such. Implicit confidence therefore can be placed in them by persons who take Whisky on medical advice, for health's sake or for dietetic reasons, and connoisseurs in the delicate fragrance and flavours which are found in old and well-bred Whiskies only will not be disappointed. Profits there must be, but the interests of customers and not profits are the first consideration, and my desire is to meet modern competition and extend business by specially good value and willing service.

Efforts were made to 'cultivate a large export trade' by advertising in the *Over Seas Daily Mail*, and when this produced few sales Matthew asked the editor for a list of subscribers 'so we might follow up the advertisement by a letter'. In the lead-up to the Royal Commission on Whisky, the press had noted that the export trade 'now amounted to seven million gallons per annum', and since the People's Budget 'killed the home trade' with its rise in duty, many whisky companies were looking for new markets overseas.

The firm's Letter Books for 1908/9 reveal a steady effort to establish agencies in North America, where the rapidly developing u.s. economy offered a lifeline to the depressed home trade. In November 1908 Matthew was negotiating with George Steiger, who was planning to establish a wine and spirits agency in New York, Eric Steele from Didsbury, who was seeking to do the same in Vancouver and British Colombia, and A.F. Henderson of Glenalmond House, a long-standing customer of Gloag's, who was proposing to begin exporting to South Africa. In all three cases, it was The Famous Grouse which was being offered as the export brand.

Evidence for agencies elsewhere is less clear.

Orders sent to India, for example, seem to have been developed by the old 'Perthian' connections and word-of-mouth recommendation.

Matthew was not confident that all these endeavours would prevent sales falling, and with regret, cut his order for the excellent 1906 Bordeaux vintage, which he had tasted on a recent visit to France.

At the end of the financial year, in January 1910, Matthew Gloag decided to retire on grounds of poor health, handing over the daily running of the business to his son Willie with a loan of £10,000.

Matthew continued to play an active role, however. A parcel of letters in the archive from Stonehaven in Kincardineshire, where he had taken other members of the family on holiday for the month of July 1910, provide an insight into his way of doing business.

Opposite:

Soon after registering 'The Famous Grouse' as a trademark (on 12th August 1905) Matthew Gloag published a catalogue promoting his 'Perth Whiskies', with strong focus on Grouse, as well as his wines.

story continued on page 111

Notes on Whisky.

THE FAMOUS GROUSE BRAND.

REGISTERED.

"As near a perfect Whisky as possible."
—*Court Circular.*

MATTHEW GLOAG,

PERTH, SCOTLAND.

ESTABLISHED IN 1800.

Telegrams—"MATTHEW GLOAG, Perth."
Telephone No. 67.

IT has been my constant aim and endeavour to produce and supply Whiskies which will be at once pure, light, delicate in flavour, easily digestible, and especially possessed of the valuable ethers which are known to sustain the action of the heart, and without which the usefulness of Whisky from a medical point of view is greatly lessened. These ethers are chiefly to be found in the costly Whiskies of the north and west of Scotland, Whiskies which are too expensive for general trade and for all but merchants having a high-class demand and customers able and willing to pay an adequate price, and it may be mentioned that all my brands contain their proportion of such. Implicit confidence therefore can be placed in them by persons who take Whisky on medical advice, for health's sake or for dietetic reasons, and connoisseurs in the delicate fragrance and flavours which are found in old and well-bred Whiskies only will not be disappointed. Profits there must be, but the interests of customers and not profits are the first consideration, and my desire is to meet modern competition and extend business by specially good value and willing service. It is further submitted that when customers will take the trouble to deal direct with the original and first-hand purveyor, avoiding intermediate profits and commissions, they receive better Whisky and better value than otherwise. My Whiskies have been analysed and favourably commented on (without payment or any consideration) by *The Lancet*, commended by the Press and by a large number of esteemed customers, and also examined and been awarded the Certificate of the Institute of Hygiene (see page 5).

MATTHEW GLOAG.

PERTH WHISKY DE LUXE.

The Famous "Grouse" Brand.

41/-

per Dozen.

—

Carriage Paid. . .

"As near a perfect Whisky as possible."

—*Court Circular.*

FOR EXPORT:

21/- per dozen, *Free on Board.*

WHISKIES FOR EXPORT.

Special attention is paid to this department and to Bottling in Bond. Free on board prices will be quoted on application, for any of the qualities listed on pages 6 and 7 for Export under Bond, in Casks and Cases.

GLOAG'S PERTH WHISKIES—*contd.*

For Persons to whom Whisky stored in Sherry Casks is objectionable, the following Anti-Gout and Anti-Diabetic qualities, free from sweet, colour, and wine flavour, are recommended as fulfilling Medical requirements in a highly satisfactory manner:—

	Per Doz.
No. 1 Anti-Diabetic Whisky,	
Seven Years Old, - - - - - -	42/-
No. 2 Anti-Diabetic Whisky,	
Ten Years Old, - - - - - -	48/-

Parcel Post.

Attention is respectfully directed to the convenience of receiving by return of post Single Bottles delivered to destination in the remotest parts of Great Britain, at the dozen rate, plus 6d (two bottles 8d), to cover postage, and it is submitted that the value supplied is well worth the small extra expense for postage.

Terms.

Net Cash. *Remittance or reference respectfully requested with new accounts.*

Free Delivery.

Railway Carriage is paid on One Dozen Bottles, or any larger quantity, assorted or otherwise. Customers are requested to add the word "unexamined" when signing Carrier's Receipt Book, and to immediately report any loss or breakage at their own Railway Station, as well as to the sender.

Empties.

Address Cards should not be removed from return Casks, Jars, and Special Returnable Cases.

Orders.

All Orders, whether large or small, receive immediate and careful personal attention.

It is a special favour when quite convenient to customers to order *two dozen bottles or more in one consignment,* as a saving in carriage is thereby effected. This, of course, is of their kindness.

NOTES ON WHISKY.

AS the subject of Whisky is one which closely concerns the health of those who use it, and which is therefore worthy of some study and attention, the following few notes may be of interest. Scotch Whisky may be divided into two classes, viz. :—"malt" and "grain." The former is made from malted barley. The barley after being "malted," *i.e.*, allowed to sprout, is dried in a kiln over a fire which consists of coke or peat or both. When coke is used there is no flavour communicated by the fuel. When peat is used its smoke impregnates the grain and flavours the Whisky in proportion to the quantity used. After being dried the malt is ground small and passed into the mash-tun as grist, and thence into the "still," water is added for the mashing process, and yeast to promote fermentation. When the starchy water has been converted into saccharine, the result is distilled several times until a pure spirit is obtained, and the spirit is Whisky. In distilling malt a pot-still is used, and as the pot-still sends over not only alcohol and water but also flavours, oils, and essences yielded by the materials from which the mash was made, it is obvious that to obtain a good result only the very best materials must be used, viz., the finest barley well ripened, carefully malted, and treated with the utmost cleanliness and skill to avoid mustiness, etc., the best quality of sound peat, pure air and a supply of pure soft water. Fortunately there are many distilleries where these requirements are carried out, but as there are exceptions, it is the function of the experienced merchant to discriminate and to see that his customers are safeguarded. The process of manufacture being complete the Whisky is stored in casks to mature. Genuine age is of vital importance in the production of a Whisky to be at once pleasant to the palate and wholesome in its use, and as age means rent, interest on capital, loss of quantity by evaporation, etc., and as the duty to be paid is 11/- the gallon at proof, it is obvious that if really fine Whisky be required a fair price must be paid for it. "Grain" Whisky is made from a mash which consists usually of 75% of unmalted corn and 25% of malted barley. A modern patent "Coffey" still is used. The still is so contrived as to prevent many of the impurities such as "furfurol," "fusel," etc., from passing over with the distillate, and the result is a highly rectified pure spirit, milder in flavour and with fewer impurities than pot-still Whisky. When well matured in sherry casks or other suitable wood, and afterwards blended with old pot-still Whisky, the product is a lighter, softer, and more easily digestible Whisky than any pot-still Whisky by itself. There is the public evidence in a recent trial, given by Dr. John Glaister, Regius Professor of Forensic Medicine of the University of Glasgow, an authority on the subject, and of other medical men, that patent-still Whisky by itself is "purer and less harmful than pot still," and this fully coincides with experience.

4

MATTHEW GLOAG'S PERTH WHISKY.

Copy of "Lancet" Report of July 3rd, 1897.

"The flavour of Whisky is entirely a matter depending upon the skill in blending, while its wholesomeness may be measured by the time the spirit has been allowed to mature. The above Whisky, though of full alcoholic strength, possesses a delicate and soft flavour, and is free from any excess of colouring matter and extractives.

"It is clearly a wholesome and well-blended Spirit, possessing age, and is desirably smooth and mellow to the taste."

INSTITUTE OF HYGIENE.

No.
1381.

Date of Issue.
15th May, 1906.

This is to bear witness that The "Grouse" Brand Scotch Whisky of Mr. Matthew Gloag of Perth, N.B., has been passed by the Examining Board of the Institute of Hygiene as fulfilling the Standard of Purity and Quality required by them. A Certificate has been granted in these terms, and the Executive Council have signed and affixed the Seal of the Institute thereon.

Issued this Fifteenth day of May, 1906.

(Signed) J. GRANT RAMSAY,
Director & Hon. Secretary.

W. G. M'DOWELL, L.R.C.P., &c.,
Medical Director & Registrar.

Devonshire Street, Harley Street, London, W.

---

*"We cannot deny that Alcohol is a food in the strict sense of the word."—*Dr. Robson Roose.

"Admitting as we must that Alcohol is to some extent a food, we know that it is not taken for purposes of nutrition by the great mass of those who use it in moderate quantities. Persons who are honest and intelligent say they take it because they like it ; because it makes them more comfortable ; because they enjoy their food better than when plain water is taken ; because it helps them to sleep, etc. Now all these are perfectly valid reasons, and as such ought to be respected. They are not to be thrust aside by the assertion that such an auxiliary is a dangerous one, and that its good effects are much overrated, and, if not, are more than counterbalanced by others of an opposite character. Experience is unshaken by such assertions, and is strongly reinforced by the fact that alcohol in some form or other is in common use among civilised nations. It may well be asked—Is such experience to go for nothing?

"For persons compelled to lead a sedentary life, a little alcohol taken with meals may be not only pleasant, but often extremely useful. It is found to help digestion, and to brace up and sustain flagging functions. In old age alcoholic stimulants are often very serviceable, especially in relieving sleeplessness attended with slow and imperfect digestion. The late Dr. Carpenter, the most sensible and the most intelligent Champion of the Temperance Cause, found it desirable in his old age to take a little Wine, and declared that he was the better for it."—Dr. Robson Roose, *in the "New Review."*

5

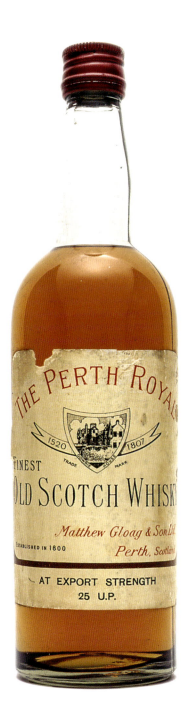

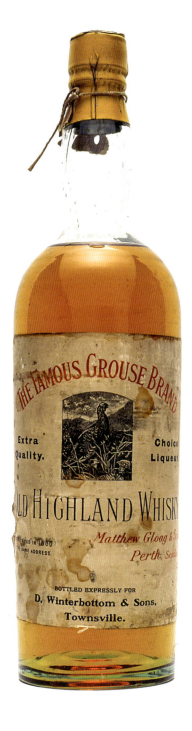

Opposite:
A selection of rare bottles held in
the company archive.

Like his uncle and his grandfather before him, Matthew had kept a close eye on the running of the shop and had dealt personally with all mail-order custom. He kept up with his customers and made them feel valued, and there is no doubt that the goodwill thus generated was good for business, when existing customers—very many of them belonging to the higher reaches of society—recommended Gloag's to friends, who became new customers.

So, as well as family news and advice on replacing staff, Matthew scans the pages of *Farm Topics* and *The Scotsman* for news about customers—of the 'births, deaths and marriages' kind—which Willie should follow up. He is instructed to amend the address-book entry for 'Mr Struthers' to 'Sir William Struthers'; to send a letter of welcome (with a price list) to the new owner of Faskally Estate and a gift to the newly born son of a loyal customer.

Matthew Gloag III, the creator of The Famous Grouse, died on 5th November 1912, aged sixty-two, at his house, St Albans, Perth, leaving £16,260. He instructed his executors to sell his interest in the family firm to Willie, allowing him a reasonable time to repay the outstanding loan of £10,000 he had made to him in 1910.

Perth in the 1900s.

CHAPTER IV

MATTHEW WILLIAM

GLOAG

(1882–1947)

"GROUSE" BRAND WHISKY.

For all purposes we recommend our "Grouse" Brand Whisky in preference to others.

SIX REASONS WHY YOU SHOULD TRY IT.—

It has the lightness and delicacy of well-bred whisky.
It does not vary in quality.
It is thoroughly matured.
It is a blend of all that is best.
It is in every respect a gentleman's whisky.
It is moderate in price.

25/- for six bottles, or **48/-** per doz., net cash, carriage paid.

MATTHEW GLOAG & SON, PERTH, SCOTLAND.

Established in the year 18co.

There can be no better summary of the characteristics in whisky
esteemed by consumers during the late Edwardian era!

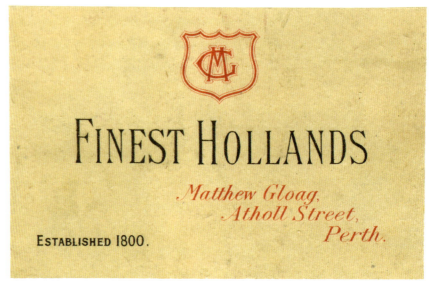

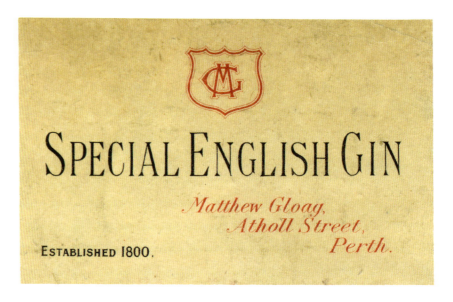

Willie Gloag's labels were inspired by French wine labels.

The effect of the 1909 People's Budget would be spread across the whole of the coming and subsequent years: profits from spirits could be expected to fall. As soon as his father put him in control of the firm, Willie Gloag determined to spread the risk by expanding the fine wine side of the business, where duty was not so punitive.

The cellars of Bordeaux House contained some remarkably good vintages, including 1897 Ch. Lafite, 1896 Ch. Mouton Rothschild, 1906 Ch. Clos Saint–Emilion Phillipe, 1884 Moselle Berncastler, 1884 Cockburn port and pre-Phylloxera Cognacs from 1848, 1865 and 1875. On his first day in control of the firm, Willie wrote to Deinhard & Co. of London, who specialised in German wines, ordering new labels for his Hocks and Moselles.

He did not ignore The Famous Grouse, redesigning the standard newspaper advertisement to place the game bird in a large capital 'G' and adding 'Six reasons why you should try it'.

Willie's tactics, based on the firm's reputation for quality, did well to hold the turnover during 1911 at a little below £10,500, earning a profit of £1,456.

Encouraged by this, he laid in more stocks of wine, publishing his first list in 1912. This contained twenty different clarets; the cheapest were Ch. Framont, Médoc 1907 (13/- for a twelve-bottle case, delivered) and Côtes de Fronsac 1907 (15/- the case); the most expensive, Ch. Cos d'Estournel 1893 (60/- the case) and Ch. Lafite (72/- the case).

There were six Sauternes, including Ch. d'Yquem 1887 (72/- the case), sixteen red Burgundies, including Romaneé-Conti, Clos de Vougeot and Chambertin (72/- the case), five white Burgundies and three Australian Burgundies—which Willie recommended as 'greatly superior to the many brands available at or about the same price'.

There were twenty-five different ports, headed by Cockburn's 1884 (105/- the case—the most expensive wine on the list), twenty-one sherries, eleven Hocks, fourteen Moselles, and seventeen Champagnes, including Moët et Chandon (66/- the case) and Pommery et Greno sec (100/- the case).

The twelve brandies listed ranged in price from 48/- to 250/- the case, the latter for a Cognac from the 1836 vintage. The Famous Grouse was given prominence, with discounts for large orders placed direct with the firm, and a 'special offer' for bulk purchases in five, ten or twenty-gallon casks. There were no additions to the whisky list, with The

Glenlivet 1892 continuing to be the most expensive.

Willie did not allow the death of his father in November 1912 to upset his planned Christmas promotion. A postcard was sent to customers headed 'The Famous Grouse Brand for Christmas Presents', with the forthright declaration:

There is no better whisky than the Grouse Brand. It is delicate in flavour and the cream of the finest Highland and Old Grain Whiskies, matured by long age in bond. It is guaranteed to be over eight years old, but as a matter of fact it is nearly ten. It represents the very best value for money that it is possible to supply.

The price was 6/- (30p) the bottle or £6 for a five-gallon cask, carriage paid. Supporting literature, published earlier that year, advertised Balmenach-Glenlivet 1897, 'unblended Old Highland Whisky' at 4/6 a bottle and a thirteen year old Cambus, 'Pure, Unblended Old Grain Whisky' at 4/- the bottle. It is interesting to see that Grouse, a blended whisky, was more costly than 'Old Highland' malt.

Such tactics increased trade from discerning drinkers of good wines and spirits throughout the British Isles. Orders were often small and infrequent: typical was a Mrs Campbell of Lyme Park, Disley, Cheshire, who sent for two gallons of Grouse in September 1911, followed by a dozen and a half bottles of Madeira in December, but did not place another order until Christmas 1912, when she requested that a case of The Famous Grouse be sent to a friend. Heartened by the recovery in demand for whisky, Willie issued a new price list, repeating his father's business philosophy from *Notes on Whisky*.

During 1913 he introduced another 'special offer': a free bottle of 'Hennessy Vintage 1893 Liqueur Cognac' for every case of whisky ordered and adding a postscript to each letter saying 'Grouse is the whisky we use at home and personally prefer for all purposes to any other'.

Realising that he could not keep up this level of trading single-handed, Willie invited his younger brother, Alistair, to join him in the family business.

He was immediately sent to Bordeaux to learn about wine-making from the Calvets. The bundle of letters in the archive from Alastair reveal his progress, not only in understanding wine-making and 'the preservation and care of wine', but also in wine tasting—'I am onto racking white wines and tomorrow I am to have a morning tasting white wines (most interesting)', visiting châteaux—and learning French from his landlord in the Rue Narjac, 'who is a professor at some college'.

Alastair was made very welcome by the Calvet family, and they were clearly very friendly with Willie (in an April letter Alastair tells his brother that M. Jean Calvet would be in Perth in a few days time: 'I told him that you would expect him to stay the weekend'). Almost every letter reports lunch or dinner with either Jean or George Calvet; on 5th May he writes:

I had dinner with M. George Calvet last evening and enjoyed it very much. Seven courses and five wines. I was not sure whether I would be able to stand after dinner. I went home singing: he is awfully kind, so is Mrs C.

Alastair had been specifically asked by his brother to buy as many sherry butts as he could find for the maturation of whisky, and he began searching as soon as he arrived in April. On 19th April he writes:

I have made enquiries about sherry butts and I think they will be very difficult to get anywhere… I went to see [an Englishman, who is in the cask business] and

he told me they were very hard to get and that there was a tremendous demand for them. One time before to get them and he only collected 6 in 12 months. The first ones cannot have been very fresh: he says he will let me know if he hears of any.

On 21st April:

If sherry hogsheads are any use to you I can get you 20 and perhaps a few more at 25f [£1] each. Please let me know by return if you want them because they will be sold. If you should want them I understand they are fresh emptied. It is the Chief Maître who has found them for me.

On 25th April:

I have followed out your instructions and Mr Manderfield was good enough to accompany me to see the casks this morning. They seem quite nice strong casks, branded 'A. Sancho, Xeres'. I think they are all Amontillado but there are no scribe marks that we could see.

On 11th May:

I saw your casks on the quay yesterday. They do not look anything wonderful but I hope you will be pleased with them. Two of them look as if they had been leaking a little round the edge of the flat and had a bit of straw caulked in, but the others seem very sound. The wood looks very good where they have scraped the cask for the MG&S [i.e. Matthew Gloag & Son]. *It is one thing to see them in the cellar and another in broad daylight. I am enclosing a small circular on 'Sanchos'. I have not the least doubt that they are genuine sherry casks.*

The demand for ex-sherry casks, and the paucity of supply, led to a—sometimes dubious—specialist trade in used casks from outside Spain. Alastair writes on 8th June:

I am glad they [the casks] *are satisfactory, the only reason I doubted them was because I thought they were too many and too cheap. When whisky began to boom and there was a demand for sherry casks there was (and is) a man called Mc … something who was a carter in Glasgow who could not even write his name but who made his fortune dealing in casks.*

He continued to seek out casks until his return

Opposite: A Spanish bodega. The sherry casks Alastair and Willie were looking for were not 'ex-solera'—they will not have been used to mature the sherry—they are 'transport casks', used to ship the fortified wine, which, of course, was made in Andalusia, Spain. Until about 1960 American oak was favoured for transport casks, and after this Spanish oak. We have seen that since the 1860s 'sherry wood' had been highly esteemed for maturing Scotch whisky, and there were plenty of transport casks arriving in the U.K. to supply the demand from distillers and blenders, many of whom were discovering the benefits of maturation for the first time. During the 1860s, Britain was importing eighty-seven per cent of Spain's total sherry production. Until the mid-1870s the number of casks being imported continued to rise, from just under 250,000 butts (1860–65) to 350,000 butts (1870–75), but after 1870 the market for sherry began to shrink. Between 1880 and 1885, the number of butts arriving and available to the whisky industry was 150,000— just at the time when quality blended Scotch was taking off. So it is not surprising that the Gloags were having difficulty in sourcing good ex-sherry casks to keep up the quality of their whiskies.

to Perth in October, but his main activity, apart from working in Calvet's cellars, was visiting châteaux all over the Bordeaux and Burgundy regions, recommending wines that Gloag's might buy, and, in July, to Cognac. A typically enthusiastic letter dated 23rd July reads:

I am very busy. I was at Cognac Friday and Saturday, Sunday Royan, took a boat across the Gironde to Point de Grave and from there to Lesparre where I spent two days with a broker going all over the Bas Médoc and tomorrow morning I am off to St Emilion till about Sat'y. Things are on the move.

They were most awfully kind to me at Cognac and taught me all about eau de vie and tasting. I tasted about 30 different Cognacs, all in about an hour, specially arranged for me, first plain then with some water. I would very much like if you could do business with them. This place is very nice and well kept. I try not to be indebted to any one but they at Cognac drove me everywhere. Paid my hotel, lunched and dined with me all the time. Champagne and Cognac (108 years old)—I pinched a sample bottle and I am going to compare it with yours when I get home. I learned a lot and am going to go back at the vintage.

He goes on, significantly:

I am beginning to understand the wine business here and the more I understand the more I see the faults both with the peasants, brokers and merchants. When you can get through about 100 casks of claret a year it will be worth your while to buy direct from the owner of the property without broker or merchant. I will be able to tell you lots of things when I get home, but perhaps you already know as much as I do.

A scandal he mentioned the previous month may well have influenced the above advice. On 30th June he wrote:

There is a big row on here just now, but nobody is supposed to know and nobody does know much but apparently the Maison Delure (a big firm here) [actually 'Delare', a leading firm of brokers] has been 'dickieing' the wines. Nobody knows what they have been doing exactly. They say putting [in] water and colouring and sugar, etc., but suffice that I believe he offered a big sum to the proprietors to withdraw their claims. It will perhaps be in the papers soon.

Alastair returned to Perth in the autumn of 1913 to manage the wine side of his brother's business.

When war was declared on 4th August 1914, Alastair Gloag immediately volunteered. Willie Gloag, now a captain and Commanding Officer of the Perth company, 6th (Perthshire) Battalion, The Black Watch, also volunteered to serve in Kitchener's 'New Army'.

He was posted to the 10th Battalion, The Black Watch, which was raised at the regimental depot at Queen's Barracks, Perth, in September 1914, and was commissioned on the twenty-third of that month.

The Battalion trained in various camps in England, as part of the 77th Infantry Brigade, initially in Wiltshire, then Bristol, and finally at Warminster, before being sent to France on 17th September 1915— a week before 'The Big Push': the largest battle of the war so far, around the village of Loos, which opened at 3 a.m. on 25th September.

On 5th November 1915 orders were received that the 77th Infantry Brigade, including the 10th Battalion, The Black Watch, was to be moved to Salonika, after the declaration of war on Bulgaria and at the request of the Greek prime minister. The Battalion travelled to Marseilles and sailed to Egypt,

and after a brief stop at Alexandria, continued to Salonika, arriving there on 24th November 1915.

The Salonika Force dug in until the summer of 1916, then in July the Battalion moved to Sarigol, where Willie's Company attracted the attention of the enemy and suffered outbursts of shelling. Later that summer he was appointed major, and by December was acting as the Battalion's Second-in-Command.

The most important action of the Macedonian campaign was the (first) Battle of Doiran on 8th May 1917, and here Major William Gloag played an important part, leading an attack on the enemy lines, on account of which he was mentioned in dispatches by the General Officer Commanding, Sir George Milne.

In February 1918 he was transferred to a staff post with the 26th (United States) Infantry Division in France, as ADC to Major General Gay, its Commanding Officer. In September 'The Yankee Division', as it was known, took part in the offensive at St Mihiel, on the River Meuse, then moved into position for the last major offensive of the war, at Meuse-Argonne, fought from 26th September until the Armistice on 11th November 1918.

story continued on page 128

THE BATTLE OF LOOS

BY 1915 A STALEMATE HAD BEEN REACHED ON THE WESTERN FRONT, with both the German and Allied armies dug in along a line of trenches that stretched from the Channel to Switzerland. Marshal Joffre, the Allied Commander in Chief, was determined to break the deadlock with a massive frontal assault on the German positions in Northern France, but the British High Command, led by Field Marshal Sir John French and General Sir Douglas Haig, were less enthusiastic. Ammunition was low, the British Expeditionary Force would not be at full strength until 1916, the battle ground was unsuitable and the objectives of the attack—to drive the Germans out of France—were unreasonable.

In spite of repeated requests for a change of plan and delay, the British were obliged to support their French allies and committed six army Divisions to the offensive. By the time the attacks were called off on 13th October 2,013 officers and 48,367 other ranks had been killed or wounded, with 867 officers and 21,627 other ranks missing. Casualties were particularly high among Scottish units: the 8th Battalion, The Black Watch, lost 511 officers and men on the first day alone. Nothing had been gained, and the war of attrition resumed.

Willie's 6th Battalion, recently arrived in France, was initially held in reserve. After the first assault, Haig urgently demanded of Sir John French that they be brought forward, but French delayed giving the order until 9.30 a.m. All day the Battalion moved up through shattered communication trenches full of wounded men, stretcher bearers and signals runners, and on tracks and roads full of traffic and under shellfire, arriving at the front line trench at 6 p.m. They remained at the front until, exhausted, they were withdrawn on 29th September.

Sir Douglas Haig was adamant that the opportunity to follow up the early success in the battle and break through the enemy lines had been lost because of Sir John French's mishandling of the reserves. They had arrived too late to provide the punch that was necessary. Through Lord Kitchener he obtained the resignation of the Commander in Chief and was himself appointed to the role on 10th December.

David Simpson,
piper of The Black Watch,
leads the charge at Loos,
but is killed almost immediately.

During Willie and Alastair Gloag's absence on military service, the business was managed by a 'Mr Rigg', assisted by Willie's wife, Nellie, and overseen by the firm's accountants, J. & R. Morrison & Co.

The archive tells us nothing about Mr Rigg, but he was clearly very important to Gloag's business. In a letter dated 4th November 1916, sent to Major Gloag in Salonika, Morrison's are very concerned that Mr Rigg might be drafted. He was young, unmarried and certified fit for military service; his case had been before the Military Tribunal in Perth before and he had been granted 'conditional exemption', but they were nervous that this might be revoked at any time. Mr J. Morrison reported:

The Tribunal last night dealt with your case quite exceptionally … the Chairman intimated that we should look for a substitute.
I explained could not be appointed without your authority and that if they were going to take Mr Rigg they should arrange for your having reasonable time in the Country to enable you to find someone. The Military Authorities and Tribunals are now dealing very drastically with many cases and it would be well that you advise us what to do if Mr Rigg is definitely called up.

In another letter of the same date, Mr Morrison writes that he has spoken to A.J. Cameron, Master Blender with John Dewar & Sons about a 'substitute'—an insight into how whisky firms helped one another in times of difficulty:

He will do anything he can to assist … and will let you have a man who might be as suitable as any … [a Mr Finlay] … He has poor abilities but I think thoroughly honest and very correct and attentive to his work and might be able to keep things going if matters come to a crisis.

The archive does not reveal whether or not Mr Rigg was called up and Mr Finlay employed.

These were hard times for many, but Matthew Gloag & Son's business prospered during the war years—so much so that Mr Morrison was advising, in 1917, that the firm should 'keep down sales as much as possible' to avoid the wartime Excess Profits Tax which had been introduced in December 1915 by the Finance Act, starting at fifty per cent, then ascending for seven years.

Within months of the outbreak of war it became impossible to buy French wines, and although sherries and ports continued to be shipped, the price of all imports increased rapidly. Gloag's was fortunate in having a well-stocked cellar and Mrs Gloag—not unreasonably, and in line with other wine and spirits merchants—increased her prices.

By 1918 her cheapest claret, Ch. Fromont, from the Médoc, had doubled, and 'good sherry' rose from 36/- to 78/-.

As we have seen, David Lloyd George, Chancellor of the Exchequer—and after December 1916 Prime Minister—was fanatically opposed to alcohol. In a speech at Bangor in February 1915 he claimed that munitions workers were drinking their wages and shirking their jobs: 'Drink is doing more damage in the war than all the German submarines … We have got great powers to deal with drink, and we mean to use them.'

Next month he proposed to the Cabinet that all liquor be prohibited for the duration of the war, then he proposed that the state buy up all breweries, distilleries and licensed premises—it was estimated that this would cost between £225 and £230 million, not including the distilleries! Then he considered taxing alcohol out of existence—in his late April budget he proposed that spirits duties be doubled

Matthew William Gloag.

1916. 56 gns. **NAME** The Right Hon. The Earl of Moray.
1918.   **ADDRESS** Kinfauns Castle. Near Perth

1914							1914						
Apr.	14	To Balance Brought Forward		10	13	6½	June 20	By Cash		38	2	6
"		3 dozen Talisker £7.10/- ᵛ 3 dozen Hollands £5-14/-		13	4							
"		1 Bottle Italian Vermouth 2/- ᵛ (to Kinfauns)			2							
"		2 dozen Perrier-Jouet £8-8/- ᵛ (to Doune Lodge)		8	8							
"		1 " Hollands £1-19/- ᵛ 1 dozen Perrier-Jouet £4-4/-		6	2							
"		1 " ½ Bottles Perrier-Jouet £2-4-6 (to Donibristle)		2	4	6						
April	21	1 Track Double Aum 10/- to Kinfauns			10		1914 April 30	By Cash		1	10	-
"	24	1 Empty Port Pipe 20/-		1	"		June 5	" Cash			10	-
June	4	1 " Double Track Aum			10		"	" Balance		2	11	6½
"	20	Balance		2	11	6½	Sept. 21	By Cash	½	6	6	6½
July	15	1 dozen Niersteiner Riesling 34/- 2 dozen ½ Bottles Do 3 15 (6641)		3	15							
Sept.	21	6 bottles unsweetened Gin		1	-	6	1915 Jan. 14	By Cash		4	4	-
Nov.	24	12 x ½ Bottles Nuits St. Georges 19/6 8 Bottles Do. 24/-		2	3	6						
"		4 Bottles Cockburns 1900 20/- (7244)		1								
1915 Jan.	28	1 dozen Nuits St. Georges 36/- 12 x ½ Bots Do. 19/6		2	15	6	" 31	By Balance		4	5	6
"		½ " Cockburns 1900 Port 30/- 60/- (7693)		1	10							
"	31	To Balance		4	5	6	Apr. 12	By Cash		4	5	6
May	7	Gray House :- 4 + 3 dozen cases 10/-			10			" Balance				
"		1 Gross Straw Envelopes 2/3 ᵛ carriage 1/-			3	3		Cart. Forwd.		2	2	6
"		Time & expenses of man 10/-			10							
"		Dramaway Castle :- 3+1 dozen cases 4/6			4	6						
"		3 dozen Wine quarts 4/6 ᵛ 50 Wine Corks 2/-			6	6						
"		Wine Cork presser 5/3 ᵛ 3 dozen straws 6d wax 6d			6	3						
"		carriage & postage 2/-			2							

and those on wine quadrupled, but was obliged to back down on account of adamant opposition from the Irish M.P.s, who held the balance of power in the House of Commons.

In the end he had to make do with the Immature Spirits Act, which required that whisky be matured for at least two years (increased to three years in 1916), a measure which had the support of the whisky industry. Lloyd George wrote in his memoirs:

One by one I was compelled to abandon, for the time being, these proposed taxes, and could only retain one insignificant but quite useful little restriction in the shape of a prohibition on the sale of spirits less than three years old, the object being to prohibit the newer and more fiery spirit.

In 1915 Lloyd George set up the Central Control Board (Liquor Traffic), under the chairmanship of The Viscount D'Abernon, with wide powers to meddle in the 'Drink Trade', as he called it.

Among many other measures, in 1915 the Control Board directed that whisky could be sold at strengths down to 65° Proof (37.2% ABV)—50° Proof (28.5% ABV) in munitions areas—and could

not be sold at above 75° Proof (42.9% ABV). At these low strengths the liquid becomes hazy. As the Government chemist reported:

Practically every self whisky [i.e. single malt/grain], *and particularly every malt whisky, becomes opalescent or cloudy when reduced even to the old limit of 25° under Proof* [i.e. 42.6%. Most whisky was bottled at 46% or above]—*that the defect was inherent in the whisky, that it was got rid of with extreme difficulty, and in some cases not at all, and that it increased with increase of dilution.*

The Wine and Spirits Brands Association also found that:

the successive filtrations necessary to secure bright spirit have the result of very materially destroying the characteristic flavours upon which the reputation of the several brands has been built up.

At first the Control Board was persuaded to fix the bottling strength at 75° Proof (in 1916), but this was reduced to 70° (40% ABV) in January 1917. This is still the commonest strength at which whisky is sold.

story continued on page 136

Left:
Gloag's made a special offer of
'our fine Whiskies in casks, sent carriage
paid, complete with nickel-plated tap,
and the cask bored half-way up,
so that it can be always kept half-full.'

Opposite, top:
15th December 1923:
Country Life *endorsed the idea*
of buying a cask and keeping it topped up.

Opposite, below:
A 1923 advertisement.
Gloag's were not alone in
continuing to sell by the cask
during the 1920s.
Happy days, when whisky cost
70/- per gallon
[£3.50p per 4.5 litres]!

MAKING GOOD WHISKY BETTER.

Many of the people who know that wine matured in cask goes on improving after it is bottled are not aware that in spirits once bottled no appreciable improvement takes place. Messrs. Matthew Gloag and Son of Perth, for this reason, recommend their customers to purchase their well known "Grouse" Brand whisky in small casks of convenient size, which effects a saving of some shillings a gallon in cost. The cask should be kept at least half full, and the old whisky which will thus always remain in the cask plays an astonishing part in improving the supply added. Messrs. Gloag have been established for over a hundred years, and their advice as to how to make good whisky better is only part of the policy of quality-before-everything which they have always maintained.

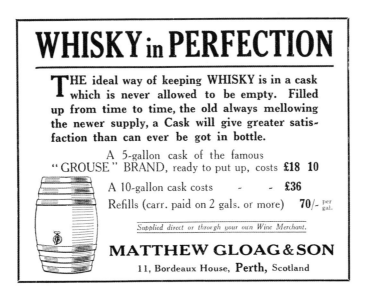

WHISKY in PERFECTION

THE ideal way of keeping WHISKY is in a cask which is never allowed to be empty. Filled up from time to time, the old always mellowing the newer supply, a Cask will give greater satisfaction than can ever be got in bottle.

A 5-gallon cask of the famous "GROUSE" BRAND, ready to put up, costs £18 10

A 10-gallon cask costs - - £36

Refills (carr. paid on 2 gals. or more) 70/- per gal.

Supplied direct or through your own Wine Merchant.

MATTHEW GLOAG & SON
11, Bordeaux House, **Perth**, Scotland

The Viscount d'Abernon of Esher's caricature by 'Spy' (Leslie Ward) in Vanity Fair *on the 20th April 1899, captioned 'Eastern Finance'.*

'An upper class drifter, who had been everything from a dragoman at Istanbul, to a Guards Officer, to a Conservative candidate and a Liberal candidate, as both of which he was rejected by the electorate' (Ross Wilson).

He was also a dedicated teetotaller and published Alcohol—Its Action on the Human Organism *in 1918.*

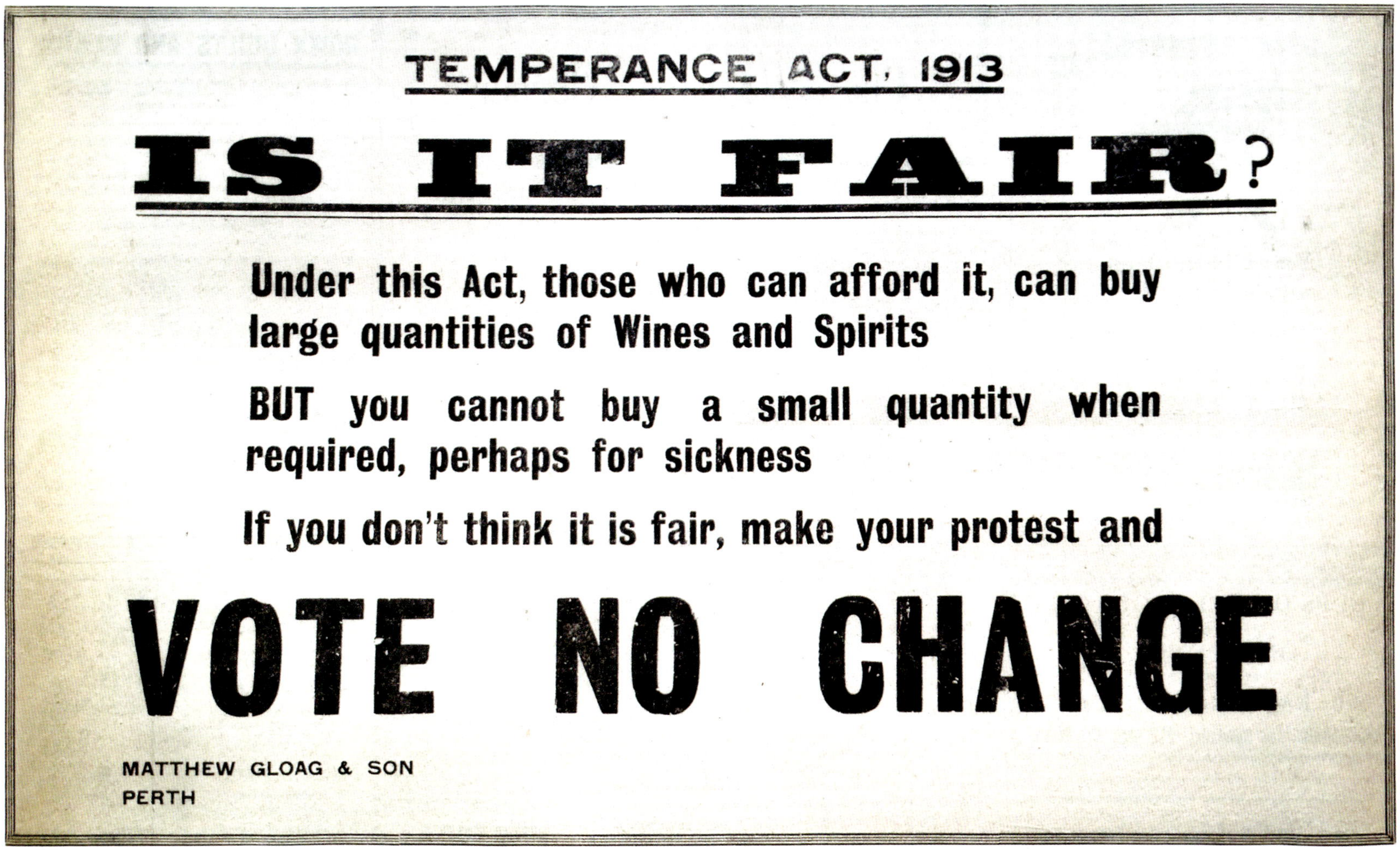

TEMPERANCE ACT. 1913

IS IT FAIR?

Under this Act, those who can afford it, can buy large quantities of Wines and Spirits

BUT you cannot buy a small quantity when required, perhaps for sickness

If you don't think it is fair, make your protest and

VOTE NO CHANGE

MATTHEW GLOAG & SON
PERTH

The Temperance (Scotland) Act 1913 entitled voters in small local areas to hold a poll on whether alcohol should be 'permitted' or 'prohibited' in their area, by a simple majority of votes cast.

In 1916 the Board also prohibited distilling which was not licensed by the Ministry of Munitions, required pot-still production to be no more than seventy per cent of the average of the previous five years and prohibited grain distillers from making whisky—all their spirit had to be for munitions.

In 1917 releases of whisky to the home trade were limited to fifty per cent of what it had been in 1916 and pot-still production was banned.

All this 'meddling' increased the price of Scotch—during 1917 it quadrupled (to 80/- a gallon). The price of a dozen bottles of The Famous Grouse rose from 48/- in 1914 to 60/- in 1916 to £108/- in 1918, at which time all Gloag's whiskies were offered at this price. In spite of these increases, business was good, especially from pre-war customers now serving in the armed forces, who recommended their favourite brand to their brother officers and messes, encouraging them to order direct.

The firm abandoned the sale of single whiskies, but continued to lay down stocks for blending: large amounts of new-make grain whisky (from Caledonian, Cambus, Carsebridge and Cameron Bridge distilleries) and smaller quantities of The Glenlivet, Glen Rothes, Glendronach, Cragganmore and Highland Park.

The cover of the 1923 list.

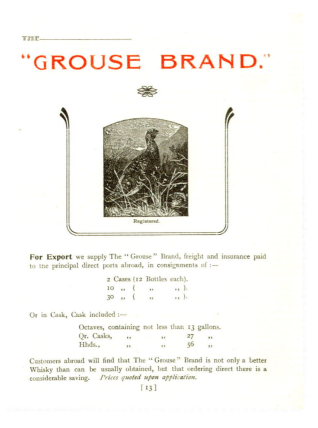

From Matthew Gloag's 1917 price list.

As we have seen, in 1917 Willie Gloag's accountant was advising that profits be reined in to avoid tax: although volume sales had declined, profits had exceeded £14,000—an unprecedented achievement. During the following year profits were held in check and finished at less than £700.

Upon his return from war in 1919, Willie was determined to enlarge the business and take advantage of the expected boom in the economy; that year he invested over £14,000 in wines and spirits, of which £4,000 was used to replace stock lost in a fire. Sales were now almost three times their pre-war level, at £32,000, and profits advanced to £6,500. This remarkable performance, accomplished with little advertising, reflected the loyalty of the firm's customers, nearly all of whom received their orders by rail or post.

This level of business was sustained into the 1920s, when an effort was made to establish the firm's own-label port, Conquistador, nationally, alongside The Famous Grouse. At the same time, the extensive pre-war wine list was reduced—only four clarets were offered, five Burgundies, a Barsac, a Sauternes, a Graves and four Champagnes, but no German wine. This reflected the problems of supply,

ARE YOU A JUDGE OF GOOD WHISKY

How do you judge good whisky? By its purity, lightness, its delicate appeal to the palate. No biting tang. No crude roughness to trouble the throat. Just a smooth, stimulating drink that connoisseurs and doctors too, with confidence, recommend — that's the standard set by "Grouse" Brand Whisky.

Ask for it from your wine merchant, but if difficult to obtain send **25/-** to Matthew Gloag & Son, Perth, for 2 bottles for trial, post free.

GROUSE WHISKY
Matthew Gloag & Son, Perth

Obtainable abroad from :—

S. RHODESIA - The "GROUSE" Agency, Box 678, Salisbury.
KENYA - - Jardin, Phipson & Co., Ld. Nairobi & Mombasa.
Etc.

GIBRALTAR M. Baglietto.
JAMAICA - H. M. Kalphat, Kingston.
BERMUDA - J. E. Lightbourn & Co., Hamilton.
Etc.

since the French trade had been severely dislocated by the hostilities and prices were unattractive.

Two Australian wines, sold under the Aussie brand name, were featured prominently, but priority was given to The Famous Grouse, which Professor Oram considers a decisive shift in Gloag's business away from wine.

It would be a rocky road. As he had privately promised, Lloyd George, still Prime Minister (until 1922), began to increase duty. Excise duty had remained at 14/9 per proof gallon since 1909. In the spring of 1918, with the end of the war in sight, Bonar Law, the Chancellor of the Exchequer, doubled it to 30/-, so the price of a standard bottle was now 9/- (40p). The price hike did not affect the industry immediately, since the restrictions on the amount of whisky which could be released to the home trade were partially relaxed and home consumption increased slightly.

Encouraged by this, Austen Chamberlain, Bonar Law's successor, raised duty to 50/- in 1919 and prohibited the whisky trade from passing the whole increase on to the consumer by fixing the price of a bottle at 12/- (60p). Again the pill was sweetened by home trade clearances being further eased to

seventy-five per cent of what they were in 1916, and again consumption increased.

In July 1920 Chamberlain again 'returned to the docile cow for a further augmentation this year of 22/6 per gallon', in the words of William Ross, Managing Director of the Distillers Company. Now duty stood at 72/6 per gallon, and the price of a bottle of Scotch at 12/6 (62½p), almost three times what it had been in 1914, giving rise to the well-known music-hall song by Will Fyffe:

Twelve an' a tanner a bottle,
That's what it's costing today;
Twelve an' a tanner a bottle—
Man, it taks a' the pleasure away.
Before you can hae a wee drappie
You have to spend a' that ye've got—
How can a fella be happy,
When happiness costs such a lot.

Gloag's middle-class customers were not as badly affected by the price rise as the average music-hall visitor, and sales of The Famous Grouse continued to climb, supported by imaginative promotions aimed at appealing to changing drinking fashions—such as

story continued on page 144

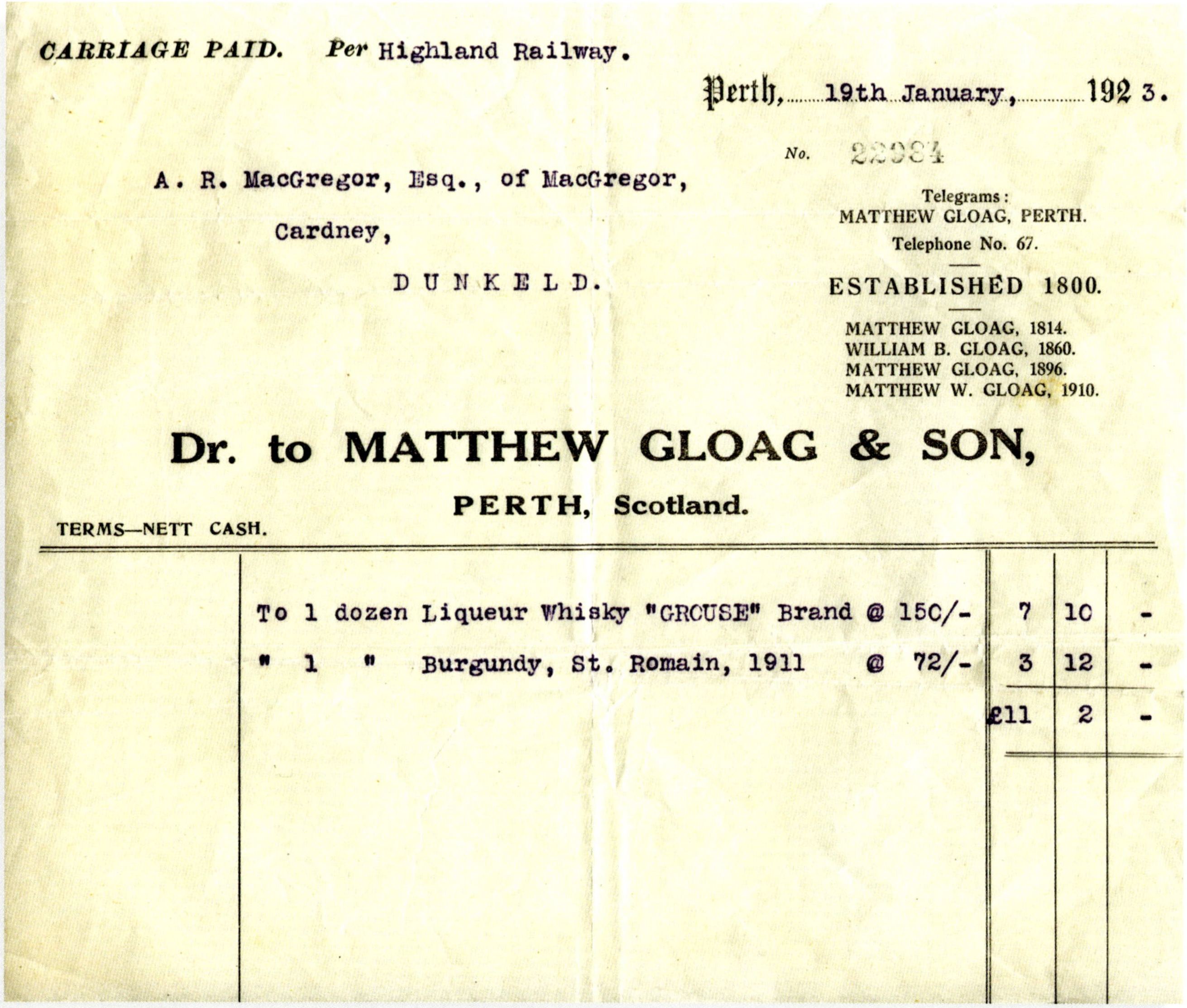

CARRIAGE PAID.   Per Highland Railway.

Perth, 19th January, 1923.

No. 22984

Telegrams :
MATTHEW GLOAG, PERTH.
Telephone No. 67.

A. R. MacGregor, Esq., of MacGregor,

Cardney,

DUNKELD.

ESTABLISHED 1800.

MATTHEW GLOAG, 1814.
WILLIAM B. GLOAG, 1860.
MATTHEW GLOAG, 1896.
MATTHEW W. GLOAG, 1910.

Dr. to MATTHEW GLOAG & SON,

PERTH, Scotland.

TERMS—NETT CASH.

	£	s	d
To 1 dozen Liqueur Whisky "GROUSE" Brand @ 150/-	7	10	-
" 1 " Burgundy, St. Romain, 1911 @ 72/-	3	12	-
	£11	2	-

'Twelve and a tanner a bottle' [12/6d or 51.5p]

A 1930 advertisement.

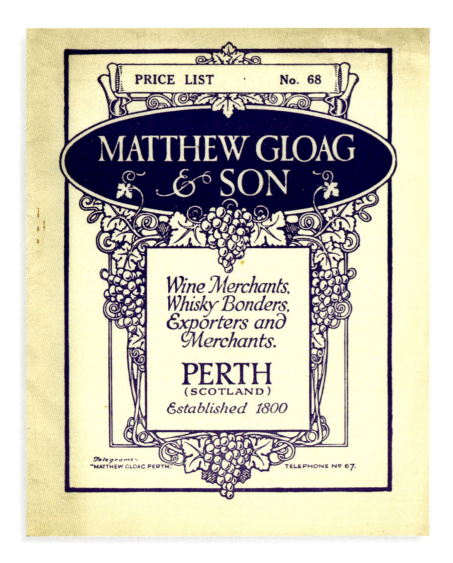

Front and back of the 1927 price list.

THE FAMOUS GROUSE BRAND

ESTABLISHED 1800

One Reason

why the "GROUSE" BRAND WHISKY is so much better than ordinary brands——Nothing but Old Scotch Whiskies of the very highest grade are allowed to enter into its composition.

Usual Strength - **150/-** per doz.
Pre-war Strength **166/-** per doz.

Obtainable either through your own Wine Merchant, or direct from

MATTHEW GLOAG & SON
11, BORDEAUX HOUSE, PERTH, SCOTLAND

An advertisement in October 1927.

1931 Matthew Gloag & Son
price list cover.

the publication in 1924 of a booket *CUPS—How to Make; Why to Take*. Casks of Grouse were reintroduced in time for Christmas 1923, at £18/10/- for a five-gallon keg (£12 more than in 1914). Perth Royal returned to the list at the end of the year, with testimonials from all over the country:

'I congratulate you on the excellent quality of the Whisky. I shall certainly recommend it to all my friends.' Wolverhampton

'Yours is the best I have tasted for a long time.' Leeds

'I consider this whisky by far the best I have tasted since pre-war days.' Weybridge

'There are hills, heather, pure air etc., here, but no Whisky to compare with yours.' Rothesay

In 1925 duty on wines produced within the Empire was lowered. Gloag's seized the opportunity to step up the promotion of Aussie Imperial Dessert Wine, with slogans like 'Buy within the Empire', 'Restores the Ailing and Puts Fresh Life into Everyone' and 'To Resist Influenza and to Keep in Vigorous Health'.

From 1st January 1920, 'the manufacture, sale, transportation, import and export of intoxicating liquors' was banned throughout the United States.

The Scotch whisky industry's initial reaction was dismay. With the high rate of taxation and the Great Depression at home, export markets were becoming increasingly important, and the fear was that the 'dry rot', as it was termed, would spread to other markets.

However, it soon became apparent that the demand for Scotch was undiminished—indeed, increased—and by making use of ports in neighbouring territories, cargoes could be brought to within striking distance of the United States. Exports to Canada, Mexico, Latin America, the West Indies (particularly the Bahamas) and the small French islands off Newfoundland, St Pierre and Miquelon, rose dramatically—and what happened to the goods after they arrived in such places was 'of no concern' to the exporters.

The other tactic employed by Willie Gloag to combat the depressed home market was to step up his export trade and expand the number of overseas agents, rather than rely on direct sales from Perth. This was especially necessary if the Prohibited

1931: Famous Grouse label for agents in Malta.

market of the United States was to be supplied, and he appointed new agents in Canada, Trinidad and Jamaica. Agencies were also established in places like Malta, Shanghai and Tientsin, to meet the needs of ex-pat communities.

The promotional cards issued to such agents

story continued on page 150

CUPS

How to Make, Why to Take
With Something about a few Appetisers & Other Matters

by

W. TEIGNMOUTH SHORE
author of "Charles Dickens & His Friends,"
"My Cook Book," etc.

PUBLISHED BY

MATTHEW GLOAG & SON
PERTH, SCOTLAND

CUPS

SITTING under the trees in the garden, watching the energetic folk playing tennis or while waiting for a game; in the golf club-house; after making a century or while admiring some other batsman doing so; up the river on a sunshiny afternoon; at a picnic—what is more soothing, comforting and cooling than a well-made CUP? It cheers the heart, refreshes the body, stimulates conversation, and does no manner of harm. And remember:

> "There are five reasons why men drink:
> Good wine, a friend, because I'm dry,
> Or least I should be by and by,
> Or any other reason why."

But there are Cups and Cups; good, bad and indifferent. The only worthy Cup is the Good Cup. Away with all others! Don't insult yourself or your friends with any but the best. What's worth making at all is worth making well; otherways it's worthless.

THE RIGHT WAY

The right way to make a worthy Cup is to use the right ingredients and the proper quantities; and to take pains. Otherwise pains may come after drinking it! Only too many people offend their friends' palates and tempers with, say, Claret Cup which is made just anyhow and of anything. It is not necessary, indeed it is little short of crime, to use a vintage Château claret for a Cup; but what you do put in should be sound stuff, not "swipes"! So, also, with every ingredient in every Cup. Be good, and you'll be happy! And don't mix your Cup a minute or two before you're going to drink it; if you do so the various flavours will not have amalgamated or, so to speak, matured; no, take time as well as pains.

Most Cups should be concocted at least an hour before they are swallowed. Remember this, however, if you put in any cucumber peel—an abomination in a Cup, *I* think—pick it out after ten minutes or so, or you will *bitterly* rue it! This also, don't be too lavish with your sugar. Be as sweet as you like, of course, but not too sweet, or you will be cloying. The object of a Cup is to refresh and allay thirst; a sugary drink will not do either.

Then there is the mightily important question of temperature. Rule one—never put ice into a Cup; put your jug, or other vessel, into ice, or set it in a cellar cool. Rule two—don't make your Cup icy cold, thereby destroying its flavour. *Cups should be drunk cool*, then they are tasty and really refreshing. If you have no ice, wrap the jug in a damp cloth and set it in a shady place and a draught; that'll do it. If you are going to drink your Cup at dinner or at supper, its temperature should be just a few degrees lower than that of the dining-room, no more. All this sounds like heresy; it isn't, it's orthodoxy. Only those who don't value beautiful flavours make their Cup—or wines— icy cold.

Straws are as a rule to be avoided; you don't want to spray the back of your throat, that's not where you *taste* a drink; I'm even eccentric enough to imbibe a Cocktail without a straw. But I admit that to straw or not to straw is to a certain extent a matter of personal taste.

So, if you'll take advice, or if you are already a complete Cup maker, we can sing with rare Ben Johnson

> " *Nor shall our cups make any guilty men;*
> *But at our parting, we will be, as when*
> *We innocently met.*"

Or perhaps you will prefer the advice of Master Abraham Cowley :

> " *Fill up the Bowl then, fill it high—*
> *Fill all the Glasses there ; for why*
> *Should every Creature Drink but I?*
> *Why, Men of Morals, tell me why?*"

THIS LITTLE BOOK

The object of this little book is both to help those who do not know and to make the knowers even more knowing. It mainly consists of well-tried recipes for Cups and other entertaining and profitable quenchers ; some for mere males, some for the ladies, some for the children ; a few for all three—in moderation and discretion. All said and drunk, is not discretion the better part of drinking? In moderation,

> "*Drinking makes wise, but dry fasting makes glum.*"

As for the right occasion do we not read in Don Quixote :

> " *I drink when I have occasion,*
> *And sometimes when I have no occasion*"?

It is not so much the " when " as the " what," so let us :

" *Drink down all unkindness,*" as is said in *The Merry Wives of Windsor.*

A Cup of Sack, so beloved by Sir John, is not recommended, but here follow some Cups that " meet the occasion.". Take your choice.

CUPS

How can a Cup be defined? I know not and the dictionary helpeth not. One which I consulted gave the illuminating information that a Cup is the liquor contained in a cup or drinking

7th July 1931: advertising sketches by F. Wilson, 101 Hatton Garden, London.

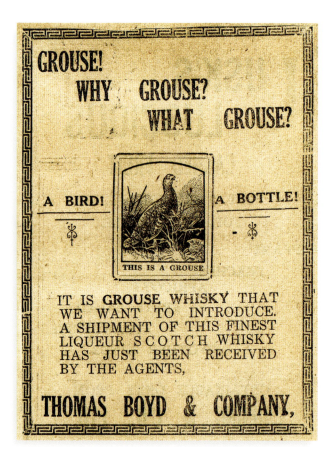

A charming advertisement

from Trinidad.

boldly declared 'There is No Finer Whisky Available' and claimed that Grouse was 'specially suited for the Tropics'. Thomas Boyd of Port of Spain, Trinidad, ran a cheeky newspaper campaign in October and November 1930 with the headline:

GROUSE! Why Grouse? What Grouse? A Bird! A Bottle! When you can get a Drink of the Now Famous Grouse Whisky it's nothing short of An American Tragedy for any man, young or old not to look happy!

About the same time, H.M. Kalphat, the agent in Kingston, Jamaica, ran a print campaign under the headline: 'Mellow as a Night of Love', and with the strapline: 'One Grouse and you want No Other'! So successful was this that in early January 1931, supplies of Grouse ran out. Mr Kalphat gained considerable further publicity by chartering a plane to fly in supplies from Black River, eighty miles away.

The collapse of the New York Stock Market in October 1929 precipitated the largest global economic depression of the twentieth century. Between 1929 and 1933 Britain's world trade was halved, the output of heavy industry (the backbone of the British economy) fell by a third and at the

story continued on page 155

GLOAG'S "GROUSE" WHISKY BY AIR.

QUICK WORK IN THE WEST INDIES.

The Only Way.

The Air Way.

To overcome a temporary shortage in Kingston, Jamaica, this aeroplane flew to Black River and back, 180 miles in less than two hours, bringing fresh supplies of "Grouse" Whisky. 3rd January, 1931.

L. to r. :—Capt. HOLLAND, Mr. H. M. KALPHAT, Major G. E. BEDFORTH, Mr. C. S. MORRISON,
Pilot.　"Grouse" Agent.　of Matthew Gloag & Son, Perth.　Solicitor, Kingston.

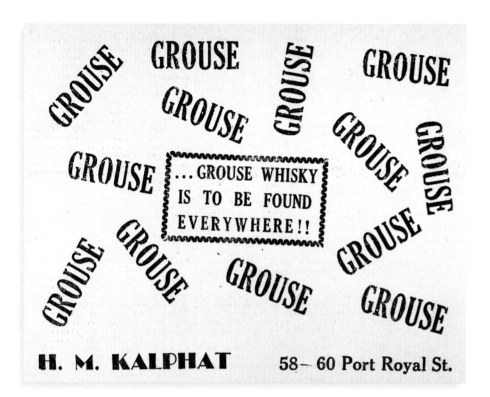

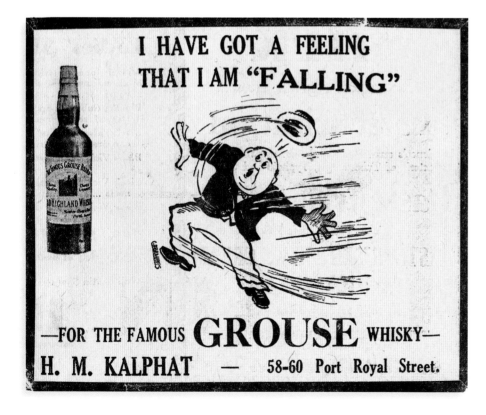

A MELLOW LIQUEUR HIGHLAND WHISKY

"GROUSE" BRAND "GROUSE" BRAND

M. GLOAG & SON   PERTH, SCOTLAND

A GAME BIRD   A GAME WHISKY

SUPPLIERS

"GROUSE" BRAND   "GROUSE" BRAND

H. M. Kalphat — 60 Port Royal St.
Kingston.

Hilton & Hilton .... Montego Bay
Hendriks & Co. .... Black River
E. L. Delvaille .... Sav-La-Mar

...THE MAN OF THE MOMENT
IS NONE OTHER THAN THE FAMOUS MR. "GROUSE"

"I Am Always In The
Very Best Of Company
They Take Me Up For
What They Can Get
Out Of Me;
Am I Swell-Headed?
I Should Say So—
I Can't Keep My Cap On"

TEL. No. 3065
H. M. KALPHAT
58-60 Port Royal St.

"GROUSE"

"GROUSE WHISKY"

A bird famed in English literature for the sport
it provides to the marksman. Found on the
Scottish moors, and in desolate marshes in the
North of England.

Famous in all the leading hotels and clubs everywhere for its smoothness. Made in Scotland,
sold all over the world, yet within every man's
reach.

Obtain your supplies from:—

H. M. KALPHAT, 60 Port Royal Street, Kingston.

Hope & Co.,   Morant Bay.
Hylton & Hylton,   Montego Bay.
Hendricks & Co.,   Black River.
E. L. Delvaille,   Sav-La-Mar.

JUST ONE DRINK
.....that's all it needs to make YOU a new man.

ONE DRINK —— THAT'S ALL.

GROUSE  WHISKY

NEEDS.

One drink will transform you into a new man — full of vitality, and
power—But like every good thing in life—it must be kept up.
DRINK "GROUSE" WHISKY ALWAYS—AND BE A "NEW MAN."

H. M. KALPHAT,
58–60 Port Royal Street.

— Also Supplied by:—
HILTON & HILTON ......Black River   HOPE & CO. ....Morant Bay
HENDRICKS & CO. ....Montego Bay   E. L. Delvalli..................Sav-La-Mar

deepest point of what became known as the Great Depression, in the summer of 1932, registered unemployment reached 3.5 million, and many more had only part-time employment. In the industrial areas of the North of England, Scotland, Wales and Northern Ireland, seventy per cent of the population were out of work.

Willie Gloag continued to advertise Grouse, and during 1931 introduced Pintail to meet the surprising increase in demand for sherry. Between 1927 and 1933 sherry exports increased by fifty per cent (to 100,000 hectolitres)—the majority to the U.K.

In spite of Gloag's ambitious efforts to hold sales, in 1931 the firm recorded its first loss since 1897.

The setback was temporary, however, and the abandonment of the Gold Standard in September 1931 made it easier for exporters (the Gold Standard had been restored in 1925, leading to an exchange rate of $4.86 to the pound; now it fell to $3.40) and laid the ground for gradual economic recovery.

In 1933 Prohibition in the United States was at last repealed. Probably in preparation for this, Willie Gloag employed an export manager for the first time—a man who would play an important part in the success of the firm in years to come, Charles

A 1935 promotion.

story continued on page 158

The Bodega at Jerez, where "PINTAIL" Sherry is matured.

"FOR THE GUEST THE BEST"

Spain has one product that she offers to the world, supreme of its kind—a pale, dry, exquisite Sherry.

You cannot be wrong in offering a glass of "PINTAIL" to your guest for the little "11 o'clock" and before or after meals. He will certainly appreciate your good taste

6/-

Per Bottle

Pintail
A FINE **SHERRY** DRY

SHERRY

versus

COCKTAIL

Sherry is more and more recognised as a much more healthful appetiser than the Cocktail, and is equally suitable for drinking before, during, and after a meal, and it is the only Wine the flavour of which *is not adversely affected by smoking.*

6/-

Per Bottle

Pintail
A FINE **SHERRY** DRY

It is in the emptied "Pintail" casks that the famous "Grouse" Brand Whisky is matured.

May be obtained through Wine Merchants everywhere, or direct from

MATTHEW GLOAG & SON,   PERTH,   SCOTLAND.

521

A 1935 advertisement for Pintail Sherry in The Tatler.

Several factors contributed to the success of sherry during the 1920s, and particularly late in the decade. First, shippers now favoured quality over quantity. Second, the Sherry Shippers Association pursued steady generic advertising campaigns in the press. And third, the largest houses, Pedro Domecq and Gonzales Byass, abandoned the previous practice of shipping in bulk and began to market their own brands in bottle.

LAW OFFICES
JOHN S. WISE JR.
20 BROAD STREET
NEW YORK

CABLE ADDRESS
"PLOVERWISE"

June 21, 1922.

Messrs. Matthew Gloag & Son,
Perth, Scotland.

Gentlemen:

        Your most seductive catalogue
came several days ago, but having the misfortune
to live in a land where the Presbyterians

    "Compound for the sins they are inclined to
     By damning those they have no mind to."

I can't get any more of your good liquor into this
land, but will you please send a dozen bottles of
old Grouse to my friend

        John Baker,
         Kindowie,
          Boyndon Road,
           Maidenhead,
            Bucks, England,

and advise him that it is sent with my compliments,
and let me have the bill.

        Yours very truly,

        [signature]

JSW. AEP

Prohibition came into force in the U.S.A. on 1st January 1920 and lasted thirteen years.

XMAS, :: :: **1927**

OVERLEAF are a few suggestions for CHRISTMAS CASES of Wines and Whisky, at special prices, during December.

Some Sparkling Wines, and a fine Port, are offered on the back page, and enclosed is a selected list of a few very rare and choice Wines and Spirits.

Everything quoted is of our usual highest grade quality, and will give great satisfaction to recipients. Cases containing half the quantities are offered at half the prices, carriage paid.

Please order at earliest, to ensure prompt delivery. Order form is attached, and extra addresses can be written on the back of it.

MATTHEW GLOAG & SON.

BORDEAUX HOUSE,
PERTH, SCOTLAND.   *Estab. 1800.*

A reminder that wines still formed a large part of Gloag's business in the 1920s and 30s

Mactaggart, who had been trained in the London offices of Thomson McLintock, Chartered Accountants, and subsequently worked for Pullars of Perth, the well-known dyers and dry cleaners.

In the home market Willie augmented the firm's long-standing mail order system by approaching quality wine merchants and persuading them to take stock for retail sale. To this goal, he used a sales pitch which says much about the way Scotch whisky was perceived at the time:

Scotsmen the world over use it 'neat' to warm them when cold, diluted to refresh them when warm, to revive them when exhausted, as a medicine in sickness, as an aid to digestion, as a sedative for sleeplessness, and, universally, to celebrate the meeting with, or parting with, friends, confident that, used in moderation, it will suit the occasion as nothing else will do, and with nothing but good effect.

He supported his pitch to wine merchants with a new advertising campaign in magazines like *The Field* and *Country Life*, under the heading: 'No Party is Complete without Grouse Whisky', using a range of illustrations, from a shooting party on the Glorious

story continued on page 164

158

The next five pages show advertisements that appeared in Country Life *during 1933.*

The natural Complement
of a Perfect Day.

GLOAG'S
"GROUSE"
BRAND WHISKY

No party is Complete without

Gloag's "Grouse" Whisky

No party is Complete without

Gloag's "Grouse" Whisky

Twelfth to a bridge party. The advertisements listed agents in Rhodesia, Kenya, Tanganyika, Malta, Gibraltar, Trinidad, Barbados, Bermuda, Granada, Jamaica, China and Japan.

Local trade remained an important part of the business, with parcels of whisky and wine being delivered by message boys on heavy bicycles as far away as Glenfarg and Tibbermore, and by private carriers further afield. One member of staff recalled:

Mr Gloag called all the message boys 'John'. They were sort of Jacks-of-all-trades. Did all kinds of tasks—like laying and lighting [the] fire in the office, as well as deliveries and posts. That's how they all started, then moved their way up ... if they behaved themselves and got on with it.

Richard Oram interviewed Vic Scott and Jack Kidd in 1994, both of whom started as message boys (in 1929 and 1933 respectively).

Jack Kidd told him:

You started as a message boy, aged fourteen. At sixteen you started your time at a trade. As a message boy, I was paid 10/- [50p] a week and I got two bob

pocket money. And I could get the bus from Scone into Perth, go to the pictures, go and have a fish supper, a wee bottle o' lemonade and a Saturday Post 'cos we had no wireless, get the bus home and still have change out of 2/-!

In 1931 Willie introduced his son, Matthew Frederick ('Fred') Gloag, to the business, aged twenty-two. Just as he had been sent to Bordeaux at the start of his career, so Freddie was sent to stay with M. Duverne of J. Calvet et Cie in Beaune.

Unlike Willie, who thoroughly enjoyed his time in France in 1900, poor Fred was miserably homesick. M. Duverne wrote on 25th August 1931:

Mrs Olivier came to Beaune Sunday afternoon, telling me that your son, although she had tried to make his stay as agreeable as possible—was home sick and desirous to go back to Perth! His intention was categorical!
It was impossible for me to leave for Dijon as we had a customer visiting us on that very day, but I wired you at once thinking that you might give your son your instructions before his departure from Dijon....
It is true that the beginnings in a foreign country are

rather difficult and I am sorry that I could not find a more pleasant boarding house. I think that your son ought to take in Perth French lessons during a few months and it would, then, be for him less difficult to stay in France later on.

Give him my kind regards and I hope that neither you nor he shall be angry with me!

It would seem that Fred took M. Duverne's advice to heart, since he returned to Bordeaux and Calvets the following year, to lay the foundations of his knowledge of French wines.

In 1935 Charles Mactaggart made the first of many trips to the United States, with instructions from Willie to 'get to know people'. First he fostered good relations with established clients in the West Indies, then he appointed new agents in New York, the first stage in developing a nationwide agency system focused on the sales of Grouse, which was by now Gloag's principal product. On his return journey he fell victim to malaria and was hospitalised in the Dutch colony of Curaçao. During his convalescence he recruited an agent there. He preferred to travel by sea, and would never fly by night, since he believed the pilot could not see in darkness.

Sales reached a new peak of almost £110,000 in 1935, with a record profit of £11,370.

To meet the growing volume of exports, Willie Gloag planned to build a large bonded warehouse further along from Bordeaux House on the opposite side of Kinnoull Street, costing some £16,000. Before construction could begin, a church dating from 1821, a fire station belonging to Pullars of Perth, and other properties had to be demolished. When it opened in January 1936, the new bond contained the very latest plant for blending and (for the first time) semi-automated bottling. A booklet, published to mark the occasion, described it:

The frontage to Kinnoull Street is 110 feet, and the depth of the warehouse is 150 feet. Massive oak doors give entrance to the spacious Receiving Floor, where casks are examined on arrival from the distilleries. On the ground floor are the Blending Vats in which the 'Grouse' Brand is put together; at one side is a roomy electric lift for the conveyance of casks to the upper floors, and ahead is an automatic fireproof door leading to a lofty warehouse for the storage of casks. On this level also is the Bottling Compartment, white-tiled, well lighted, comfortably warmed,

story continued on page 168

BONHARD HOUSE

In 1935, sales reached a new peak of almost £110,000,
with a record profit of £11,370.
In 1936, Bonhard House was bought as the Gloags' family home
and construction of the new bond in Kinnoull Street
was begun.

and spotlessly clean. Here the 'Grouse' Brand goes through the operations of filtering, bottle filling by vacuum machine, closing (with up-to-date rolled on pilfer-proof seals), labelling, polishing, wrapping, packing, and eventual dispatch to all parts of Great Britain, and overseas.

The first manager of the bond was a Mr Japp.

[There were] great big Clydesdales, and they used to back in with the loaded up trailer, blocking the way out. Mr Japp would say 'Go', but I'd say I can't get past the horse. And he'd say it won't touch you, and I'd have to pass in front of this big Clydesdale.
Mr Japp was a nice person. He was retired for a while. He wrote with a dip pen and ink, and when he retired all his notes were thrown out, because folk thought he'd finished … and when he came back he had a job getting them … He was brought back out of retirement because his replacement got the heave.

With these excellent facilities Gloag's was well placed to take advantage of the revival in the whisky trade in the late 1930s, but the storm clouds were gathering over Europe and sales were held back over the next two years as stocks were accumulated in anticipation of the outbreak of hostilities.

It was apparent to Charles Mactaggart, with his accountant's training, that the way the firm was structured—as a partnership—was ill-suited to its increasing size. He advised Willie Gloag to convert the business into a limited liability company, spreading some of the equity around the family to reduce exposure to death duties.

Matthew Gloag & Son was registered as a limited company in April 1939, with Willie Gloag as chairman, Fred Gloag and John Wylie as directors and Charles Mactaggart as company secretary. John Wylie was a lieutenant colonel in The Black Watch during World War I, and had served in the same battalion as Willie. He had been brought into the business by Willie to manage the bonded warehouse. The capital of the company was £62,500, divided into 42,500 £1 ordinary shares and 20,000 £1 preference stock. Willie held nearly all the ordinary shares, and thus retained a clear controlling interest in the new company.

The new bonded warehouse on Kinnoull Street in 1936.

The casks came from the distilleries by rail and were carried to the bond by horse and cart.

MACKAY DECORATORS (PERTH) L^{TD}

TELEPHONE No. 227

DECORATIONS & FITMENTS
DESIGNED & CARRIED OUT
IN ANY STYLE OR PERIOD
MODERN OR HISTORIC

REGISTERED OFFICE
18 MAIN STREET PERTH

SKETCHES ESTIMATES &
SUGGESTIVE COLOUR SCHEMES
PREPARED FOR SINGLE ROOMS
OR ENTIRE BUILDINGS

Messrs. Matthew Gloag & Son,   June, 1936.
33 Kinnoull Street,
PERTH.
per Messrs. Erskine Thomson & Glass.

1935/36.
Nov/Feby. To work done on New Bonded Warehouse, as per
            estimate of 24th October, 1935.   205   7 10

            extra work done :-

            TWO VATS.
            Preparing and varnishing sides 3 coats.   3 10   -
            Preparing and oil-painting undersides 2
            coats white.   1   2   6
            Oil-painting hoops black.   12   6
            Lettering "CONTENTS. 2352 GALLONS" white and
            black outline.   18   6   6   3   6

            SMALL MOTOR.
            Cleaning and oil-painting 1 coat.   4   6

            BOTTLING ROOM.
            Cleaning and oil-painting small pump 2 coats
            red.   2   6
            Preparing, sizing and varnishing 2
            Instruction Boards.   2   6
            Preparing, staining and varnishing legs and
            sides of 4 Tables.   10   6   15   6

            OFFICE SAFE.
            Preparing and enamelling 1 coat.   7   6

            EXCISE OFFICE, MAIN OFFICES & ENTRANCE HALL.
            Preparing and varnishing 1 coat back of all
            panelling and window shelves.   4   5   6

            ALL IRON DOORS IN BOND.
            Steel-brushing and priming 1 coat.   2   9   6

                                    Carry Forward.   £219 13 10

Messrs. Matthew Gloag & Son,
Kinnoull Street,
PERTH.
3rd August, 1936.

To Erskine Thomson & Glass.
Chartered Architects.
Perth.

(PARTNERS — W. ERSKINE THOMSON, F.R.I.B.A. & J.G.L.GLASS, L.R.I.B.A.)

1934		NEW BONDED WAREHOUSE & OFFICES IN KINNOULL STREET, PERTH.	£	s	d
March.		To in terms of instructions received from Mr. W. Gloag, taking measurements and levels of ground at corner of Kinnoull Street and Union Lane, Perth; preparing Plans of the site and existing buildings to be demolished............................	10	10	0
"		Do. do. preparing sketch plans of proposed new Bonded Warehouse and Offices, cubing cost, and submitting same to Mr. Gloag for approval............			
August		Do. do. preparing completed working drawings of new Bond to sketches approved of by Mr. Gloag, comprising Plans, Elevations and Sections............			
"		Do. do. preparing copies of above Plans to submit to Excise for approval, and handing same to Mr. Gloag................................	3	3	0
Sept.	3	Do. do. issuing Schedules of Quantities for Demolition of existing Buildings, on site of new premises, to various Contractors, obtaining offers, and submitting and advising on Tenders received......			
"	17	Do. do. accepting offer of Messrs. Brand & Son for Demolition Work............................			
Nov.	20	Do./			
		Carry Forward.............	13	13	0

J. McCOWAN—116.   TELEPHONE 933.   A. GUILD—933.   April 1936.

ELECTRIC LIGHTING, HEATING
MOTORS, FANS, TELEPHONES,
BELLS and COMPLETE
COUNTRY HOUSE PLANTS.

OFFICE and SHOWROOMS
31, HIGH STREET.
(OLD SHIP CLOSE).

C.M.A. CABLES ARE
USED EXCLUSIVELY
IN ALL OUR
INSTALLATIONS

M^cCOWAN & GUILD
ELECTRICAL ENGINEER'S

THE
ELECTRICAL
CONTRACTORS
ASSOCIATION
OF
SCOTLAND

PARTNERS:
JAMES McCOWAN
ARTHUR GUILD.

31, HIGH STREET
PERTH

Messrs Erskine Thomson & Glass,
Chartered Architects,
George Street,
Perth.

1935/36.

Item	Electric Lighting and Power Installation in New Bonded Warehouse, Kinnoull Street, for Messrs M.Gloag & Son.	£	s	d
1.	Supply and erect main switchboard complete as specified.....................................Sum	15	14	3
2.	Supply and erect meter board stained and varnished to accomodate Corporation meters,............Sum		7	6
3.	Allow for tailes and meter bites.............Sum		6	6
4.	Allow for fixing all bolts, brackets etc.....Sum		5	—
5.	Allow for "earthing" main switchgear in manner specified.....................................Sum		2	6
6.	Supply and erect the following M.E.M. Dist.Boards as specified................:-			
	(a) Office Lighting. Cat.No. 154 M.P. 1 @ 26/-	1	6	—
	(b) Bond Lighting. Cat. No. 153 M.P.. 3 @ 21/-	3	3	—
	(c) Bottling, and Cooperage Lighting.Cat.No. 154 M.P.............................. 1 @ 26/-	1	6	—
	(d) Office and Rest Room Heating, two Boards. Cat. No. 156 M.P................... 2 @ 29/3d	2	18	6
	(e) Bottling and Cooperage, 230v Power, Cat.No. 158 M.P............................. 1 @ 38/6d	1	18	6
7.	Supply and erect main switch-fuses below each Dist. Board.......................... 5 @ 11/-	2	15	—
	c/ford.	30	2	9d.

40 SOUTH METHVEN STREET,

PERTH, 13th June, 1936.

To J. Nairne Campbell, F.F.S.

Surveyor.

TELEPHONE No. 831.

Messrs. Matthew Gloag & Son,
Wine & Spirit Merchants,
PERTH.

NEW BONDED WAREHOUSE & OFFICES, KINNOULL ST., PERTH.

1936.			£		
June	13.	Fee for remeasuring, pricing and making out final accounts of Mason, Brick & Synthetic Stone, Carpenter & Joiner, Steel, Plumber, Plaster & Concrete, Tile & Terrazzo, and Glazier Works, Re-inforced Concrete Floors and Fireproof Doors - 1¾% on £10,256. .. ..£	179	9	6
		Making calculations and preparing statements for 19 instalments - ⅜% on £9,290.	34	16	-
		Typing face copy and three carbon copies of final measurements - 90 pages in all. 3/3	14	12	6
			£ 228	18	-

Paid with
Thanks.

for J. Nairne Campbell

A view of the new warehouse from Kinnoull Street.

Casks arriving.

Maclennan of Lowrie's erecting a vat. Sandy Moir, the Master of Works, looks on.

The cooperage.

Taking off a blend with patent filler. A. Morrison, J. Wylie and D. McLaren.

Casks coming into the receiving floor. A. Morrison, D. McLaren and Stewart LNER.

The middle floor with bottling vat.

M.F. Gloag and Mr Sterry on the receiving floor, checking casks and testing strength on arrival.

The Bottling plant.

A busy bottling room.

Cases leaving the warehouse.

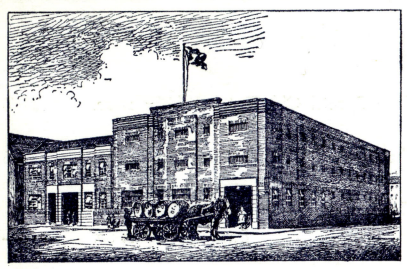

Trade price list for 1936.

MATTHEW WILLIAM GLOAG,
outside Bonhard House.

A fine gentleman … I never heard any member of staff say anything against him. He was someone we respected … On occasion I used to go to Bonhard House [his home] *when he was unwell to do some work for him. I enjoyed having lunch with his wife and him. They made me feel like I was one of the family—very nice people … He was so kind to his staff. We used to have outings to Edinburgh which he paid for. If there was a good show on in Edinburgh, he'd give my predecessor money and book seats and go and have a meal afterwards … Mr Gloag was friendly with Mr Hogarth of Delvine, who had a nine-hole golf course where we were invited to go any time we felt like it … Those were very enjoyable days. Being with Gloag's was something I enjoyed—and obviously quite a lot of people would have liked to have been employed by them.*

Mrs Fleming

[After 1942] *Mr Willie Gloag was hardly there. He was ill a lot of the time. Everyone got a bottle of whisky when he returned to work in 1947, but he died in April. He was very superstitious. Wouldn't allow anything green in the place—clothes, anything. He thought green was an unlucky colour. His chauffeur used to work in the bond when he had nothing else to do.*

Mrs Mary Gray

C. Stanley Todd. 1984

CHAPTER V

MATTHEW FREDERICK

GLOAG

(1910–1970)

Matthew Frederick Gloag and Edith (Isla) Irving on their wedding day on 3rd September 1939 the same day Britain declared war on Germany.

As had happened twenty-five years previously, war clouds were again gathering over Europe, just when the whisky industry was pulling out of the depressed years of the 1920s and early 1930s.

With the deteriorating international situation, blenders and brokers scrambled for new-make spirit and mature whisky, anticipating that distilling would be controlled when war was declared. Gloag's customers also laid in stocks of The Famous Grouse to prepare for coming shortages, and during 1939 sales of the brand reached record levels. The directors were careful to conserve their stocks, however, and as a result, when war was declared on 3rd September the company held reserves to last for an estimated twelve years.

Duty was immediately increased by 10/- a gallon, and by a further 15/- in 1940, raising the price of a bottle of standard blended Scotch from 12/6 to 16/-. In April the Ministry of Food was re-established under the direction of Lord Woolton, a prominent businessman, with the task of guaranteeing adequate nutrition for everyone. As well as introducing food (and alcohol) rationing, the Ministry ordered that whisky distilling be cut by one third.

At the same time, the government required the

Top: 12th October 1938. An advertisement on the back page of Tatler.
Below: 15th May 1937. An advertisement in The Accountant.
Opposite: 1st September 1938. An urgent need.

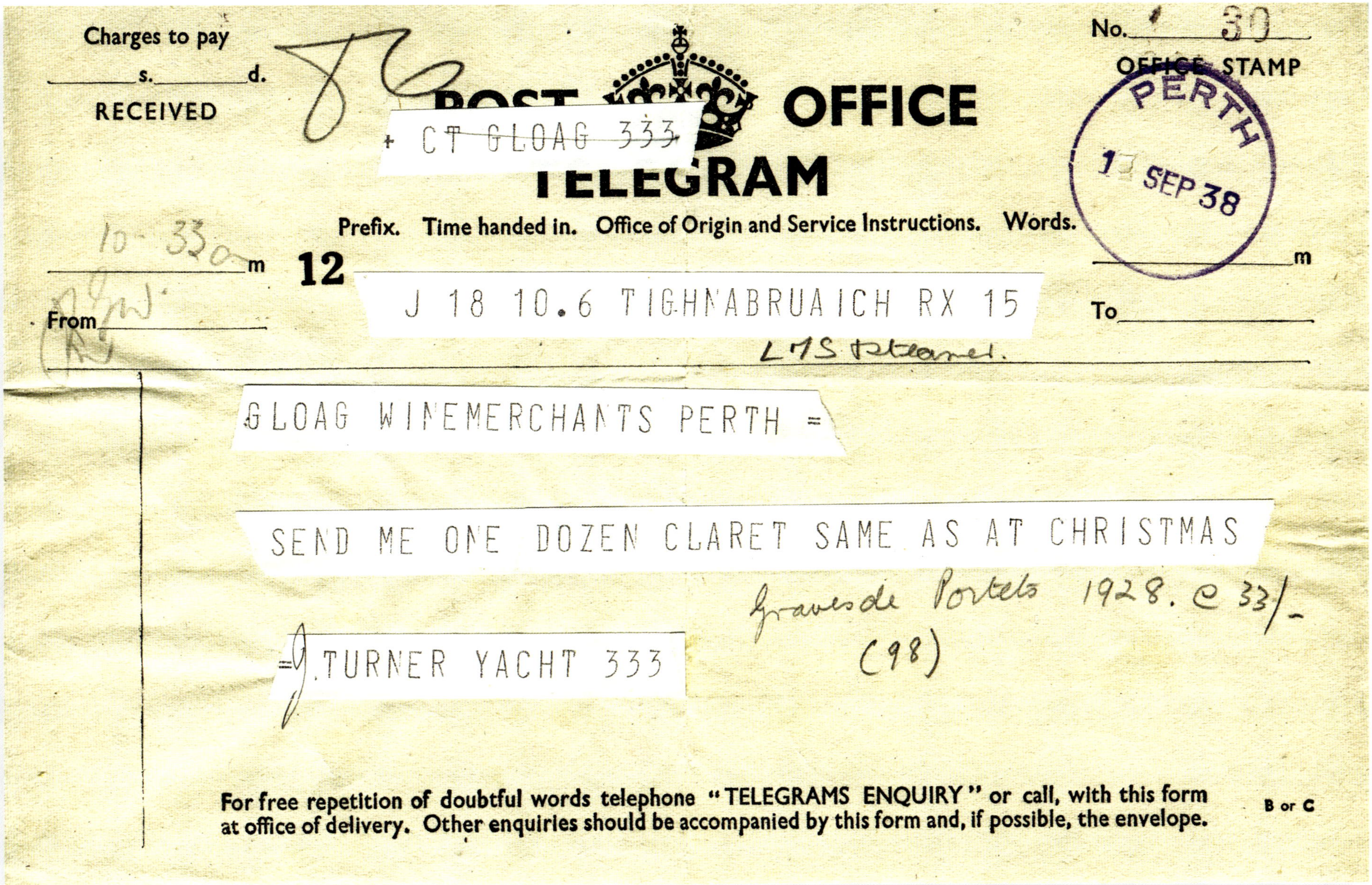

Charges to pay

____ s. ____ d.

RECEIVED

10 · 33 a.m.

From ____

POST OFFICE TELEGRAM

+ CT GLOAG 333

Prefix.   Time handed in.   Office of Origin and Service Instructions.   Words.

12

J 18 10.6 TIGHNABRUAICH RX 15

LMS steamer.

GLOAG WINEMERCHANTS PERTH =

SEND ME ONE DOZEN CLARET SAME AS AT CHRISTMAS

Graves de Portets 1928. @ 33/-

(98)

= J. TURNER YACHT 333

No. ____ 30

OFFICE STAMP

PERTH
1? SEP 38

To ____

For free repetition of doubtful words telephone "TELEGRAMS ENQUIRY" or call, with this form at office of delivery. Other enquiries should be accompanied by this form and, if possible, the envelope.

B or C

whisky industry to step up exports to the United States in order to improve Britain's dollar earnings and offset the cost of war materials purchased there. The Whisky Association immediately cut supplies to the home market by twenty per cent of the pre-war level (increased to fifty per cent in 1941). Exports to the U.S.A. increased by one-third (to seven million gallons). Matthew Gloag & Son's exports trebled during the course of the year.

During 1941 the shortage of imported grain, owing to the U-boat blockade, obliged the patent (grain) distillers to close down for the duration of the war; the number of operating malt distilleries fell to seventy-two. In October 1942 malt distilling ceased, since the Ministry of Food refused to make any barley available for distilling.

In that year's budget, duty was increased by £2 per gallon, adding sixty per cent to the price of a bottle, and when a further £1 was added the following year, the price stood at double what it had been in 1939.

Fred Gloag joined The Black Watch in May 1941, originally as an NCO, but he was commissioned 2nd Lieutenant in August. Later in the year he was injured in the London Blitz, so was seconded to the

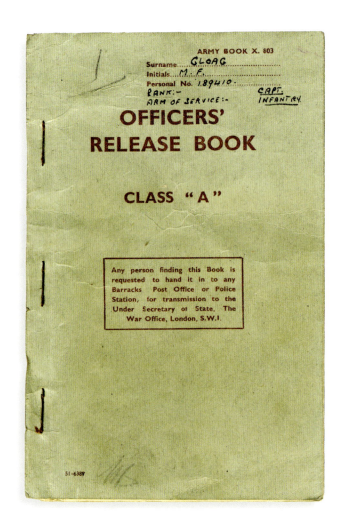

Fred Gloag's Officers' Release Book.
By 1945 he had been promoted to Captain.

Opposite: A reassuring letter to customers.

THE FAMOUS GROUSE BRAND

REGᴰ

Telegrams: 67 PERTH.   Telephone Nº 67.

MATTHEW GLOAG
& SON LIMITED

DIRECTORS:
MATTHEW W. GLOAG.   MATTHEW F. GLOAG.
JOHN WYLIE.   CHARLES D. MACTAGGART.

PERTH,
SCOTLAND.

ESTABLISHED 1800

MATTHEW GLOAG. 1814

WILLIAM B. GLOAG. 1860

MATTHEW GLOAG. 1896

MATTHEW W. GLOAG. 1910

WHISKY SUPPLIES.

As difficulties are accumulating, owing to shortage of staff and materials etc. we regret that we shall no longer be able to deal with orders to the Trade on the same scale as heretofore. But having ample supplies of Whisky, should no unfortunate occurrence overtake our stocks, we propose to supply, circumstances permitting, to our pre-war customers on the same scale as in the last pre-war year, 1st September 1938 - 31st August 1939, spaced over the year on the same lines. It may be possible to do more than this but it seems unlikely.

It will help us in keeping the flow going if customers would let us know early in the month if they desire to take up the quantity corresponding to that supplied in the corresponding month of 1938 - 1939.

Cases should be returned promptly, with senders name and address clearly marked on them.

MATTHEW GLOAG & SON LTD..

Intelligence Corps—although he was allowed to continue to wear his Black Watch insignia. On 15th November 1945 he was promoted to Acting Captain. Charles Mactaggart joined the Royal Air Force and other members of staff joined their units.

Jack Kidd (1919–2013), who started with the company as a message boy in 1933, said:

Most of the staff went off to the war, and only three men were recruited to the firm—Simpson, McNaughton and Haley—to help out.
Mr Fred was a Captain and most of the men were away at the war. Willie Hatton was paid £2 a week to be the Fire Guard on the roof, watching for bombs.

Jack enlisted as a Military Policeman. In 1940, soon after the evacuation of Dunkirk, he was captured at St Valery, along with many others from the 51st Highland Division and spent the rest of the war in a prisoner of war camp in Poland. When he was finally released at the end of 1945, he weighed just six stones.

It took him several months to get back to Perth, but when he arrived he was delighted to discover that the company had continued to pay half his wages and his National Insurance Contributions for the entire duration of the war, without knowing whether he was alive or dead. Furthermore, the jobs of all Gloag's employees who went to war were protected, so they could return to them on de-mobilisation. Jack remarked: 'When we came back from the war, we just took over where we left off, although we weren't as busy because of the shortage of spirits'.

Jack credited his survival in the POW camp to parcels of food sent in by the Red Cross, so in 1952 he joined the Red Cross. In 1984, the year after he retired after fifty years' service with Matthew Gloag and Sons/Highland Distillers, he was presented with the British Empire Medal (BEM) and in 1988 was awarded the Badge of Honour by the Red Cross.

After the war, Fred Gloag continued his involvement with the military, serving as a lieutenant and, after March 1949 captain in the Territorial Army. From February 1949 his commission was fixed for three years 'in view of this officer's medical category', which was 'B.E.—fit for base camp duties'. In August the following year he applied to be put on the T.A. Reserve List.

Shortage of staff put considerable pressure on the remaining directors, Willie Gloag and John

Wylie, and both fell ill as a result, and were obliged to work part-time. So when Charles Mactaggart was invalided out of the R.A.F. in 1942 and returned to Perth, he was soon managing the company's affairs almost single-handed.

With the restrictions on distilling, he acted quickly to confine exports to hard currency markets which would be useful at the end of the war. Despite the huge increase in the home market price, trade remained buoyant, and because of the large stocks that had been amassed prior to the outbreak of war, Gloag's was able to meet the demand from established customers throughout the conflict. Willie's prudence in accumulating stock during the late 1930s was paying dividends.

Throughout the U.K. demand far outstripped supply, and the price of mature whisky fillings soared. In 1942 the stock of a deceased dealer in Glasgow achieved an average price of £11/1 a gallon for whisky distilled in 1936 and 1937 at a cost of 5/- the gallon. By 1944 the situation was even worse: an unpublished *History of the House of Dewar* remarks:

During the course of the year limited quantities of

whisky changed hands at fantastic prices on the open market. Young whiskies were fetching up to £16 per gallon, against a pre-war price of roughly 14/-.

At an auction in Belfast in late 1944, the agents for a London nightclub paid £20/10 a gallon (plus duty of £7/17/6 per gallon) for a whisky blended in 1936.

The limited supply of Scotch to the home market led to a thriving black market. The Whisky Association (which had changed its name to the Scotch Whisky Association in 1942) assumed a remit to protect consumers by regulating retail and wholesale prices, as well as 'protecting and promoting the interests of the Scotch whisky trade'. They fixed the price of a standard bottle of Scotch at 25/9 (£1.29), but by early 1944 the black market price was four times this, and many spirits dealers were selling their rationed stocks for as much as their customers would pay.

The S.W.A. retaliated by banning wholesalers and retailers who exceeded its fixed prices from receiving stock from its members, and began to buy up any whisky which came to auction, whatever the price, selling it on to its members at the fixed price.

No whisky at all was distilled during the 1943/44 season, in spite of the industry pressing the Ministry of Food to be alert to future prospects:

We have repeatedly ... pointed out the extreme importance of our trade from a national point of view in the export markets of the world ... With stocks as they already are, well below the danger point, my members visualise great difficulties ahead in the post-war period in regaining the ground they have lost in these export markets unless matters are so arranged that stocks to meet these export demands are built up at the earliest possible moment.

Under such pressure, and with victory in sight, the government agreed in August 1944 to make a limited amount of grain available for distilling in the coming year. Thirteen grain distilleries re-opened, producing just over six million gallons of spirit during the 1944/45 season. When, in January 1945 more grain was released on the understanding that a proportion of mature stocks would be reserved for export, thirty-four malt distilleries re-opened, producing almost 3.2 million gallons during the season.

In April 1945 Prime Minister Winston Churchill—who was himself a whisky enthusiast—wrote the famous memo:

On no account reduce the barley for whisky. This takes years to mature and is an invaluable dollar producer. Having regard to all our other difficulties about export, it would be most improvident not to preserve this characteristic British element of ascendancy.

By the end of the war, as Professor Moss writes:

Scotch whisky makers had endured forty-five years of adversity ... Although the experience of this long recession in demand had halved the number of distilleries in operation, it left the industry in a strong position to meet confidently the challenge of peace-time trading.

Denied the home market by government order and high duty, the whisky distillers had no alternative but to exploit overseas sales. This they were in an excellent position to do.

The Labour Government which swept to power in the election of July 1945 took no heed of Winston Churchill's advice, in spite of it being patently obvious that whisky was an essential 'dollar earner', necessary for repaying war loans.

The Lord President of the Court of Session, Lord

story continued on page 202

199

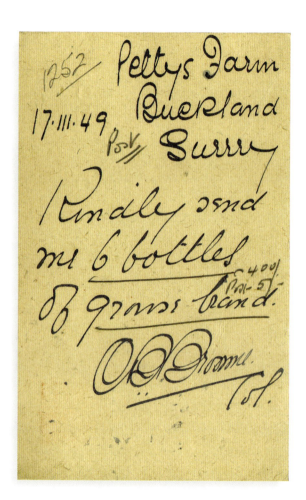

By 1949, the price of a bottle of Scotch was 35/-, making it 'a luxury' only the wealthy could afford.

PROFITEERING

The Lord President of the Court of Session, Lord Normand (above, seated and wearing a wig) , observed from the bench in December 1945 that the high prices whisky commanded:

'…presented to astute people a strong temptation to exercise their ingenuity for the purpose of escaping excess profits tax.'· [The latter had been reintroduced in 1939]. 'The procedure adopted by those who saw their opportunity, whom I shall call the promoters had a common pattern. [They] approached the shareholders of a company which held a desirable stock of whisky with an offer for their shares [so as] to obtain control of the company… The promoters [after various transactions] designed to obscure, then sold the stock for a great profit in the brokers' market, after arranging that this eventual profit should be available to finance the purchase of shares.'

Normand, observed from the bench in December 1945 that the high prices whisky commanded:

Presented to astute people a strong temptation to exercise their ingenuity for the purpose of escaping excess profits tax. [The latter had been reintroduced in 1939.] *The procedure adopted by those who saw their opportunity, whom I shall call the promoters had a common pattern.* [They] *approached the shareholders of a company which held a desirable stock of whisky with an offer for their shares* [so as] *to obtain control of the company… The promoters* [after various transactions] *designed to obscure, then sold the stock for a great profit in the brokers' market, after arranging that this eventual profit should be available to finance the purchase of shares.*

The new administration's slogan was 'Food before Whisky', and its tone was distinctly anti-alcohol, although the Manufacture of Spirits Regulations 1945 (which came into force on 1st January 1946) doubled malt-distilling capacity by the simple expedient of allowing brewing and distilling to be done concurrently, and permitting malt distilleries to work on Sundays.

This measure was academic until 1954, since there was simply not enough barley available to increase production. Food rationing continued—indeed it was expanded to include bread—and the amount of barley allocated to distillers was made conditional on their selling three-quarters of their product in export markets. Yet stocks of whisky in bond had fallen from 144 million proof gallons to 84 million proof gallons, while demand, both at home and abroad, had never been stronger: the very fact that Scotch was scarce added to its desirability.

Jack Kidd recalled how word reached a funeral cortege that Gloag's had a case of half bottles.

So the cortege arrives at the door and every person, including the driver of the hearse, came to get a half bottle. The body was left lying! They all came into the shop! It was as scarce as that, and once the case was finished, that was it.

In the season 1946/47 spirit output fell to 9.1 million gallons (in 1938/39 it had been thirty-eight million gallons). Meeting export targets from the much depleted mature stocks required rationing releases to the home market at twenty-five per

cent of their pre-war level, and to rub salt into the wound, Hugh Dalton, the Chancellor of the Exchequer, increased duty by twenty-one per cent in 1947, while his successor, Sir Stafford Cripps, added another £1 next year. Excise duty now stood at £10/10/10 per proof gallon, and the price of a bottle of standard blend at 35/- (of which 24/3d was duty). The home market quota was reduced to twenty per cent of the pre-war level. Henry Ross, Chairman of the Distillers Company, commented ruefully that 'Scotch is now regarded as a luxury instead of being within the reach of everyone, as it had been in the past'.

Companies like Gloag's neighbour, Arthur Bell & Sons, which relied heavily on the home trade, were hit hard by the drastic increase in the price of a bottle of Scotch; Gloag's were cushioned to an extent by the fact that their home market customers were principally found among the upper echelons of society.

Despite Willie Gloag's continuing absence due to ill health, the company was still a tight-knit family business. Everybody knew everybody and 'mucked in' to do what needed to be done, taking pride in their work and in their company. As Richard Oram writes:

Opposite: The Gloag family in the grounds of Bonhard, the family home, in 1955. On the bridge there are Matthew Frederick Gloag and Isla his wife. Their eldest daughter Susie is standing holding the family dog called Whisky. Seated are the Gloags' other children Felicity and Matthew.

[Matthew Gloag & Son] *was a small, self-confident, self-conscious business which had its set niche in the market and which time had largely passed by. It is quite clear* [from interviews with staff he conducted in 1994] *that working practices from the mid-nineteenth century had been carried over to the late twentieth century.*

Many of the staff who began their working lives at Matthew Gloag & Son during the post-war years—and many of them happily remained there until they retired—had never heard of the company. It was small and discreet, 'a posh type of company' as one put it. But it had a high reputation with the Perth Commercial College, from which all the secretarial

staff were recruited, and was considered 'one of the premier places to look for a job'.

All staff began 'at the bottom' and worked their way up the small hierarchy, learning a diversity of trades, helping out and 'mucking in'.   Sylvia McPherson, who joined in January 1960 and worked in the export department in the bond, told Dr Oram:

You really got a lot of training, because you did everything… I came from the Commercial School and I could type—a little!—and I had shorthand and some book-keeping, but you started off with things like writing out the labels which you stuck on the cases of whisky—the name of the ship, the dock—all handwritten.

You filled in a book for the carrier with the weights— you had to work out all the weights in your head because you didn't have a calculator in those days. You had to work out X cases at Y pounds—they were all wooden cases, and I can remember that they weighed 41lbs each.

This was the junior's job, writing out labels and all that, and then you moved on to Customs & Excise documentation and export documentation. So you actually ended up doing everything…

There was this 'phone … and I was petrified of the 'phone when I started because I'd never used one …the 'phone would ring and you'd pick it up, but it was only someone from the office… Vic Scott, he was always ordering the whisky from the bond, and he'd say '50 IQ'—IQ was an Imperial Quart or 40oz, if my memory serves me right—then he'd start going on about quarts and pints and quarters, and I was at a total loss! Then you had to 'phone the Customs & Excise, and turn this little handle to get through to them.

The business had three components: the office in Bordeaux House, the shop—also within Bordeaux House—and the bonded warehouse and bottling hall across the road on Kinnoull Street.

Willie and Fred Gloag had their room in Bordeaux House. Adjacent to it was the 'head office'—known, by those who worked in the bond, as 'The Other Side'— comprising the formidable Miss Smith, a typist, a filing clerkess, a book-keeper and an office junior.

Miss Smith was very precise. Very correct in style and manners. Very nervous. She was probably only in her thirties, but she seemed old to us girls. She dressed old and acted like she was older. Her ideas were very old-fashioned: every letter had to go into a letter book—she didn't like the new-fangled filing systems.

story continued on page 211

Burgundies (Contd.)

See page 18 St Emilion 1950 in case

Quantity	Description	Price	Ordered	Insured	Recd.	Rotation	No.	Cont.	Ull.	Fined	Bottled	Run	Seal	Bins
1 hhd.	Macon Superieur 1952	£32.15			10/6/54	54/206	39	48	47	4/6/54 47		28/9/54	23 10/12 dz qts.		57
1	do						40	51	50	11/6/54 50		28/9/54	25 8/12 dz qts.		57
1	do						41	48	47	11/6/54 47		28/9/54	23½ dz qts. 2 dz pts.		57
1	do						42	50	49	11/6/54 49		28/9/54	24½ dz qts.		57
1	Beaujolais Superieur 1952	£45.15					43	48	47	11/6/54 47		1/10/54	23½ dz qts.		42
1	do						44	50	49	11/6/54 49		1/10/54	24 8/12 dz qts.		42
1	Moulin a Vent 1952	£64					45	50	49	11/6/54 49		2/10/54	24½ dz qts.		43
1	do						46	49	48	11/6/54 48		2/10/54	24 dz qts.		43
1	Nuits St. George 1952	£86.5					47	50	49	11/6/54 49		5/10/54	23 11/12 dz qts		132
1	do						48	49	48	11/6/54 48		5/10/54	24 dz qts.		132
1	Alose Corton (bchd)	£74	1/4/54		21/10/54	54/1121	24	47	46	22/10/54 46		23/11/54	23½ dz qts.		65
1	do						25	50	49	22/10/54 49		23/11/54	24 11/12 dz qts.		65
1	Vosne Romanee 1953	£85			29/5/56	56/513	16	48	47	3/5/56 47		4/7/56	23 8/12 dz qts		4 n/c
1	Vin De Marque 1953	£24			17/9/56	56/757	9750	48	47	14/9/56 47		16/10/56	23 8/12 dz qts 10 ?		47 47
1	Beaujolais 1955	£44			18/5/57	57/389	14	49	48	29/6/57 48		12/7/57	25 ½/12 dz qts		77
1	Do 1955	£44					15	49	48	29/6/57 48		12/7/57	25 ½/12 dz qts		77
1	Fleurie 1956	£62					16	49	48	29/6/57 48		15/7/57	25 2/12 qts		79
1	Do 1955	£62					17	49	48	29/6/57 48		15/7/57	25 5/12 qts		79
1	Moulin à Vent 1955	£86					18	49	48	29/6/57 48		11/7/57	25 7/12 qts		78

During the 1950s the company bought wine by the cask and bottled it in the cellar of Bordeaux House. See over.

The cellars of Bordeaux House.

The counter of the shop in Bordeaux House.

Nothing could be done in a rush. Everything had to be just perfect.

Georgina (Gina) Harley (employed 1950):

I remember one day, I was the office junior and one of my jobs was to stick stamps on the envelopes. I'd done them all just before I went for my lunch, but when I came back in the afternoon she'd unpicked them all! I had just stuck them on, but she wanted them to be straight—the edges in line with the edge of the envelope. So I had to sit and stick them all back on—straight!

Mrs Isobel Johnstone (employed 1950):

She was very, very conservative. Before I started, she always wore a hat. All the girls had to wear hats. She lived in another generation altogether ... She thought the sun rose and set on Mr Gloag, which it did in my estimation too.

Vic MacDonald (employed 1960):

I remember the first time I actually used the 'phone—I saw her [Miss Smith] *going out and thought I'd make a quick call. She came back in and caught me. 'Are you using the telephone, Victor?' Yes. 'Well, I'll let you off this time, but the next time I want your money down on the table'.*

And I remember Mrs Johnstone, the cleaner, saying: 'Good morning, Miss Smith. You don't look terribly well today. Are you alright?'

'Yes'. And then about an hour later she was away home. We all had a good laugh!

The shop was managed by Peg Strachan, who had been there for 'years and years', and knew all the regular customers. She was assisted by Willie Findlay, another old-stager. Like the company, the shop was very discreet—Willie Gloag was superstitious about cleaning the windows, although inside, everything was immaculate and highly polished.

A long counter ran the length of the room, backed by barrels and behind that, shelves of wine and whisky. It looked not unlike a pub. Indeed, Vic MacDonald recalls:

When I started serving at the counter, these chaps came in, older men. They stood and looked at each other and one said, 'Well, what are you wanting, Jim?' 'Oh, I'll have a half and a nip.' They thought it was a pub!

Gloag's had given up selling groceries in 1945 and focused exclusively on wines and spirits. Until 1954, when rationing ceased, the shop had a sign on the counter reading 'Whisky Quota Finished Today'.

Mary Gray remembered:

Vic used to favour some people more than others, and Dan [who later became the cellarer] used to favour others. It depended on who was there, whether you got whisky or you didn't. We used to get a lot of Poles—from the base at Errol—queuing up for their half-bottles of whisky.

Beneath the shop, the cellar was run by Dan McLaren for many years, assisted by a man named Clerk. Mrs Johnstone, the office cleaner, recalled:

The cellars were immaculate. There was a winding wooden stair going down to them… They were some-thing to be seen. If visitors came to see Mr Gloag and he wasn't ready for them, they'd go to see the cellars…

If they were having a wine tasting it was like the Holy of Holies. Sandy Simpson [the cellarer] used to have wrought-iron candlesticks, with candles in them… you'd hold the bottle to the flame to see the colour. It used to be lovely when they were bottling Demerara Rum. It always smelled of Christmas… made me think of Christmas puddings… They also bottled sherry: Pintail, Amontillado and Tio Pepe.

The cellars were also prone to occasional flooding recalled Vic MacDonald:

The first time it was through the drains down in the far corner of the cellar. It was amazing the amount of water that came in, and it was the drainage system that caused the problem… [the lower parts of Perth, closest to the Tay, were flooded] I was listening to the radio and thought I'd better go down and see… but there was nothing round this area. But I thought I'd better check the cellar anyway, so I went down and it was flooded. It was spouting up.

Until after 1970, there were two floors of flats above the office at Bordeaux House—a couple were let to members of staff, and one to the Grand

Temperance Hotel! When The Famous Grouse took off in a big way the rooms were used for storage, and then converted into offices.

At the rear of the building was a small courtyard, where bottles were washed and recycled. 'Old Macdonald' was responsible for washing the bottles in an antiquated manually operated machine, and was assisted by message boys and anyone else available. Although everyone in the company had allotted tasks, in truth all the staff mucked in to help where required, and there were no 'fixed grades' of employment.

Until the early 1950s bottles were returned, washed and re-used. Glass was precious, and customers received a returnable deposit. Washing was done in an old-fashioned machine in the yard behind Bordeaux House. Mrs Isobel Johnstone said:

You used to fill up the cages with the bottles. If you didn't fasten it tightly, sometimes they would fall out… I remember one customer—a very up-market gentleman—who used to bring his bottles back. But he used to buy them in the supermarket because they were cheaper.

Mary Gray:

I can remember going out on a cold morning carrying the cases of empties to be washed. All frosty and very heavy. On the really cold days, though, we'd sit round the boiler and tell fortunes while we changed the seals in the bottle caps. During the war, see, we used Bakelite caps that were re-usable—for the home trade just. They had a wee rubber seal inside and that had to be changed each time they were re-used.

In the bond office, Charles Mactaggart, Export Director, shared a room with Colonel Wylie, Director and Company Secretary, until 1957, when John Wylie died. The office looked after exports, stock management and shipping. Four secretaries worked in the office. Mary Gray recalls:

Lieutenant Colonel John Wylie was a Director. He was very military. He used to check everywhere for dust. He'd run his finger down the bannister and say, 'Has this been dusted today?'

story continued on page 217

CHARLES MACTAGGART (opposite right)
Export Manager (1935–1982)

*I liked him, but he was a wee bit eccentric. He was
the boss… very mannerly, very gentlemanly.*
Hazel Anderson (1969–2000)

*Charlie Mactaggart was a shrewd man.
He could be really chatty and friendly, but he was
just getting information out of you about other
people. He liked to know about everything that
was going on. He had a really bad temper—he
had a bad stomach which made him like that—but
he was always very sociable with the ladies.*
Mary Gray (1942–1984)

They were still so formal in those days [1960,
when she joined the company]. *They called you
by your surname. I don't think Mr Mactaggart
ever used my Christian name… It even took
Mr Sherriff a long time to call me by my
Christian name. Everybody was called by their
Christian name then* [1974, when she moved
to Bordeaux House to work for Alick Sherriff],
*but I don't think Mr Mactaggart even knew it!
We were very much in awe of him… Everything
had to be just so. When he dictated letters you
didn't dare change a comma or anything—he used
to dictate even where the commas went! He
punctuated for you—and if you changed it…!*
Sylvia McPherson (1960–2000)

The Excise office in the bonded warehouse. From left to right: Mr Sterry, J. Wylie and M.F. Gloag.

Mrs Isobel Johnstone:

I always remember his feather hat, kept up in the attic… It must have been from his regiment. It was good in the bond. If you had a cold you just went upstairs to the blending and had a snifter.

Upstairs was the blending room and the bottling hall, managed by Mary Gray. Close by was the Customs & Excise office, manned by Mr Boyd. Until the 1980s, all distilleries, blending halls and bonded warehouses had to have a resident Excise Officer. They had very considerable power. As Mary Gray remembered:

You had to do just what they wanted. They had to be present when the bond was opened, so you couldn't get in before 9 o'clock. If you wanted to do overtime you had to put it in a book. If you wanted the bottling hall opened, you had to put in a letter of request.

The job of the message boy had changed little since before the war.

Vic MacDonald, who started work in 1960 at the age of fifteen:

You swept the floors and there were two fireplaces—I cleaned the fireplaces—and all the brasses and that sort of thing. Friday was your busy day when you went away with your message bike… It was a blue bike that I had, and it had big wooden boxes in front of the handlebars, and you used to go round the shops and whatever.

The main local customers for wine were hotels.

We used to get the carriers on a Friday, three or four different carriers, and it was all the hotels up north— Pitlochry, Aberfeldy—they went round all the hotels.

And the message boys delivered cases to local bars and hotels:

At that time it was all still the cobbled streets. And if it was one box at a time it was quite all right. But I remember the first time that they put two boxes on— in my basket—and I thought I could never manage. Going down Mill Street, on the cobbles, with two boxes on top!
[Gloag's also had two-wheeled and four-wheeled hand carts.] *I've seen me out with the two-wheeled barrow. That was the first time I was sent up to the*

Waverley Hotel—cobbles—and we're talking about twenty-odd of these wooden boxes. How was I going to manage that! So they said, 'We'll give you a shove up to the top.'... Then that was you left. And if somebody nicked a case there was nothing I could do, because you were on your own.
We had a customer in Bellwood Park over on Dundee Road... the bond had a four-wheel barrow with a big handle... so I would go over to the bond to get their barrow and go over to Bellwood, and it was like that [indicates a steep hill].

The mail order business still operated in the 1960s. Wine lists were regularly send out to customers by post, and orders were also posted, or sent by bus—'we used the buses a lot'—plus the local carriers. Larger packages were sent by train.

As was the custom of everyone 'mucking in', Vic also helped with bottling:

At the time when I came in, we bottled all the wine ourselves. That was really beautiful. You had all your casks and things set up, and all your bottles: sherries, ports, clarets, Burgundies—you name it. And at that time we had a big barrel up here and we used to bottle
and sell whisky ... there was a step you went up and you stood on a big flat box and you had to rummage in the barrel, you know [with a valinche?]... Vic Scott was my boss. He was really good, because he showed you everything. How to do all the measuring and bottling.

Automation came to whisky bottling in the 1950s—bottle filling, labelling machines, capping machines—but the company continued to bottle its own wines. Vic Macdonald remembers, in the 1960s:

The different wines had different colours—red, green and blue—different caps. For vintage ports you had a wee pot on the stove and you put the wax in and boil it up and dip the bottle in ... Then you used to stamp it— with the vintage—and wrapped them in green tissue for Burgundy and red tissue for claret.
The last thing I remember bottling was rum.

Vintage port was stored in the old R.B. Smith's bond, which Gloag's had used before building their own bonded warehouse in the 1930s. In the 1960s the company was still offering 'wee barrels—about a gallon or a half gallon'.

By the late 1940s, prices for mature whisky were

The advertising office in the bonded warehouse.

at exorbitant levels, and the directors of Matthew Gloag & Son became concerned about the colossal estate duties payable on the basis of these unrealistic valuations, should Willie Gloag die. So great was their concern that early in 1947 they sought legal advice about what precautions they might take.

In fact, Willie's health rallied briefly, and he was able to return to work in February, when all the staff were given a bottle of Grouse to celebrate. Alas, it was not for long: Major Matthew William Gloag died at Bonhard House, Perth, on 28th March 1947 aged sixty-five. His son, Matthew Frederick Gloag, became chairman of the company.

Fortunately, Willie Gloag's holding of 41,000 ordinary shares in Matthew Gloag & Son were valued on the (correct) assumption that the whisky stocks held by the company would be used for blending and not sold rashly in the inflated open market. However, since they were valued at £82,000, some shares had to be sold to institutions to pay the estate duty, depleting the company's slender financial reserves. Indeed, Fred Gloag was obliged to continue paying off the death duties for many years.

As his forbears had done—right back to the first Matthew Gloag—Fred Gloag devoted much time to developing personal contact with his customers, drawing attention to special offers, congratulating them on the births of children, commiserating them on deaths in the family and generally assuring them of their value to Gloag's—no matter how small their orders.

He was a connoisseur of wine and took a special interest in this side of the business, regularly hosting customers at his home. In truth, wine was the driving force of the company until after 1970.

Fred Gloag was very popular with his staff, although a somewhat shy and distant figure. A member of the family remembered him as 'very private and actually quite reclusive, but once you got to know him he was absolutely charming, polite and caring—very traditional and a proper gentleman, but a strict father'.

Gina Harley, who began with the company in 1950, recalled:

I remember when Milnathort Station was being closed—that was Dr Beeching—and I only found out afterwards that they'd been selling off all their equipment. I was really annoyed because they had a

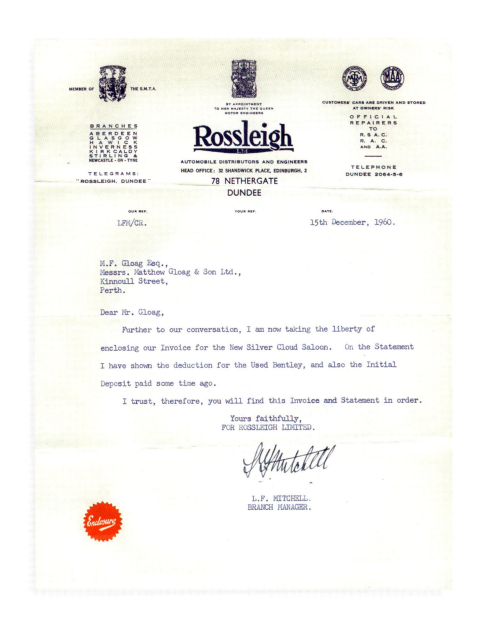

Letter to Fred Gloag from Rossleigh in Dundee, enclosing their invoice for his 1960 purchase of a Rolls-Royce Silver Cloud Saloon.

parcel cart that I would have liked for the Girl Guides—to collect jumble, and things like that—but it had gone. When I came into the office I was talking to Mr Gloag… After lunch he called me in and told me to go to Perth Station. He'd bought a parcel cart for me and I had to go and choose one!… That was Mr Gloag for you.

But more than one member of staff was uncertain whether his heart lay in business. Again, Miss Harley remarked:

He wasn't really interested in business. It was his livelihood, but I think he did it out of a sense of duty to the family. His real interest was in the army. That's where he was always happiest—he kept up his interest in The Black Watch and went to all their functions.

Mrs Fleming, who worked for Gloag's from 1927 to 1947, starting on 7/6 (37½p) per week as a junior, rising through book-keeper to become Willie Gloag's secretary commented:

I don't really think Mr Fred was cut out for the office. He got on fairly well, but it never seemed to be his forte. Army and cars were his two great loves. He was

very nice… quiet. And his wife was quiet, but I never knew her very well. It was a super firm to be with.

He was certainly very keen on motor cars; always attended the Motor Show in London and drove a Bentley. His chauffeur/handyman drove him to work each day in the family Land Rover, however, which he believed to be a very safe vehicle in the event of an accident.

The impression gathered from the staff interviews in 1994 is that of a close-knit family business, with 'Mr Gloag'—he was never referred to as 'Fred'—at the helm, where everyone knew each other and was proud of working for the company. Although much smaller than its neighbours, Bell's and Dewar's, it is clear that Gloag's staff felt a cut above the other companies. Vic Macdonald:

I always had the impression that the folk who worked for the likes of Dewar's were just a number on a wage

Opposite: A gathering of Gloag staff at Bonhard House.

packet. Gloag's was always that close-knit, family sort of thing, where everybody got on. They were a lot bigger…there were six or seven hundred people at Inveralmond [Dewar's operation]. But at Gloag's you were all down here [at Bordeaux House] or through the back—close-knit—great laughs!

Vic Scott, who joined the firm in 1929 as a message boy and rose to become manager of the bonded warehouse, put it this way:

You see, Gloag's was a private firm, Bell's and them were bigger things, and we never compared ourselves to them. We were—to be snobbish—something special. It wasn't just Grouse, it was The Famous Grouse. That was instilled in us by Willie Gloag. You'd see it in all the papers, all the adverts.

Sylvia McPherson, who joined in 1960, recalled:

We all felt part of the family. You really did. Because as far as you were aware they treated everybody the same. You knew everybody… What they did on the first day was take you round and introduce you to everybody… Only Mr Gloag, Mr Sherriff and Mr

THE FAMOUS GROUSE BRAND

Telephone Nº 2333-4.

MATTHEW GLOAG
& SON LIMITED
PERTH. SCOTLAND

ESTABLISHED 1800
MATTHEW GLOAG. 1814
WILLIAM B. GLOAG. 1860
MATTHEW GLOAG. 1896
MATTHEW W. GLOAG. 1910
MATTHEW F GLOAG 1947

BLENDED SCOTCH WHISKY 86.8°

DIRECTORS
JOHN WYLIE
MATTHEW F. GLOAG
CHARLES D. MACTAGGART

8th November, 1958

The Right Honourable Baron Akers,
No. 1, Threadneedle Street,
Grouse-On-The-Rocks,
California, U. S. A.

Dear Baron Akers,

    Since I last wrote you, matters have taken a turn for the worse.

    Few indeed, besides yourself, recognize the steady deterioration of American/Scottish diplomatic relations. As you know, we had hoped for improvement. But I must inform you now that the situation could easily become serious enough to require immediate mobilization of The Black Watch and the Edinburgh Constabulary, with even more drastic measures in the offing.

    The next step might well be cancellation of overseas Bagpipe Concerts, and an embargo upon the export of haggis.

    Or worse - restraints upon further shipments of the "Ultimate Experience" Scotch Whisky - THE FAMOUS GROUSE BRAND.

    We must all work together to avert this catastrophe.

    If you will do your utmost to dissuade your American friends from the barbaric practice of referring to THE FAMOUS GROUSE BRAND Scotch Whisky as Scotch "Whiskey" (that is, with an "e") I will, for my part, undertake (in the interest of The Greater Good) to supply a case

BALFOUR, GUTHRIE & CO., LIMITED, SAN FRANCISCO   EXCLUSIVE U.S.A. PACIFIC COAST IMPORTERS

THE FAMOUS GROUSE BRAND

Telephone Nº 2333-4.

ESTABLISHED 1800
MATTHEW GLOAG. 1814
WILLIAM B. GLOAG. 1860
MATTHEW GLOAG. 1896
MATTHEW W. GLOAG. 1910
MATTHEW F. GLOAG 1947

MATTHEW GLOAG & SON LIMITED

PERTH. SCOTLAND.

DIRECTORS:
MATTHEW F. GLOAG
CHARLES D. MACTAGGART

REG⁹

BLENDED SCOTCH WHISKY 86.8°

PAGE TWO

8th November, 1958

history which illustrates the folly of employing superfluous

letters. (By some incredible oversight my former secretary

neglected to include this page in my recent letter to you.

Please accept my apologies).

Whiskey (with an "e") is, I am told, a distillate of

sorts concocted in the hills of your Kentucky county.

Now, I daresay one might eventually acquire a taste for it,

but it is by no means to be confused with an exquisite Scotch

such as THE FAMOUS GROUSE BRAND, which has been Whisky since

1800 and, in spite of its great age, will never lapse into

a life of "e's".

Getting back to the superfluous, kindly consider for

a moment the consonant "P", as used in the word "Ptarmigan".

Then read the attached label carefully. Notice that nowhere

do we refer to THE FAMOUS PGROUSE. Yet it will be rewarding, as

you gratefully sip the contents of the bottles we are sending to

BALFOUR, GUTHRIE & CO., LIMITED, SAN FRANCISCO   EXCLUSIVE U.S.A. PACIFIC COAST IMPORTERS

THE FAMOUS GROUSE BRAND

Telephone Nº 2333-4.

ESTABLISHED 1800
MATTHEW GLOAG. 1814
WILLIAM B. GLOAG. 1860
MATTHEW GLOAG. 1896
MATTHEW W. GLOAG. 1910
MATTHEW F. GLOAG 1947

MATTHEW GLOAG & SON LIMITED

PERTH. SCOTLAND.

DIRECTORS:
MATTHEW F. GLOAG
CHARLES D. MACTAGGART

REG⁹

BLENDED SCOTCH WHISKY 86.8°

PAGE THREE

8th November, 1958

your Pacific Coast (confound that secretary, she's done it again!)

to ponder the dismal thought that THE FAMOUS GROUSE BRAND might well

have been "The Famous Ptarmigan Brand", but for Three (3) Things:

Thing No. 1:   There is no such thing as a famous
               ptarmigan - undoubtedly because of
               the psilly way it pspells its pname.

Thing No. 2:   "The Famous Ptarmigan Brand Scotch Whisky"
               is too long to fit on the label.

Thing No. 3:   Our printers - a thrifty lot - would
               never set up a letter (P) that wasn't
               going to be pronounced anyway. Extra
               ink, you know.

Observe, please, the likeness of the proud and uncompromising

Grouse (nee ptarmigan) on the label. Note also that THE FAMOUS

GROUSE BRAND has had the same address since 1800. This is A Signif-

icant Fact.

And now, permit me to close with the immortal lines:

      "Let your 'Bird in the Hand'

      Be THE FAMOUS GROUSE BRAND."

                              Cordially,

BALFOUR, GUTHRIE & CO., LIMITED, SAN FRANCISCO   EXCLUSIVE U.S.A. PACIFIC COAST IMPORTERS

MATTHEW GLOAG & SON,
PERTH.

Loading Port on the Douro.

FAMED FOR PORTS.

Port arrived in Perth by the butt and was bottled at Bordeaux House.

*Mactaggart were what you would call real bosses…
Before Matthew* [Fred's son, Matthew Irving Gloag]
*worked in the office with me—he did that for a short
time—he'd be working in the bond, loading lorries. His
sisters sometimes helped out. I'm sure I can remember
Mr Sherriff up on the bond roof doing something…
They just mucked in.*

At busy times everybody helped in the bottling
hall (except Mr Mactaggart!), making cartons,
capping bottles and so on, even senior staff. Vic
MacDonald, who also joined the firm (as a message
boy) in 1960, mentioned:

*Mr Morrison, he was the foreman over there. And
there was Mr Boyd, he was the Customs & Excise. He
had his office in there. And there was Jack Kidd, he was
foreman. Mr Sherriff used to come along and help as
well. And Matthew's sister, Susan, was in one night as
well… When he was a young boy, when his Dad was
here, Matthew and his pal used to sometimes come
down and sort of… tried to help us out.*

Christmas and New Year were particularly hectic,
but the staff was generously rewarded.

22nd May 1958: Country Life *advertisement.*

Jack Kidd recalls:

We used to work two nights, but we got double time. And the men got two hundred cigarettes, the women got a box of chocolates and the laddies got a big tin of caramels. That's over and above your wages. And for your holidays you got double pay. A fortnight's holidays! I think we were one of the few firms that got a fortnight in those days.

By the 1950s the Christmas bonus was eight weeks' wages—'an awful lot of money'. Sylvia McPherson never forgot her first bonus—a £20 note. Full of excitement she met with a friend and opened the wage envelope: neither of them had ever seen a £20 note before. For the summer holidays, the staff received their month's wages, plus two weeks' bonus for the holiday.

There were various Christmas gift packs of two or three mixed bottles—'a bottle of sherry and a bottle of port; a bottle of whisky and something else'. All had to be individually wrapped, then packed in two bottle hampers and sent off by post.

The immediate post-war era was a period of recovery and rebuilding, especially in Europe, which had been shattered by the war. People worked hard and respected the values and business practices they had been brought up with.

By the late 1950s and throughout the 1960s, society was changing rapidly, and with it business and management. Both were based on economic success: in 1957 Prime Minister Harold Macmillan summed up the general view with the words: 'Most of our people have never had it so good'.

Between 1950 and 1973 the annual real GDP growth of developed economies averaged around five per cent. And the fact that people had more money in their pockets was reflected by the success of Scotch whisky, both at home and abroad.

Until 1953 annual export targets to hard currency markets were agreed with government, under the so-called 'Strachey regime'—named after the Minister for Food, John Strachey (1946–50). Distillers had been granted unrestricted access to cereals in 1950—as one minister succinctly put it: 'the country needs

Opposite: Matthew Irving Gloag
in San Francisco in 1967

story continued on page 233

RAYMOND MIQUEL was employed by Arthur Bell & Sons as an 'efficiency expert', to look into Bell's operations and procedures. He was twenty-five years old, and after National Service with the R.A.F. and a brief spell in an accountant's office, had received some training in time-and-motion studies and accounting with a Glasgow firm of management consultants.

A comparison between the two companies in this period is instructive.

Raymond Miquel had no experience of the whisky trade, so cast an objective and highly critical eye over what he found. 'I thought I'd gone back to the Middle Ages', he said after visiting Bell's warehouses in Leith. 'I didn't think people worked like that in 1956'.

He set about improving the warehousing and bottling operations and then the delivery procedures from Perth. To the bewilderment of some, and the scorn of others, he produced an 'organisation chart'. Many of the changes he introduced were unpopular to begin with, and many were ahead of their time.

He concentrated on the home sales force, expanding and reorganising it, and driving the men hard—Miquel himself was a workaholic, with an iron will (at the time he joined Bell's he was running a hundred miles a week) and unlimited ambition, but he was very aware of the importance of inspiring and leading his employees. The year after he joined the board (1962), the company's profits exceeded one million pounds—an achievement which Bell's chairman, W.G. Farquharson, had pronounced impossible only five years before.

By 1965 Miquel was deputy managing director, by 1968 managing director and, on the death of Farquharson in April 1973, chairman and managing director. That year the company's profits had exceeded three million pounds, and output had topped a million cases.

The company built its strength in the home market, where sales trebled between 1967 and 1973 and export sales more than doubled. Profit in 1973 was over £4 million.

Raymond Miquel

Telephone Nº 2332 (3 LINES)

THE FAMOUS GROUSE BRAND

MATTHEW GLOAG
& SON LIMITED
PERTH.
SCOTLAND.

REGᴰ

DIRECTORS:
MATTHEW F. GLOAG
CHARLES D. MACTAGGART.

ESTABLISHED 1800

MATTHEW GLOAG. 1814
WILLIAM B. GLOAG. 1860
MATTHEW GLOAG. 1896
MATTHEW W. GLOAG. 1910
MATTHEW F. GLOAG. 1947

Mr John Sullivan, Executive Vice-President,
    Empire Liquor Corp, NEW YORK, 54, U.S.A.,   August, 1960.

Dear Mr. Sullivan,

        At the request of Fred Seggerman I am writing to you to set out
some information concerning our Famous Grouse Brand Scotch Whisky.

        The Famous Grouse is a Blend of only the finest single Whiskies
that are distilled in Scotland including the rarest Speyside Malts which are
all matured by us in either freshly emptied Sherry Casks or Refill Sherry
Casks. These Sherry Casks are specially selected so that no woody flavour
will communicate itself to the Scotch Whisky.

        Then our Scotch Grain Whiskies are matured in Casks made from
the finest American White Oak which we import from Birmingham, Alabama, and
these Casks are also dressed with Sherry before we fill them. We absolutely
refuse to mature any of our Whiskies in the already used American Bourbon an
Rye Casks which are very cheap and are used in thousands by many of our
competitors, but the result is we feel an inferior product.

        Even after blending Grouse Whisky in our Oak Vats we run it back
into Casks to marry for another year because we know this gives it a better
finish.

        The Average age of our Grouse Scotch Blend is around 7 years and
in this respect quality is the first essential even before age, because a
secondary Scotch Whisky can never really become first class merely by ageing
Then the fine light body and exquisite non-smoky flavour of Grouse is really
the result of using the best single Whiskies available.

        Matthew Gloag & Son Limited is an old family business and it has
been run by the same family in direct succession since 1800 so we enjoy the
cumulative blending experience of five generations of the same family in
direct succession. We do not engage in mass output and Famous Grouse is one
of the few remaining custom made scotchs. If we thought we could produce a
better one we would certainly do so.

        The Undoubted High quality and fine character of Famous Grouse has
found great favour in many parts of U.S.A. to-day and it is now the Bar Scot
in the more exclusive Clubs of San Francisco, Boston and other large cities.

                Yours sincerely,

                Charles D. Mactaggart.
                    Director,
            MATTHEW GLOAG & SON LTD.,

All the whiskies used in The Famous Grouse blend were matured in sherry casks in 1960.

food, dollars mean food, and whisky means dollars'.

Led by America, there was a phenomenal increase in the demand for Scotch during the decade. In 1960 exports to the u.s. stood at twelve million proof gallons; by 1968 it was thirty-three million. Two million gallons of Scotch were being exported to Italy by 1970, and the amounts to France and Germany were even higher. Gloag's had appointed Armando Giovinetti as their agent for The Famous Grouse in Italy in the late 1950s, on condition that he 'did not sell too much', since Charles Mactaggart was concerned that they did not have sufficient stock. In the early 1960s, Giovinetti also obtained the agency for Glen Grant single malt, and by 1970 Italy had become that brand's leading market. By 1977 sales of Glen Grant had reached 200,000 cases a year.

To meet the demand, output across the industry increased slowly until 1963/64, then began to accelerate rapidly from 29 mpg (million proof gallons) to 51 mpg in 1967. Scottish Malt Distillers, the production division of the mighty Distillers Company, increased the number of stills in their fifty distilleries by more than half between 1959 and 1967, and their example was followed by many independent distillers.

By 1959 there was enough mature whisky in bond to allow first the Distillers Company and then other blenders to take their standard brands off quota in the home market; deluxe whiskies, like Johnnie Walker Black Label (12YO), remained on quota until 1962.

Although the u.k. remained the largest market, sales were depressed by increases in duty in 1957 (price of a standard bottle now 37/6), 1964, 1965 and 1968 (twice). Duty per 26⅔ fluid ounces (75cl) bottle now stood at £2.20, twice what it had been in 1960. Duty on wine was also increased, and this further damaged Matthew Gloag & Son's home trade.

Charles Mactaggart redoubled his efforts to sell The Famous Grouse in hard currency countries such as the United States, Canada and South Africa. A letter from him in August 1960, addressed to the Executive Vice-President of the Empire Liquor Corporation, in which he provides 'some information concerning our Famous Grouse Brand Scotch Whisky', also gives an insight into what he—and presumably the company as well—considered to be the key contributors to its flavour and distinctive qualities. (The letter is reproduced opposite.)

The whisky industry was generally conservative

story continued on page 236

ALICK SHERRIFF, Sales Director

Alick Sherriff arrived in 1956. He was a very nice man. He started at the bottom, working in the bond. He worked his way right up through the company and ended up at the top.
Gina Harley (1950–1993).

He was very good-looking and a real gentleman. The girls over the road in Pullars used to fancy him!
Mary Gray (1942–1984).

Mr Sherriff was a very nice person. He started in the bond. I used to charge him 6d a week for his tea. He was very well thought of. He was one of the Queen's bodyguards—the Royal Company of Archers.
Mrs Isobel Johnstone (1950–).

Such a strong, strapping-looking man. A real gentleman. It was tragic what happened to him.
Sylvia McPherson (1960–2000).

Alick Sherriff's tasting notes from 1958.

*Matthew Frederick Gloag
in the garden of Bonhard House.*

and suspicious of change, and this was especially true of the Distillers Company, the largest and most influential company in the industry.

But even measured by the prevailing business practices of the day, Matthew Gloag & Son was 'old-fashioned', as might have been gathered from the description of its operations—although it has to be said that this approach found favour with those who worked in the company.

Sylvia McPherson recalled:

By 1970 [Matthew Gloag & Son] was an extremely old-fashioned business. I remember speaking to friends working in other places, it didn't seem so formal where they were. But I don't know if there was anything wrong with being formal.

*Armando Giovinetti, left,
with Major Douglas MacKessack
owner of Glen Grant distillery.*

Although sales of The Famous Grouse rose rapidly in the hard currency countries (the United States, Canada and South Africa in particular), the company's home trade was badly hit by the rises in duty and the quota system, which, although it was gradually relaxed after 1954, continued until 1959.

In 1954 the government lifted the restrictions on importing barley, and for the first time in fourteen years distilling was able to return to pre-war levels. The directors of Matthew Gloag & Son resolved to employ all their resources in building up stocks to meet the steadily increasing demand: over the next ten years the company's stocks of mature whisky trebled in size, while sales more than doubled. Profit advanced to about £120,000 in 1956/57, six times what it had been in 1939/40.

In 1958, the company's capital was raised to £180,000, largely by capitalising reserves to reflect the value of assets more accurately, but there was still not enough cash to restore the home trade to its pre-war level.

Alick Sherriff, who was made Sales Director in 1961, found the going tough during the boom years of the 1960s—for most of the decade he was only able to hold sales more or less level.

The board of Matthew Gloag & Son was never tempted to buy market share by sacrificing quality in order to reduce prices. The key customer base in the home market continued to be the upper middle class, as it had been from the start. The modest advertising budget of a little over £2,000 was devoted to quality periodicals like *Country Life*, *The Field*, *The Illustrated London News*, *The Commonwealth Journal* and *The Diplomat*. Such tactics maintained customer loyalty and yielded healthy profits; the small band of shareholders had nothing to complain about.

Fred Gloag's death on 11th January 1970, aged fifty-nine, was very sudden. His secretary, Gina Harley, recalled:

In 1968 it was young Matthew's twenty-first birthday [he had joined the company the year before]. *The staff all clubbed together and bought him a pen, so Mrs Gloag invited us all out to Bonhard for a drink. I remember talking to Mrs Gloag and she was saying that her health wasn't too good and that she was going to see a doctor. That's when they found out that she had cancer.*
Mr Gloag was so upset. Every day I had to arrange for a bouquet of flowers to be sent to her room, and

Mr Gloag was always in touch with the hospital. Every morning I would have a conversation with him about Mrs Gloag. He got himself very depressed, and that helped bring down his health too. He was determined to keep trying. He was positive he would find someone who would find a cure for her.

And then one Sunday Mr Sherriff 'phoned to let me know that Mr Gloag had died. And I thought, 'Surely he means Mrs Gloag', but no.

I remember that he had come into the office on the Friday with his coat on and had sat on a radiator, complaining that he couldn't get warm. He thought he'd the flu, but he died on the Sunday.

Edith Gloag followed her husband three days later, on the night of his funeral.

Gina Harley (joined 1950):

Mr Fred was like a father to us. He wanted to know all about his staff. He was very human, a really kind man—but I don't know if he was a good businessman. He was too nice a man to be a boss…

He always wanted to keep absolute control…to see to everything—every order received a personal letter back from him. The mail always had to go to the Post Office at 4.15, to catch the evening post. The walls on Mr Fred's office were covered in photographs and pictures, and he used them as mirrors to check if you had gone to the Post Office in time.

Hazel Anderson (joined 1969):

He was always a gentleman. He'd always stand up when you came into the room—that sort of thing.

Mrs Isobel Johnstone (joined 1950):

He was a perfect gentleman, but very superstitious about the colour green. I remember once I had a green overall and I had to change it. He didn't tell me to, but he said it to somebody else… And he didn't like the windows cleaned. I've seen Mrs Gloag passing, and she would come in and say to Vic Scott that the windows were terrible. And Vic would say that Mr Fred won't let us do it. And if you scrubbed the table, he was always sure it brought rain. But oh, he was such a nice person.

CHAPTER VI

MATTHEW IRVING

GLOAG

(1947 TO PRESENT)

Left to right: Dilly and Matthew Gloag, Lord Lansdowne and Prince Charles.

'YOUNG' MATTHEW HAD JOINED THE FAMILY BUSI-NESS IN 1965, aged seventeen, and started at the bottom—literally, in the extensive cellars of Bordeaux House—working under Sandy Simpson, the cellar master, receiving barrels of sherry, wine and whisky, checking quality, bottling and, where appropriate, racking the bottles to mature.

After two years of this, he was sent to London where he worked as a relief manager for Brown & Pank wine shops for eight months before following in the footsteps of his father and grandfather to work for Calvet et Cie (the distinguished wine shippers) in Bordeaux and learn the French wine trade.

In fact Maison Calvet's business at this time was quiet, so he moved to Château D'Angludet after meeting its owner, Peter Sichel, whose family had been in the Bordeaux wine trade for six generations. During his six months here he was given a sound apprenticeship in all aspects of making this 'Cru Bourgeois Exceptionnel' and made many friends.

Next year he worked a passage to Australia on a cargo boat belonging to the Lyle Shipping Company, with a view to expanding his knowledge of Australian wines—since at least 1910, Matthew Gloag & Son had been listing 'Australian Burgundies', 'imported direct, bottled with the utmost care by ourselves and given time to mature in bottle'. He spent nine months in the country, but was obliged to return home in a hurry when his mother was suddenly taken seriously ill.

As he writes in the Foreword to this book: 'I returned home to find my family completely caught up with the care of my mother. On one particular day, having taken her nurse to Perth railway station, I came back to find that my father had suffered a fatal heart attack on the landing outside my mother's bedroom. He was lying at the bottom of the stairs. My mother then died two days later.' Matthew I. Gloag was appointed as a director, in succession to his father, in June 1970.

In 1970, Estate Duty was running at 30% on all property over £10,000. No provision had been made for such an unforeseen occurrence and Fred and Edith Gloag's executors were faced with having to pay double death duties. Since the largest portion of the estate was Fred's shareholding in the family company, the executors and the directors—Charles Mactaggart, Matthew I. Gloag and Alick Sherriff—had no alternative but to seek a buyer for Matthew Gloag & Son, in order to pay the tax.

Alick Sherriff sought help and advice from Pat Scott, a relation by marriage and a director of The Highland Distilleries Co. Ltd., which had been supplying malts for The Famous Grouse for many years. The Highland board considered the proposal carefully for two months, then offered to buy Matthew Gloag & Son for £1.25 million: £545,000 in cash, plus an allocation of 350,000 shares in Highland (valued at approximately 31/6d each [155.25p]).

Some members of the Highland Board joined that of Matthew Gloag & Son—John Macphail, Harry Penman (Highland's Chairman) and John Goodwin, with Andrew Kettles as Company Secretary. Matthew was determined, to the surprise—he would say 'dismay'!—of the other directors, to continue on the board of directors and to work in what had been his family's firm, although the working atmosphere had changed dramatically.

Initially, he was a 'director without portfolio'. His experience was in the wine trade, and now the focus was on whisky, so he was sent on a six month tour of some of Highland's operations, to expand his knowledge of the business. Tamdhu and Glen Rothes Distilleries; with a spell at the Rothes 'Combination' dark grains plant; the Clyde Bond; North British (grain whisky) Distillery in Edinburgh. Then back to Perth, where he served his time as a travelling salesman around Perthshire—'I was given a white Triumph Dolomite … Needless to say, I was not born to be a salesman'—then a month's crash course in accountancy.

The Highland board wanted a brand of blended Scotch whisky and saw huge potential in The Famous Grouse, which at the time was perceived and positioned as 'up market', 'county', 'very Perthshire'. The key market was Scotland (home sales amounted to 44,686 cases), although 58,673 cases were sold in export markets in 1971.

The re-launch was master-minded by John Goodwin and John Macphail—the former being in charge of the day to day running of the company, the latter involved in strategic decisions. Alick Sherriff also played a major role in positioning the brand as a premium product. On his return to Perth, Matthew Gloag was made responsible for Public Relations and Advertising. All parties were determined that the quality of the blend was paramount.

Holmwood Advertising (later taken over by Saatchi & Saatchi) was re-appointed as the advertising agent to plan and execute the launch

campaign, and on the suggestion of Alick Sherriff, Ron Baird, Holmwood's creative director, adopted the reassuring slogan 'Quality in an Age of Change', a line which would serve Matthew Gloag & Son well for the next twenty-five years.

The company's key market had always been in Scotland, but now concerted efforts were made to promote The Famous Grouse throughout the United Kingdom, and, after 1974, abroad. By the end of 1973, U.K. sales had almost tripled to 101,083 cases.

The long-established firm of Deinhard & Co., for which Gloag's had acted as Scottish representatives since Fred Gloag's time, was appointed distributor for England and Wales. This was a family-owned company: Freddy and Austin Hasslacher had been contemporaries and friends of Fred Gloag; their sons, Peter and Michael, who were friends of Alick and Matthew, were now Chairman and Managing Director.

Opposite: The Famous Grouse
sponsored a horse-drawn bus in London, 1980.

Throughout the 1970s and 1980s, grass-roots sponsorship was key to winning the support of both the licensed trade and consumers, and this was Matthew's special responsibility, assisted (after 1982) by Iain Halliday, Trade Relations Manager, and (after 1987) by Jim Grierson, National Sales Manager. Such sponsorship was key to the success of The Famous Grouse in these decades: no other whisky company was so active in this area.

Matthew approached the task with enthusiasm and imagination, sponsoring a very wide variety of activities, both local and national, to support local communities, develop public relations and expand brand awareness. Matthew's ethos and challenge was based on his belief that involvement and sponsorship worked best if the sponsorship events were those that he or other members of the company had, at least at the outset, been closely involved or interested in. 'I quickly realised that if there was anything out of the ordinary to sponsor, it became my responsibility', he says, 'and the brand's success in the home market allowed Highland to back whatever promotions or sponsorships I proposed—and some were 'unusual', to say the least'.

A glance at the minutes of any of the Management

story continued on page 279

CRICKET

'One of our earliest sponsorships was an M.C.C. pre-season cricket tour of Germany, and for many years we supported Worcestershire Country Cricket Club', Matthew told me. The Western Cricket League in the South-west of England was also sponsored—the fourteen clubs played each other and were brought together at an annual awards dinner, to which many VIP guests from the world of cricket and celebrity were invited, with awards for 'best batsman' and 'most improved team' of the year. Every club was given two dozen cricket balls. This activity provided excellent trade cover and interest in The Famous Grouse, covering Cornwall to Worcestershire.

SHOOTING

Support for the North Wales Shooting School, owned by Jackie Stewart, led to the brand later sponsoring a team at his Celebrity Charity Clay Shoot at Gleneagles Hotel.

GAME FAIRS AND AGRICULTURAL SHOWS

The annual Game Fairs were held at different venues each year. The Famous Grouse supported events such as the clay pigeon shooting competition sponsored by Country Landowners Association. The Aberdeen Angus Cattle Society, the Royal Highland Show and the Royal Yorkshire Show were all regular events for The Famous Grouse.

Opposite: Roy Bignell and John Macphail with The Famous Grouse Bull.

HIGHLAND GAMES

Sir Roddy Macdonald wrote to Matthew seeking sponsorship in the late 1980s, and this lasted for seven or eight years, during which time the Skye Games gained an international following. Although a comparatively small event, it was very picturesque, held in a natural amphitheatre.

CARRIAGE DRIVING

The World Carriage Driving Championship was supported between 1974 and 1994, and the National Carriage Driving Championships continued to be supported until the mid-1990s. Alick and Sue Sherriff were much involved in this for many years, and Matthew sat on the committee of the Carriage Driving Society (with Prince Philip), while Sue was a judge in their competitions at Windsor, Scone Palace, York and Lowther. 'Prince Philip wanted to have his own event at Balmoral', remembers Matthew. 'My wife, Dilly, and I met the Queen and Princes Andrew and Edward, and were invited, at a later date, to have supper at Windsor

Castle. It turned out that everyone in the carriage driving world was also invited!' It was entirely thanks to the good relations developed by Matthew with the Royal Household that later, 'At Scone Palace, Prince Philip suggested to me that Matthew Gloag & Son should apply for a Royal Warrant'. This resulted in the Lord Chamberlain granting the company the Royal Warrant, on 1st January 1984, with Matthew as personal grantee.

Above: Carriage driving at Scone Palace, Perth.

BUCKINGHAM PALACE.

1 March 1990

Dear Dick,

Many thanks for your letter. It is sad news that Famous Grouse is backing out of sponsoring driving events, but after fifteen years I can well understand the wish to do something else.

I am sure that you realise how important the Famous Grouse sponsorship has been during the vital early years of a new sport. You have got it off to a splendid start and I know that everyone connected with the sport deeply appreciates the involvement of your company over so many years.

Yours sincerely

Philip

RACE MEETINGS

One or more leading races were sponsored at courses like Haydock Park, Warwick, Great Yarmouth, Redcar and Utoxeter, as well as Musselburgh and Perth, with prize money and liquid prizes presented by Matthew. Regional buyers and their wives were invited to the meetings and entertained in a Famous Grouse marquee or VIP suite on site.

Left: John Goodwin presenting a Famous Grouse trophy to the winning horse owner.

Opposite: Matthew Gloag presenting a case of The Famous Grouse in the paddock to the winning horse owner.

255

CURLING

'Curling was similar to bowls—we supported local clubs all over Scotland, but especially the 'Inverness Invitation', for which twelve leading rinks in Scotland were invited to come to Inverness and compete with local teams—we supplied a buffet and ceilidh dance.'

BOWLS

'Bowling was significant for us, first in Scotland only, then throughout the u.k. We supported local clubs with PoS materials and a couple of bottles for the start of the season, and sponsored local, regional and national tournaments. We also supplied coloured stickers to identify each team's bowls—a simple little thing, but very widely used.'

DARTS

'Somebody thought it would be a good idea to sponsor a darts match in Glasgow, so both Alick and I went along… There was a fight… I stood up, smashed my pint mug down and shouted: 'If you don't behave, we'll go home'. This had the desired effect, but left me with a cut hand. A useful lesson!' (Matthew Gloag).

Opposite: (Glorious) 12th August 1978, Jersey. Roy Bignell is third from left. Bowling sponsorship was significant for the brand, first in Scotland only, then throughout the u.k. The brand supported local clubs with Point of sale materials, bottles for the start of the season, and sponsored local, regional and national tournaments.

257

FLY-FISHING

Fishing competitions were sponsored. This event was part of the 'Licence to Skill' series.
Standing, left to right: Iain Halliday,
Chris Paterson (Sales Rep—West & Isles)
and Willie Miller (Regional Manager).
Front, second from left: Nicol Manson
(SLTA Committee).
Other fly-fishing competitions were supported on the River Test.

THE LADIES AUXILIARY OF THE YEAR

An especially popular event was the Ladies Auxiliary of the Year Award, known as 'the Oscars for ladies in the licensed trade', which was open to the landladies of pubs, restaurants and small hotels. Regional events were held, culminating in the final—a luncheon at The Savoy Hotel—hosted by Matthew Gloag and John Hughes. The night before the lunch, the Grouse team would meet the members of the committee and Matthew would take them all to a good restaurant. The lunch itself was held in the Savoy ballroom. 'It epitomised both Matthew and the brand's style, but it was also hugely popular, cemented our relationship with the licensed trade and generated huge support from the trade' (John Hughes).

THE R.N.L.I.

In 1987, a major on-trade promotion was launched to raise money for a lifeboat. Consumers in pubs were invited to buy a square on a large sheet for £1. There were 150 squares on each sheet, and when they had all been sold they were peeled to reveal a small grouse bird. Whoever had bought that square won a gallon of The Famous Grouse. 'It was difficult to organise, and we had to establish separate regional charities, but it gave us great exposure, and the required sum of £400,000 was raised in less than a year and paid for a Tyne Class lifeboat named The Famous Grouse.'

(John Hughes)

THE TIMES LIMERICK COMPETITION

A limerick competition was held in collaboration with The Times. This was started by Deinhard's (for their 'Green Label' wine), but soon adopted for The Famous Grouse in 1976. It was promoted by an ad beside The Times crossword: competitors had to incorporate the word 'grouse' into a limerick and the winner received a gallon bottle. The competition was judged by Denis Norden.

THE TIGER MOTH SOCIETY

The Tiger Moth Society held an annual meeting at Duxford Air Show Norfolk. Grouse took a tent and forty guests.

SAILING

Beginning in 1986, The Famous Grouse British Open 6-Metre Championship, over six days at Cowes on the Isle of Wight, under the aegis of the Royal Yacht Squadron, attracted crews from Britain, Hong Kong, Switzerland and France.

In 1987, The Famous Grouse Inter-Island Yacht Race, in the Channel Islands, was also sponsored, as was The Famous Grouse Cruiser Race in the Bristol Channel, organised by the Penarth Yacht Club, while the Cumbraes Regatta on the Clyde, which had been supported since 1985, attracted a record fleet of 153 boats in 1987.

The success of these events led to the company sponsoring the European and Classic 6-Metre Championships under the direction of the Royal Cornwall Yacht Club, at Falmouth in July 1988.

HOT-AIR BALLOONING

A request from a balloonist for a Famous Grouse Banner to trail on a flight from Hyde Park gave Matthew the idea of commissioning their own balloon. 'Its maiden flight was to be at a festival near Newbury. It was a disaster: the artwork made the balloon too heavy. But this was fixed, and thereafter the Grouse balloon was a familiar sight at carriage driving events, and also at the Skye Highland Games, where a film was made by Tom Clegg, called The Gathering. *We showed this at various gatherings of the Licensed Trade'.*

Glorious Twelfth events.

RUGBY

Relations with the S.R.U. began in 1990 with the sponsorship of a tour to New Zealand. In 1993 the brand became the exclusive sponsor of the Scottish national team itself, and remained so until 2008. In addition, The Famous Grouse was the leading sponsor of the Rugby World Cup in 1991 and 1995, but once this event had been established it became prohibitively expensive, and when sponsorship had to be shared with others, The Famous Grouse ceased to be a major sponsor. However, sponsorship at a reduced level continues to this day.

Left: 4th April 2002: Gregor Townsend with a golden Famous Grouse to mark his record-breaking sixty-sixth Cap for Scotland.

Opposite: Scotland players model The Famous Grouse kit. Standing, left to right: Tony Stanger, Andy Nicol, Kenny Milne, Derek Turnbull. Kneeling: Doddy Weir, Craig Chalmers, Gavin Hastings

The Famous Grouse sponsored Scottish Rugby's National Team for seventeen years, and to commemorate such a long association, the brand commissioned these gates for Murrayfield Stadium.

Chris Paterson with The Famous Grouse Kicking Tee Carrier.

GOLF

The Famous Grouse 'Shotgun Foursomes'—so called because players started simultaneously from all eighteen tees on the firing of a shotgun—started in 1984 and ran for nearly two decades. This was one of the first amateur golf sponsorships and was very popular with trade and general public alike. The professional organisers invited participation by golf clubs throughout the U.K. and Ireland to hold local competitions from which winning pairs progressed to one of twenty-four Regional Finals. Winning pairs from each of these were then invited to the National Final played over the Old Course at St Andrews. The Famous Grouse was the only commercial outfit ever permitted to have the Old Course closed from dawn to mid-morning, with players teeing off from the first back to the fourteenth on the firing of a shotgun by Matthew. The kudos this gave the brand was massive, and it meant a huge amount to players, who were very well looked after, including being provided with professional caddies.

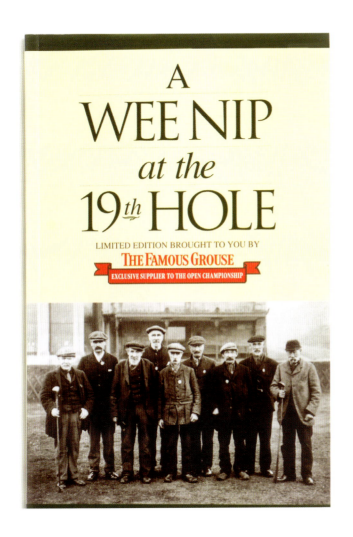

For many years The Famous Grouse was the exclusive Scotch at the Open Championship, in partnership with the Royal & Ancient Golf Club. The brand featured in 'The 19th Hole', a large marquee offering steak or smoked salmon sandwiches as well as drinks, open to the public, with half the space available for guests of Matthew Gloag & Son. This was very successful and attractive to leading sports personalities—such as Gavin Hastings, Bill McLaren, John Parrott and Peter Alliss—who mingled with the other guests.

The Ladies Golf Union's Coronation Foursomes was supported for many years. The championship was open to clubs throughout the U.K. and Ireland, with local, regional and national finals—with specially commissioned Grouse brooches for the winners. For ten years the brand had a relationship with the 19th Hole Golfing Society in Andover, whose members were all publicans, with an annual Scotland/England match.

Pool evenings were sponsored. Far left is Barry Punton, who was Regional Sales Manager for Northeast England and the Borders.

Opposite: The Famous Grouse sponsored a trade development scheme.
On the left is Eddie Johnston (Regional Manager) and on the far right, David Urquhart (Gordon & Macphail).

THIS Fiesta CAR ✴

WILL BE THE MAJOR PRIZE IN THE

FAMOUS GROUSE +
GORDON MACPHAIL
TRADE DEVELOPMENT SCHEME

Matthew Gloag at the Normandy Balloon Festival at the Château de Balleroi in Normandy (near Bayeux) in about 1980. Matthew was invited to the Château by its owner, Malcolm Forbes (of Forbes *Magazine).*

Opposite: Fred and Edith Gloag's housekeeper Mrs Anderson loading vegetables into the back of Matthew's Mini prior to his departure from Bonhard House for France in 1968, watched by Matthew's sister Felicity.

Matthew with his two daughters,
Emma and Sorcha, in 1983.

Dilly and Matthew Gloag with friends, Dawn and John Forsyth,
flying The Famous Grouse flag at a sailing event in Turkey.

Committee monthly meetings provide an idea of the diversity of causes and events supported. For example, the meeting in June 1980, lists seventeen 'PR Operations' master-minded by Matthew, from 'The Famous Grouse Taxidermy Competition' and a 'Horse Drawn Bus' in London to 'The British Helicopter Championships' and 'The World Carriage Driving Championships'.

Sponsorships ranged from local pub competitions to national sporting events—golf, bowls, darts, curling, squash, badminton, cricket, rugby—and a very diverse range of large-scale, up-market occasions, such as race meetings around the country, yacht racing at Cowes and the World Carriage Driving Championships at Windsor.

Each member of the sales team had a budget with which to support local events; larger scale sponsorships had to be cleared by the management board. And whenever there were prizes to be given out, Matthew or a member of his team would be there to present them—often in the presence of trade, local or national press. 'There was always a member of the team in attendance… The amount of extra hours the team put in was amazing' (Iain Halliday).

By the early 1990s advertising had become more

important than public relations and sponsorships and budgets were progressively diverted from the latter to the former. This change of direction and subsequent structural changes to management, not least following Edrington's takeover of Highland Distillers in 1999, led him to retire from full-time duties on 1st December 2002, aged fifty-five. Matthew was then appointed consultant to the company for life. He and his wife, Dilly, bought a house in the Midi-Pyrénées region of South West France where they spent significant amounts of time and also a cottage close to their roots in Perthshire, where they now live. While over in Perthshire for Christmas, on 15th January 2004, Matthew's arteriovenous malformation, which he had had from birth, 'exploded', resulting in severe brain injury, intensive care, rehabilitation and hospitalisation until 14th July 2005. This shocking, life-changing event and lasting disability enforced a permanent return to Scotland. Matthew's tenacity and determination, matched by the care of his family, and time has witnessed a remarkable recovery in his mental powers and his memories of the business and his working life, and despite his disability, his contribution to this book has not been

hindered at all. Bill Farrar remarked that 'Matthew was always "different" in his thinking and his ways of working—slightly quirky but always with a certain edge and style—he would add his own flavours to sponsorships and trade relations generally. During a recent visit to Matthew's house to discuss his contribution to this book, I noticed that the same "difference" that I encountered in my early years working with Matthew remains intact to this day.'

Opposite:
Matthew Gloag in the garden of his home
in the South West of France.

CHAPTER VII

THE HIGHLAND DISTILLERIES

CO. LTD

(1970–1980)

Highland Distilleries/Robertson & Baxter's

office on West Nile Street, Glasgow.

HIGHLAND DISTILLERIES HAD BEEN FOUNDED BY WILLIAM ALEXANDER ROBERTSON, IN 1887. He had arrived in Glasgow from Fife in 1855 and worked for three years for a wine and spirits merchant there before going into business on his own account, initially in partnership with Robert Thomson, and after 1861 with John W. Baxter, trading as Robertson & Baxter.

First, they acquired the agencies for a number of wines and spirits—port, sherry, claret, bourbon and rye whiskey—and then began buying and blending Scotch whisky.

Like W.B. Gloag, W.A. Robertson was a pioneer in the art of blending—indeed the *National Guardian* remarked in his obituary many years later that Robertson & Baxter soon became 'the most important business of its kind in the country'. Several leading figures in the whisky industry served apprenticeships with the firm, including Alexander Walker of Johnnie Walker & Sons (later Sir Alexander Walker) and John Dewar Junior of John Dewar & Sons (later Lord Forteviot).

In the interest of controlling how his stocks of whisky were matured and married, Robertson founded the Clyde Bonding Company in 1879, and in order to secure reliable supplies of whisky, built Bunnahabhain Distillery (in 1881), took a controlling interest in Glen Rothes-Glenlivet Distillery (in 1887) and founded Highland Distilleries Co. Ltd, to manage the two distilleries, also in 1887.

W.A. Robertson died ten years later, aged sixty-four. His obituarist reported: 'He was of a personality of outstanding importance in the wholesale trade in Scotland, and his demise creates a vacancy which will be extremely hard to fill'.

He was succeeded as chairman of Robertson & Baxter by his oldest son, James; his second son, Alexander (known as 'Nander'), became a director of Highland Distilleries.

In October 1897—within a month of W.A. Robertson's death—the Clyde Bonding Company's warehouse in Glasgow was totally destroyed by fire, along with very considerable stocks of whisky. Hard on the heels of this disaster came another—fire destroyed the malt mill, boiler and engine at Glen Rothes, reducing the distillery's output just when Highland needed it most. Prompted by R&B, the directors of Highland bought Tamdhu-Glenlivet Distillery in Knockando Parish, Morayshire, the next year.

As we have seen in relation to Matthew Gloag

& Son, the three decades following the death of W.A. Robertson were difficult years for the whisky industry. The boom of the 1890s finished suddenly in 1900. Then came World War I, followed by Prohibition in the U.S.A. and major increases in duty in the U.K.

Robertson & Baxter and Highland Distilleries weathered the storm better than some, cushioned by the fact that blending companies continued to replace stocks used up during the war. R&B's output during the year 1920/21 was the highest it had been since 1905. The price of new-make spirit rose to unprecedented levels between 1918 and 1925, and Highland's own stock climbed from 160,000 gallons to 613,000 gallons, with their value rising from £21,000 to £145,000. Shares soared in value.

In 1922, a number of R&B shareholders who were descended from the founding families intimated that they wanted to sell up. James Robertson wrote bitterly to the other shareholders:

The present inflated condition of the Scotch Whisky market [persuaded them] *to get their money into more easily realisable securities.*

Raising the money to buy them out presented a major problem for the directors. Discussions were opened with the Distillers Company, Buchanan-Dewar's and John Walker & Sons. Then James put the company into voluntary liquidation.

James and Nander immediately began trading as Robertson & Co. until 1927, when they bought back the original name from the liquidator. But the full transfer of assets and resumption of trading as Robertson & Baxter did not take place until 1937.

James Robertson was now a leading figure in the whisky trade. In 1927 he wrote to his friend Sir Alexander Walker, chairman of John Walker & Sons, which had joined the Distillers Company Limited (DCL) in 1925:

Now that the government is doing nothing to help the Scotch Whisky Trade, I am afraid that everyone—big or little—is in for a thin time… It is quite obvious to Traders in touch with the public that the consumption of Whisky will go lower this year and better trade generally will not get over the fact that the price of whisky is far beyond its intrinsic value and therefore limited to the few.

His colleague on the board of R&B, Major A.J. Wightman, launched a much-publicised attack on the inequality of whisky duty:

Is Scotch whisky, with all that its manufacture means to the Scottish farmer and worker, to disappear because of high taxation and encouragement of foreign wine drinking?... The duty of 7/6 is killing the goose that lays the golden eggs.

The Wall Street Crash of 1929 precipitated world recession, and by the end of the 1930/31 season many distillers were offering new-make spirit at less than cost in a desperate attempt to stay in business. The DCL cut its own production levels and its filling orders by twenty-five per cent for that season, then closed all its distilleries during 1932/33.

Highland halved production at Bunnahabhain and Glen Rothes, then closed the former and, as President of the Pot Still Malt Distillers Association, James Robertson urged the rest of the industry to follow suit. They did so, except Glen Grant and The Glenlivet Distilleries, which both had long-standing orders for spirit which they could not break.

Prohibition in the United States was repealed in 1933, and the fortunes of the Scotch whisky industry began to improve; by 1936 Highland was showing a healthy profit, and that year R&B was asked by the distinguished London wine merchant, Berry Bros. & Rudd, to take over the blending of their whisky, Cutty Sark.

Cutty Sark had been created specifically for the American market in 1923, and following the repeal of Prohibition was doing so well that the original blenders could not cope. In 1936 Hugh Rudd, senior partner of Berry Bros. & Rudd (and after 1943, when the firm became a limited company, Chairman) came to Glasgow to meet 'the Rolls Royce of blenders' (his words), Robertson & Baxter. They clearly had the skill and experience to take up the challenge, and through their close association with Highland Distilleries could be relied upon to find fillings for the blend. To guarantee this, Highland bought Highland Park Distillery on Orkney the following year.

Then came World War II; duty was increased, barley was rationed, and by late 1942 malt whisky distilling ceased. Nander Robertson died in 1940, and James Robertson in 1944.

James Robertson left £190,000 (£5 million in today's money) to his three daughters, Elspeth

James Robertson

(1864–1944)

The Robertson sisters: Elspeth, Agnes and Ethel.

(b. 1896), Agnes (b. 1897) and Ethel (b. 1903, and universally known as 'Babs'), almost all of it invested in Robertson & Baxter and the Clyde Bonding Company. Soon after his death, the sisters moved to Cawderstanes, a substantial mid-Victorian mansion near Berwick-upon-Tweed, which they had bought in 1943. Two years later they also bought the neighbouring farms of Edrington Mains and Edrington Castle.

It fell to the youngest sister, Miss Babs, to look after the sisters' interests in the family businesses. She was forty-one when her father died and prior to this had had nothing whatsoever to do with business, but she threw herself into it with gusto, under the loyal and experienced guidance of the companies' directors. She was elected to the board of R&B in 1947 and of Highland Distilleries in 1952. Although her sisters were not directly involved, they maintained a keen interest. Important decisions were made jointly; as one director put it 'they could not be divided and ruled'.

Soon after she had joined the board of R&B Miss Babs was approached by Samuel Bronfman, president of Distillers Corporation-Seagram Limited of Canada, a man with a tyrannical reputation and a very quick temper, who was determined to enter the Scotch whisky trade. The conversation went as follows:

'*Miss Robertson, I should like to buy your holding in Robertson & Baxter. In short, I want to buy the company.*'
'*The shares and the company are not for sale.*'
'*You have not asked me how much I would be prepared to pay.*' [In 1947, Seagram's sales topped $438 million, with net profits at $53.7 million.]
'*Mr Bronfman, the shares are not for sale at any price.*'

The reason for Mr Bronfman's keen interest was R&B's involvement with Cutty Sark. He went on to buy Chivas Bros. of Aberdeen in 1949 and his company 'multiplied itself through a rampage of acquisitions'. In 1955 he attempted to buy Highland Distilleries through an intermediary, the Glasgow broker Stanley P. Morrison, 'acting for an un-named American syndicate'. The board of Highland turned him down flat, and when it transpired that the 'un-named American syndicate' was the Seagram Corporation, Sir Henry Ross, chairman of the DCL, indicated that he would counter the bid, and Seagram backed off.

To protect themselves against hostile takeover, R&B proposed a supply/purchase agreement with its sister company for five years. Since R&B bought seventy per cent of Highland's output, the latter was happy to oblige. Early in 1956 a similar arrangement was made with Berry Bros. & Rudd and Cutty Sark's American distributor, the Buckingham Corporation, for the supply and finance of fillings, which accounted for around fifty per cent of R&B's sales.

R&B's sales had trebled between 1950 and 1952; restrictions on the importation of barley and the quota system limiting the amount of whisky which could be sold in the home market—provided producers continued to give priority to export markets—were removed in 1954. By 1957 the production of Scotch whisky was sixty per cent higher than it had been in 1939, and when, in 1959, the government finally lifted all restrictions on sales to the home trade there was a further boom. Between 1958 and 1962, R&B's profits rose from £490,000 to £1.7 million; most other whisky companies' profits quadrupled during this period as well.

The relaxation of all constraints upon the sale of Scotch in the home market in 1959, combined with the Scotch Whisky Association's decision not to fix minimum retail prices in the U.K., presented all blenders with new opportunities.

In order to boost their stocks of mature whisky—largely to support Cutty Sark—Robertson & Baxter acquired the Glasgow blending firm, Hepburn & Ross, and its well-known brand, Red Hackle. It was also decided to continue to market the brand. (It remained available until the 1970s.)

By 1960 the Robertson sisters were increasingly concerned about hostile takeover. They regarded the company's staff as part of their extended family; Miss Babs made it her business to know every employee at a more personal level than just knowing their names, and encouraged them to bring any problem they might have directly to her. She once said to Ian Good (later chairman of the companies):

People spend more of their lives here in the office than anywhere else, so if they are unhappy here, their lives become miserable … When someone in the family is in trouble, the family rallies round.

They were also concerned about what would happen to the businesses on their deaths. In 1960 the sisters were sixty-four, sixty-three and fifty-

RED HACKLE

*In February 1959 Robertson & Baxter bought
established Glasgow blender Hepburn & Ross
and its (at the time) well-known brand of
blended Scotch, Red Hackle, for £2 million.
Charles Hepburn and Herbert Ross founded the
company in 1920, after Charles had been demobilised
from The Black Watch, in which regiment he had
served as a captain during World War I. Red Hackle
takes its name from the conspicuous plume worn
exclusively by all ranks of The Black Watch. It
was granted to the regiment by King George III to
mark its gallantry at the Battle of Geldermalsen,
when the 11th Light Dragoons retreated, leaving
two field guns for the French. The Black Watch
promptly counter-attacked and rescued the guns.
Herbert Ross had died in 1957, and on the
death of his wife two years later, Charles
Hepburn decided to leave the whisky trade.*

seven, and Inheritance Tax was charged at around eighty per cent of the estate: their holdings would have to be sold to pay death duties. Having taken the advice of a leading English barrister, the sisters' entire capital was transferred to a holding company named Edrington (after one of their farms). The shares they received in return were then gifted to a charitable trust, The Robertson Trust.

The trust deed was signed by the sisters on 1st May 1961. Its two stated purposes were, first, to ensure the family businesses of R&B and Clyde Bonding should 'continue as active businesses in the control of British subjects', and second, that 'the support we have given to a large number of charities should be continued and extended'.

As we have seen in relation to The Famous Grouse, during the 1960s there was a phenomenal increase in the demand for Scotch whisky from overseas, led by the U.S.A. To meet the demand, the industry increased capacity: eleven new malt distilleries were built, five of them within existing grain distilleries; many operating distilleries were expanded and modernised; long-closed distilleries were refurbished and re-opened. Four new grain distilleries were commissioned, at Cambus (Strathmore Distillery),

Invergordon, Girvan and Airdrie (Moffat Distillery), and Montrose Distillery (now named Glenesk) re-opened.

The output of grain whisky rose from 41 million proof gallons in 1960 to 90 mpg (233.5 million litres) in 1966, and of malt whisky from 29 mpg to 51 mpg (132.4 million litres). By 1968 there was a glut of mature whisky—but this was soon taken up by the ever-increasing demand from abroad.

The same year that The Robertson Trust was established, 1961, just over one million cases of Cutty Sark were sold in the United States—the first brand to pass this milestone. All the whisky in Cutty Sark was supplied by Robertson & Baxter, and by 1963 it was clear that the company would have to lay down more stock than ever before to meet anticipated demand. In 1964, the long-established firm of blenders in Glasgow, Lang Brothers, together with Glengoyne Distillery, was acquired, principally for the firm's stocks of mature whisky. They also acquired the Clyde Cooperage Company, in 1967, to ensure a supply of casks.

They also approached the board of Highland Distilleries, who resolved to increase capacity at Glen Rothes from four to six stills and at Bunnahabhain from two to four stills; to double the size of the

Saladin maltings at Tamdhu and take a twenty-five per cent holding in a new maltings in Bridlington (they pulled out of the latter in 1968); to build substantial new warehouses at Bishopbriggs, in the north east of Glasgow. Between October 1964 and midsummer 1965, Highland's bank balance dropped from £30,000 in credit to £500,000 overdrawn.

Output from the company's five distilleries—Bunnahabhain, Glen Rothes, Highland Park, Tamdhu and Glenglassaugh (the last had resumed production in 1960, having been silent for fifty-three years)—rose to 2.6 million proof gallons (6.75 million litres) by 1964, achieved by efficiencies as well as by increasing capacity. The company was greatly assisted in controlling costs by the appointment to the board of a young chartered accountant, J.A.R. Macphail, in February 1962, who had joined R&B the year before from Arthur Bell & Sons.

But by the mid-1960s the economy of the U.K. was faltering. The Labour Government under Harold Wilson, which was returned for a second term in spring 1966, was committed to deflation by keeping interest rates high, increasing duty on whisky in 1966 and 1968 (twice) from to £14.60 to £18.86 per proof gallon, and imposing heavier corporation tax.

This exacerbated the problems facing the whisky industry in both home and export markets—the former, because, between 1960 and 1968, the price of a bottle of Scotch doubled; the latter on account of the high exchange rate. Notwithstanding these difficulties, exports rose from 12 million proof gallons in 1960 to 33mpg in 1968.

At last, in November 1967, Harold Wilson was persuaded to bow to the inevitable and devalue sterling by almost fifteen per cent. Investors were quick to see the advantages this would bring, and Highland's share price moved up sharply, with the company being tipped in the financial press as 'the leader among the smaller Scotch whisky distillers'. In 1969 Highland Distilleries was a runner-up in a competition organised by *Management Today* to find 'Britain's Champion Company'.

It was against this background that Highland Distilleries' offer to buy Matthew Gloag & Son was made. The Gloag board had no alternative but to accept, and three of Highland's directors joined it—John Macphail, Harry Penman (Chairman of Highland) and John Goodwin.

At the time, the press believed that Highland had bought Gloag's for its stocks of mature whisky,

JOHN MACPHAIL was born in Singapore and partly raised in South Africa, before being sent to the Edinburgh Academy, where he captained the shooting VIII and the rugby XV. During World War II, he served in the RAF, then returned to play for the Barbarians and Scotland (as hooker), and to qualify as a Chartered Accountant in Glasgow. He joined Arthur Bell & Sons in 1949 and, following a disagreement with Raymond Miquel (see p. 230), resigned his directorship to join Robertson & Baxter, in December 1961. He went on to become the leading figure of his generation in the Scotch whisky industry, as we shall see.

but this rumour was dispelled in early 1971 when it was announced that Highland Distilleries and its sister company, Robertson & Baxter, had made a joint venture with Gloag's to blend, develop and promote The Famous Grouse internationally, with Highland supplying malt fillings and R&B the grain stock, which was substantially greater than Highland's stock. 'The joint venture meant that we could push sales of Grouse without mucking up Highland's profits. I'm a great believer in riding the tide', commented John Macphail.

Highland could not exploit this potential alone because of the investment required in promotion and whisky stocks, especially since the business was constituted as a public company. As a private company, R&B was able to take a long-term view, and being cash rich was able to cover the costs of advertising and promotion. This investment to develop the brand was 'off the balance sheet': henceforth R&B were responsible for blending The Famous Grouse, and the price of the blend had a built-in proportion to cover the cost of their investment in advertising until it had been paid off.

The price of the re-packaged bottle was pitched between standard blends, like Bell's, and deluxe

Quality in an age of change.

The Famous Grouse Brand was relaunched as The Famous Grouse in early 1972. The new livery and the print campaign which accompanied the launch were conceived by Ron Baird of Saatchi & Saatchi, which remained the company's advertising agency until 1993. The slogan, 'Quality in an age of change' was peculiarly well suited to the uncertain political and economic climate of the mid-1970s. The artist who redrew the grouse emblem in colour, for both the label and advertisements, was a local man, Charles Stanley Todd. Later the grouse was redrawn again by the well-known ornithological artist, Rodger McPhail, from Lancashire.

ANDREW KETTLES (above) had qualified as a Chartered Accountant in Dundee, with distinction, in 1966. He was appointed Company Secretary of Matthew Gloag & Son in 1971 and Finance Director in 1973. When John Macphail became Chairman of Highland and Gloag's in 1988, he and Alick Sherriff became joint Managing Directors, and he continued in this role for three years after Alick's death in 1993.

blends like Chivas Regal, so it was perceived as a 'premium' product. The directors were determined to hold this price position—to the extent that Alick Sherriff turned down an order for 10,000 cases from a supermarket chain in northern England, owing to fears that they would slash the price.

Orders began to advance rapidly.

Change came only gradually to the offices and bond of Matthew Gloag & Son. It was seen as inevitable: the company was old-fashioned—this was mainly considered to be a strength by the staff—but the old machinery (bottle washer, bottling apparatus, etc.) was considered a weakness, and became increasingly inadequate for the scale of business.

Prior to 1971, blending of The Famous Grouse was done in the bond at Perth, supervised by Fred Gloag (and later Matthew), Alick Sherriff, Charles Mactaggart, and reduced to bottling strength (40% ABV) with local water. After the takeover, blending was done by R&B and moved to Clyde Bonding's site at Drumchapel, under the overall control of Bob Gillies, Production Director, who had previously worked for Long John International.

This was necessary for several reasons: the volumes now anticipated—and soon required—made

Château Palmer

Margaux

Appellation Haut-Médoc Contrôlée

MATTHEW GLOAG & SON, LTD.,
PERTH, SCOTLAND.

ESTABLISHED 1800.

PRODUCE OF FRANCE

Haut Sauternes.

Bordeaux.

Shipped and Bottled by
Matthew Gloag & Son, Ltd.,
Perth Scotland

Established 1800

Puligny-Montrachet

MATTHEW GLOAG & SON, LTD.,
PERTH, SCOTLAND.

ESTABLISHED 1800.

St. Emilion

PRODUCE OF FRANCE

MATTHEW GLOAG & SON, LTD.,
PERTH, SCOTLAND.

ESTABLISHED 1800

A selection of Matthew Gloag's wine labels.

it impossible to blend sufficient quantities in Perth; the increased volumes demanded a higher degree of consistency, if the brand was to take off, and R&B's stock of filling whiskies were held at Drumchapel.

Reduction and bottling continued to be done in Perth until about 1980, after which most bottling was done in Glasgow.

Odd-sized bottles were still handled in Perth and standard bottles at busy times of the year, like Christmas, until the bond closed in 1994.

The three new directors, John Macphail, Harry Penman and John Goodwin, were not permanently based at Bordeaux House, so were considered to be more remote than Willie or Fred Gloag. Vic Scott remarked:

When Highland took over, things went on just as before, but with more production… Highland didn't put their own men into Gloag's. They married themselves in gradually.

Charlie Mactaggart had retired and was replaced by Roy Bignell as Export Director (until 1986). Sylvia McPherson:

Mr Bignell was based in the main office in Bordeaux House. Of course the export department was in the bond, and he would send Hazel Anderson over with handwritten letters for her to type. And then he got an export secretary and gradually it began to change. Most of the folk coming in now have got university degrees, but we just went to commercial school.

Mary Gray added:

There weren't any machines really. That was all changed when Highland took over in 1970. Highland needed a bottling outfit and we were just right for them. A lot changed in the bond after that. We all got pay rises!
Before Highland, Mr Mactaggart would say every year that they couldn't really afford a pay increase. But in 1970 our wages went up to the same level as Highland's other places.

Many interviewees mentioned the pay rise! Hazel Anderson:

Things seemed to carry on as before after Highland

Matthew Gloag's fine wines' catalogues.

Opposite:

Point-of-sale materials were not handed out indiscriminately. They were considered to be rewards to licensees for supporting the brand, not as bribes to promote The Famous Grouse! Each rep had a catalogue of items and a budget limit, and more expensive items—clocks, barometers, mirrors—could only be earned by collecting tokens: typically twenty tokens were required, with one token issued per twelve bottle case.

took over, but we got a pay rise, and some new people were brought in, like Mr Gillies and Mr Kettles.

The company was non-union, as Sylvia McPherson recalls:

Charlie Mactaggart didn't like anybody who was in a union. They just weren't taken on. But in the bond they were always saying that if we had a union we'd get this and that and the other. So when Highland took over, the union men came from Glasgow…but gradually

not one of those who had always wanted a union showed any interest in it. After all their agitating for years, not one of them was interested—I don't know why. We got the benefits of course.

Another popular innovation was the introduction by Highland of Christmas parties. Sylvia McPherson:

We didn't have arranged parties before 1970—we just had to do it ourselves. But after 1970 we had office dances and parties…and we got Champagne wholesale!

Although changes were welcomed, members of staff who had worked for Gloag's before the takeover always felt their loyalties were towards the family business, not to Highland, and regretted the inevitable loss of closeness and family-feeling as the company grew. Mrs Isobel Johnstone, who started with the company as an office cleaner in 1950, remarked: *Gloag's staff were always great characters, but now you don't have that. It's too busy now. It's a job and you get on with it. You don't have the same laughs as you got. Gloag's was always a family company…one big family.*

The company's key market had always been in Scotland, but now concerted efforts were made to promote The Famous Grouse throughout the U.K., and, after 1974, abroad.

Branded point-of-sale materials were widely used—novel click-on optics, ash-trays, dart-boards, dominos, playing cards, clocks, barometers, pub mirrors, umbrellas, note pads, drip mats which converted into fishing caste winders… All were high quality and desirable, in keeping with the brand's positioning, and although they were aimed at the licensed trade, they promoted the brand to the consumer.

The off-trade (wholesalers and off-licenses) was not ignored, and began with small multiples, like Haddows, Agnews, Watson & Philips and Morton's, first in Scotland, then in England through Deinhard's connections. Later larger multiple grocers like Asda, Tesco and William Low, became important.

In the on-trade, the reps' goal was to 'dress the entire establishment', to which end they were given a budget and could draw PoS materials from a catalogue. As one rep told me: 'All of us proudly wore our Famous Grouse ties, and handed them out to chosen customers—as did the reps from other whisky companies, but their ties were not such good quality!'

The Gloag family's long connections with The Black Watch had led to The Famous Grouse being adopted as the regiment's 'house whisky' some years before, and through his own army connections, Alick Sherriff managed to place the brand in all the officers' and sergeants' messes of the Scottish regiments, as well as the NAAFI, which had a considerable 'halo effect' on the brand. In particular, Grouse became very popular in Germany.

By the end of 1972, U.K. sales were up forty per cent on the previous year, to 61,000 cases, and by the end of 1973, U.K. sales had almost tripled to 101,083 cases.

The optimistic forecasts for the likely level of demand for The Famous Grouse, estimated at some half a million cases a year, posed serious financial problems for Highland Distilleries, with its already over-stretched cash flow and overdraft—exacerbated by a downturn in the world economy and a rapid rise in inflation.

Although the company's Annual Returns for 1971 and 1972 continued to show a small profit, this was squeezed by the rising cost of raw materials and by the reluctance of the Distillers Company—far and

Back row: Matthew Gloag, Bill Williamson (Edinburgh), Alick Sherriff, George Walker (Fife).
Front row: Eddie Johnston (Regional Manager-East), Ronnie Stewart (Aberdeen),
Iain Cavana (Glasgow West), Bill Millar (Regional Manager-West), Bob Masson (Tayside).

away the largest producer—to pass these additional costs on to customers, either at home or abroad.

Against this background, Highland had to find funds to finance the stock for Grouse. After long negotiations, in October 1972, the Royal Bank of Scotland agreed to double the company's overdraft facility to £2 million and Highland's merchant bankers, Baring Bros. in London offered a revolving credit of £300,000. Advantage was also taken of recent investment grants and the EEC (which Britain joined on 1st January 1973) regional development grant to double the capacity of Tamdhu.

In April 1973 Harry Penman retired as chairman, John Macphail was elected to replace him and John Goodwin became Managing Director of both Highland and Matthew Gloag & Son, and spent a lot of time in Perth.

In October 1973 Egypt and Syria invaded Israel, and there followed the brief but savage Yom Kippur War. To punish America for supporting Israel, the Organisation of Arab Petroleum Exporting Countries (OAPEC) embargoed the export of oil to the U.S. until March 1984, then hiked the price substantially. At the same time the New York Stock Market lost forty-five per cent of its value, and the London Stock Market seventy-three per cent, while inflation in the U.K. was running at twenty-five per cent in 1975.

The Conservative Government attempted to control inflation through statutory price and wage restraints, but it continued to mount, and the Stock Market continued to fall. Frequent strikes crippled manufacturing and public services, unemployment rose above one million, and as the winter progressed the situation grew steadily worse, culminating in the three-day week and the General Election of February 1974 which narrowly brought Labour back into power.

Despite the desperate economic uncertainty the Highland board pressed on with its programme of capital investment—on the very day the election was announced, it was decided to increase the capacity at Glen Rothes by one third with the addition of two new stills, at a cost of £500,000.

In April 1975 the government increased Excise Duty by thirty per cent to £22.09 per proof gallon (and increased this again by £2.54 the following year). V.A.T., which had been introduced in 1973, added an additional eight per cent. At a meeting of the Highland board in June, Company Secretary R.D. Oakes intimated that the Group's cash requirement

Roy Bignell, the company's Export Director (left)

with Dick Newman (right) the Chief Executive of Austin, Nichols & Co, the American drinks manufacturer.

The Famous Grouse ice tongs.

Opposite: The Famous Grouse ceramic decanter made by Royal Doulton.

could reach £8 million by 1976. The banks were immediately approached to increase the overdraft to £3 million.

In these circumstances, the expansion of Glen Rothes was put on hold, and resources were directed towards enlarging The Famous Grouse's market share: by the end of 1975 sales in the home market had risen by eighty per cent and exports to the Commonwealth were encouraging. Following heavy promotions in the lead-up to Christmas, sales surged again by seventy per cent in 1976.

In 1974/75 Matthew Gloag & Son began to develop export markets in earnest.

Charles Mactaggart had retired in 1973 and been replaced as Export Director by Roy Bignell, assisted by John McDermott. Roy looked after South Africa, Rhodesia, Kenya, Australia, New Zealand, Japan, the u.s.a. and Canada, and John took care of Europe. 'We were trying to find distributors which were family-owned, premium-quality brand handling— people with a similar philosophy to ourselves', said Roy Bignell.

One of the first tasks was to tidy up distribution in the United States, where there were over a dozen small distributors. Roy appointed Austin, Nichols &

THE MATTHEW GLOAG GAZETTE

ESTABLISHED 1800

MATTHEW GLOAG 1814
WILLIAM B GLOAG 1860
MATTHEW GLOAG 1896
MATTHEW W GLOAG 1910
MATTHEW F GLOAG 1947
MATTHEW I GLOAG 1970

Published by Matthew Gloag & Son Ltd, Perth, Scotland
Issue No. 1, Spring 1976

WHY THE FAMOUS GROUSE IS THE FINEST SCOTCH WHISKY

GROUSE whisky has been famous by name for several years. Its fame by reputation is more recent.

Even sales director Alick Sherriff admits to being pleasantly surprised by the phenomenal rate of increase.

Selling Scotch to the Scots, in particular, has never been the easiest of tasks, but now Grouse is among the brand leaders in its own market.

Sherriff summed up the progress dramatically: "We are selling substantially more in one month than we were in the whole of 1970."

He put it down to three main factors:

☐ Concentration on the quality of the product.
☐ Avoidance of becoming another drinks trade commodity.
☐ The "freedom" of the retail liquor trade in Scotland.

The fact that Famous Grouse can now be seen on the shelves of between 60 and 70 per cent of Scottish shops is ample testimony to its acceptance.

"We have built our achievement on a high quality image", said Sherriff.

"We have taken an independent line and not followed other whisky companies."

Growth has brought a corresponding increase in the sales department's payroll.

From just one salesman in 1958, Grouse can now keep seven men fully occupied knocking on doors in Scotland.

In England Deinhard, the German wine shippers, are distributors.

Famous Grouse was given a rousing send-off for a recent visit to Moscow. Veteran actor John Laurie was at the Perth office of Matthew Gloag and Son to present a haggis and giant bottle of whisky to a Burns Federation group travelling to the Russian capital. Also in the picture above are director Matthew Gloag, travel agent Gordon Hepburn and Hamish Young, chairman of Perth and Kinross District Council. See "Eastern Bloc Promise" Page 2.

And in three years they have more than trebled sales.

Advertising has played a vital part. Famous Grouse is now promoted nationally and Matthew Gloag and Son Ltd. are spending 10 times more on advertising than they did six years ago.

However, Alick Sherriff claims with justification that his whisky sells on its own merit.

Since he joined the company in 1956 he has worked in all departments, from bottling line to boardroom.

He remembers the whisky previously being known as "Old Grouse."

"There has always been a cachet of age and quality," he added.

"I've been lucky to inherit such a soundly-based brand."

Grouse's reputation as a high grade whisky has helped spread its fame in other countries.

At one time its overseas effort was by a lone salesman who travelled simply with confidence and a case full of samples.

Now export director Roy Bignell regularly jets round the world servicing 52 markets.

He has regarded the past two years as a period for consolidation and strengthening of his distribution network.

Uncertain world trading conditions have made spectacular sales growth out of the question.

Roy Bignell prefers to wait for the economic clouds to clear before attempting to break into new markets.

"Exporting has been extremely difficult for the whole whisky industry over the past two years," he explained.

Apart from the general economic recession he mentioned the following:

☐ Discrimination against Scotch whisky by several governments. This usually takes the form of crippling duties and tariffs.

☐ A proliferation of "secondary" brands of lesser quality whisky, attractive to countries which are trading down because of high tariffs and prices.

Nevertheless, Grouse's achievements overseas have been remarkable considering that the brand was virtually unknown in many markets until recently.

Roy Bignell said: "A few people in most parts of the world had perhaps heard of it, but we did

Continued on Page 2

CHAIRMAN'S WELCOME

May I take this opportunity of welcoming you to this, the first edition of the Matthew Gloag Gazette which I hope you will enjoy.

We at Gloag's felt that this Gazette would provide an opportunity to keep the many people both at home and abroad, who contribute so much to the success of the Company, informed as to the activities of the Company and the progress of its products. As regards future editions, it will be of great assistance to us if you could contribute any items you think would be of interest.

I am happy to report that "Famous Grouse" is making very good progress in the home market, particularly so in Scotland, which is most encouraging. In addition, advances are being made in export markets such as Japan, South Africa and France, but we are still very much at the building stage and many stimulating opportunities lie ahead.

Gloag's take a particular pride in ensuring that their products are of the highest standard. We are therefore extremely careful in bringing in innovations, and will not do so unless they have been carefully researched and tested over a long period of time. Perhaps it is for this reason that it has taken us some 175 years to bring out the first issue of this publication!

*JOHN MACPHAIL
CHAIRMAN*

Orders from Moscow: Less than a week after a highly successful Burns Night in January 1975, which had been supplied with a few bottles of The Famous Grouse, Gloag's received an order for 140 cases from the Russian state drink monopoly, including Andrei Gromyko, the Soviet Foreign Minister, immediately followed by a 150-case order from the American Embassy in Moscow.

Co., owners of the well-known Wild Turkey Bourbon and the distillery in Kentucky of the same name, as national distributor. However, following the conclusion of the Vietnam War in 1975, which had stimulated the u.s. economy, America went into recession. The effect of this was felt by all Scotch whisky companies trading in this market: many consumers traded down from brands bottled in Scotland to Scotch bottled in the u.s., switched from brown to white spirits, or from spirits to wine and beer. Sales of The Famous Grouse dropped by fifteen per cent.

Later Seagram took over distribution for a few years—Edgar Bronfman was very keen on the brand.

As the leading brand of Scotch in the American market Cutty Sark was particularly hard hit, and its problem was compounded by the fact that its long-standing distributor, The Buckingham Corporation, repeatedly changed owners and became more unreliable. Sales declined dramatically, and as a result substantial stocks of mature whisky which had been allocated by R&B to Cutty Sark were redirected to The Famous Grouse.

Grouse's largest export market was Australia, where Elder Smith Goldsborough Mart Ltd held the agency. Around 50,000 cases were being sold here in the mid-1970s, but the whisky was shipped in bulk, owing to a tax on stock bottled in Scotland which doubled the price of a bottle.

Preparations were made to appoint distributors in Italy, Denmark, Spain, Sweden, Cyprus, Germany, Japan and Hong Kong. The Gloag board was keen that the slogan 'Quality in an age of change' be used in export markets, and it was taken up in most, but not in all. John Goodwin was horrified by a proposal from the Italian distributor, Cinzano, which proposed using a caricature of the Grouse bird!

Matsushita (better known as National Panasonic) was appointed distributor in Japan, undertaking to spend £260,000 on advertising there over the next three years to hit a sales target of 10,500 cases.

John travelled extensively in Europe, old-fashioned shoe leather with local sales people in the field, meeting bar owners, wholesalers, supermarket buyers and hotel owners.

Roy took on James Hodgkinson (former Rothmans salesman in the Middle East), a former major who had been involved in the Olympic Games in Australia and was now appointed to look after Grouse, Red Hackle and Lang's, especially in the Middle East. He was an excellent salesman and remained with the company for many years. In Cyprus they chose Grouse, and it went on to do very well there.

Typical was for Grouse to put up so much per case (£2) as Advertising and Promotion (A&P) budget for a year, to be matched by the distributor, though some took the view that it was our brand not theirs—but ideally a partnership to grow the brand in each market. Mostly we persuaded them to make a contribution to building the brand. Not too much advertising above the line in export markets, Ballantine's, Walker and J&B were the big European brands and spent a lot, so we had to be innovative on pack promotions (fishing flies made from grouse feathers, free miniatures, free glasses), decorated bottles at Christmas and so on. In Paris a black cab was bought from Glasgow, branded with The Famous Grouse on the door (but no mention of 'Scotch whisky' or 'express delivery service' because of strict advertising regulations in France). Burns Suppers were also sponsored in Moscow.

Jimmy Macallan, who worked in security at Prestwick Airport was also the piper who welcomed VIPs when they landed there—including Gromyko. Jimmy was also used at The Famous Grouse Burns Suppers.

The first bottle of The Famous Grouse to be sold in Duty Free was in 1974/75. A hotel group had the concession for duty-free sales at Heathrow Airport, but they had never heard of Grouse and said the price was too high. John McDermott refused to lower it, and some months later he got a call from the manager of the duty-free shop at Prestwick, which had received a lot of enquiries about the brand. Thus was the brand listed—at the premium price—and soon taken up by other duty-free outlets. In time this grew to be a colossal business; furthermore, premium pricing in Duty Free also supported on-trade sales in export markets in the same way as in the home market.

Not long after this, John McDermott negotiated sales through cross-Channel ferries which, in time, also became a huge business.

John Macphail was acutely aware that the success of the brand had been achieved with borrowed money, however, and was gloomy about the prospects for the whisky trade in general, given the alarming cash-flow problems faced by the smaller companies. In his annual statement to shareholders in 1976, he wrote: 'What the industry has to face

MOST whiskies are drinkable. Some are even very good. A few are Superb. Grouse is one of the fortunate few. Since 1800 the Gloag family have been blending and selling fine whisky. Now six generations later, the culmination is their Famous Grouse Brand Scotch Whisky. To test its fine quality, try it neat and compare it with other blended whiskies.

The FAMOUS GROUSE
SCOTCH WHISKY

Advertisement in Punch: *26th November 1975.*

up to, and the sooner the better, is to get a proper return on its investment, even if it means reduced sales in the short term'.

Apart from the high rate of duty, the key problem was the DCL's policy of keeping prices unrealistically low—'sacrificing profits on the altar of market share and damaging the whole industry in the process', as one trade newspaper put it. In 1971 the DCL commanded half the domestic market: Haig had been the leading brand of blended Scotch since the late 1920s, and the first to sell one million cases. Grouse's nearest competitor in 1971 was 400,000 cases behind. Johnnie Walker, Dewar's, White Horse, Black & White, VAT 69 and a myriad of other well-known brands were successful in overseas markets as well as at home. The company was able to adopt a policy of squeezing its competitors by keeping prices down. This was greatly resented by the rest of the trade, and during the latter half of the decade Distillers' pre-eminence was substantially eroded.

In Europe price was becoming an increasingly important factor, both for supermarket listing and for consumers. The buying power of the large European supermarket chains, through which most Scotch was sold, encouraged the growth of 'parallel exports'. These were goods bought under bond by U.K. wholesalers, with all available home trade discounts, then diverted abroad (usually to major retail chains) at a substantially lower price than that asked by the brands' appointed agents in the country in question.

Distributors were required by their contracts to spend money on promoting the brands they represented, and passed these costs on to consumers. Accordingly, they were undermined by the parallel export system.

In December 1977 the E.E.C. Commission banned dual pricing. This hit the DCL particularly hard. To protect their European agents, they increased the price of some brands in the home market (Buchanan's Black & White and VAT 69, for example) which was the kiss of death and withdrew others—including Johnnie Walker Red Label and Haig Dimple—from the home market altogether. In a futile, and somewhat arrogant, attempt to retain market share, they introduced John Barr (in a similar shaped bottle to Johnnie Walker) and The Buchanan Blend.

The Famous Grouse and Bell's both benefited hugely from these developments and increased their market share, Grouse focusing on the off-

story continued on page 318

1983: Jack Kidd retires after fifty years of service with Matthew Gloag's.
Back row: Roy Bignell, John Goodwin, Alick Sherriff, Matthew Gloag, Andrew Kettles, Bob Gillies.
Front row: Jack Kidd, John Macphail.

1983: Jack Kidd retirement party in the reception area of Bordeaux House. Bob Gillies is on the far left, Gina Harley is second to his left. Mr Kidd is in the centre in the striped suit, wearing his recently acquired British Empire Medal; his wife is to his right. Charles Mactaggart is to Mr Kidd's left. Directly behind him is Jim Cryle, then Vic MacDonald and Robin Butler (at the top of the stairs).

trade and Bell's on the on-trade. In April 1978 John Macphail was able to report a fifty per cent rise in sales in both the home and export markets (to 850,642 and 223,260 cases respectively) and an eighteen per cent rise in profit, compared with an industry-wide decline of seventeen per cent. He also told shareholders that the Price Commission had agreed to a small rise in the price of a bottle of Grouse, which would help the company's margins but should not affect the continuing growth in sales.

By the end of the year, pre-tax profits were over £4 million; the shareholders were rewarded with a dividend of £2.22p per 20p share and a one-for-one bonus issue, raising Highland's issued capital to just over £12 million. It was announced that the plans to expand Glen Rothes would be extended: now a completely new still house would be built, with four new stills, bringing the total to ten.

These were remarkable achievements, given the economic situation in the country. Labour, now led by Jim Callaghan, clung to power, although unemployment was at a post-war high of 1.5 million people and during the Winter of Discontent in 1978/79 Britain came to a virtual standstill with numerous strikes in the public sector. In March 1979

a vote of no confidence proposed by Tory Opposition Leader Margaret Thatcher precipitated the collapse of the Labour Government and in the election in May that year, the Tories were returned.

At the end of 1979 it was announced that The Famous Grouse was the most popular Scotch whisky in Scotland, narrowly topping Bell's. Sales in Scotland had increased by seventeen per cent during the year, and by seventy per cent in England; over a million cases had been sold in the home market and 221,000 cases overseas.

In line with what other whisky companies were doing, during the autumn of 1979, Bunnahabhain was first released as a single malt (at 12YO); Tamdhu, which had been launched as a single in 1976 (at 8YO) was repackaged, now bottled at 10YO, and Highland Park, which had also first been released by Highland in 1979 (as a 12YO; earlier bottlings had been done under licence) was relaunched in a distinctive bottle, with a small advertising budget to support it, owing to the cost of promoting The Famous Grouse, although this distinguished malt quickly won favour among aficionados.

The demand for blended Scotch during the 1960s and early 1970s, and the shortage of mature stock

RAISE YOUR STANDARDS.

The Famous Grouse, Scotland's legendary scotch, is setting a new standard for premium Scotch whisky.

Smoothness is only part of the legend.

Discerning scotch drinkers (who drink scotch because they prefer it) will find in The Famous Grouse all the characteristics that combine to make the final result as close to perfection as Scotch whisky can be.

The Famous Grouse.

Isn't it time you raised your standards?

SCOTLAND'S LEGENDARY SCOTCH.

From the house of Matthew Gloag & Son, established in 1800.

BLENDED SCOTCH WHISKY, 86 PROOF. IMPORTED BY THE CARRADALE IMPORT CO. LTD., SAN FRANCISCO, CA.

post-war, meant that all the malt whisky distilled went into blends. By the late 1970s the situation had changed. Amalgamations had narrowed the malt distillers' traditional customer base—the blenders—while high duty and changing fashions were reducing demand. To make matters worse, the stocks of mature whisky had never been higher: four times what they were in 1960, in excess of a billion gallons.

A partial solution to the problem was to bottle and promote their malts as single whiskies. The first company to do this was William Grant & Sons, who began to promote Glenfiddich Pure Malt in 1963/64. It sold surprisingly well—in both 1970 and 1971 sales rose by fifty per cent. The DCL followed reluctantly with Cardhu in 1965, then got cold feet and withdrew any advertising budget for the brand.

But interest in malt whisky was stirring by the mid-1970s. Hugh MacDiarmid, the eminent Scottish poet, wrote in 1974:

Only a few years ago it would have been useless to ask for a malt whisky in most of the English bars and even in Scotland, south of the Highland Line. Quite recently it has become a very different story. I had occasion recently to do a lot of motoring in the Upper Tyne valley, and in all the little pubs I visited, patronised by only a few shepherds and gamekeepers outside a little tourist traffic in the season, I found that every one stocked malt whiskies, and not just one of them but several, so that customers could choose which ones they wanted. Even more surprising to me was the bar in the Student's Union of a north English university, where I found between thirty and forty malts available.

The same year, bottled malt sales moved up by sixty-one per cent in volume to 700,000 gallons, while value advanced by fifty-two per cent to £4.24 million. Distillery owners began to follow William Grant's lead, albeit still in a small way, and with limited promotional support.

Arthur Bell & Sons introduced Blair Athol and Dufftown (both at 8YO) in 1972, and added Inchgower 12YO in 1975. Whyte & Mackay did the same with Dalmore, Tomintoul-Glenlivet and Old Fettercairn around 1978; Glenfarclas appointed Saccone & Speed as agents in England and Wales in May 1979. Laphroaig 10YO and Tormore 10YO, at the time both owned by Long John International, were 'freshened up' in 1979. Invergordon Distillers did the same with Bruichladdich and Tullibardine, and made plans to 'strongly advertise these malts to the trade' in 1980.

Although sales of single malt amounted to less than 1% of the world market for Scotch in 1978, demand grew faster than the industry anticipated, both at home and abroad. In 1980 a symposium of whisky companies anticipated that exports of single malt would increase by 8–10% per annum over the next five years. In fact it was twice that.

In 1982, Tony Lord, the editor of *Decanter* magazine wrote:

As recently as ten years ago only about thirty malts could be bought as singles, but fortunately the rapidly increasing appreciation of single malts for their individual character has seen this number nearly double.

The 're-discovery' of single malts would have far-reaching effects on the whisky industry in the decades to come.

THE ECONOMIC TURMOIL of the mid-1970s encouraged amalgamation, led by large brewing companies like Watney Mann, Allied Breweries and Whitbread, and by overseas distillers, like Seagram, Hiram Walker and Pernod-Ricard. It was rumoured in the Stock Market that all independent whisky companies might be taken over. The increased involvement of powerful multinationals in the whisky industry, combined with the drop in demand for blended Scotch in the u.s., reduced the number of customers for fillings at a time when many distillers had recently expanded their production capacity.

In May 1977 Hiram Walker Gooderham & Worts, the massive Canadian distiller, attempted to take over Invergordon Distillers Ltd for £20 million. This was turned down by the board of Carlton, which owned seventy-six per cent of Invergordon, but observers now speculated about a possible attempt on Highland, and the board became concerned about some unusual share transactions, whose ultimate ownership remained obscure.

Hiram Walker had entered the Scotch whisky industry in 1935 with the purchase of George Ballantine & Co., and of Glenburgie and Miltonduff distilleries. They had built a large grain distillery in Dumbarton, and by 1979 also owned a further five malt distilleries. On 7th December they offered to buy Highland Distilleries for 130p per share. The Highland board turned the offer down, and set about mobilising public opinion in their support. John Macphail and John Goodwin realised that the only hope was to bring in the Monopolies and Mergers Commission, and marshalled support: within a fortnight Scottish M.P.s on both sides of the House were calling for an inquiry.

In Bordeaux House there was grave concern:

We just couldn't believe it at first. I remember Mr Sherriff announcing it to us... Everybody was horrified. Especially people who had been with the company a long time.

But, as John Goodwin remarked:

Support from the staff of R&B, Gloag's and Highland was one hundred per cent. Nobody leaked any information about any aspect of the business. A terrific show of loyalty towards the management.

In January 1980 John Macphail issued a strongly

worded report to shareholders, telling them 'Why you should reject Hiram Walker's offer' and urging them to:

KEEP HIGHLAND INDEPENDENT

Don't give up:

Your fine quality malt whisky distilleries.

Your investment in The Famous Grouse—over 20 times bigger in the home trade than when Highland bought it in 1970, and still expanding fast.

Export growth still to come—and remember exports count for 85% of all Scotch whisky sold.

Over two and a half times as much whisky was laid down in 1979 for future growth as was sold in that year.

Your stake in the success of Cutty Sark—one of the top three brands in the largest export markets and outperforming the industry in the others.

Your shareholding in Highland. The market price has increased by over 500% over the past 5 years.

On 25th January the Secretary of State for Trade & Industry referred the bid to Monopolies and Mergers. When the Highland board presented their case to the Commission in May they stressed that acquisition by the Canadian group would have a ruinous effect 'on the ability of one of Scotland's few indigenous growth industries to control its own destiny and take decisions favourable to investment and job opportunities in Scotland'. In this they were supported by the Scottish Trades Union Congress and the Scottish Development Agency, and especially the Scottish Labour Party.

The Commission then asked for a presentation from Robertson & Baxter, and Ian Good explained the relationship between Highland, Robertson & Baxter and Berry Bros. & Rudd, pointing out that the tri-partite agreement would be terminated if Hiram Walker were successful.

On 27th June the Commission disallowed the takeover, on the grounds that 'the efficiency of the Highland business and of the R&B business would be adversely affected by the merger'. The Highland board breathed a sigh of relief.

This was the first time 'the tartan ring-fence' had been used. John Macphail, John Goodwin and Ian Good saw very clearly that the takeover would be the death of the companies and 'a disaster for Scotland'—and in this they were supported by all the parties.

But it was a close-run thing.

CHAPTER VIII

THE
HIGHLAND
DISTILLERIES
PLC

(1980–2000)

BETWEEN THE END OF WORLD WAR II AND THE MID-1970S, the global market for Scotch whisky increased at a compound rate of around 9% per annum. To meet this seemingly insatiable demand, production had more than doubled to over 100 million proof gallons per annum (260 million litres), and the amount of whisky being held in bond more than quadrupled to well in excess of a billion gallons.

By 1980 commentators were talking about a 'whisky loch', similar to the 'wine lake' that had built up in Europe at the same time. Production far outstripped demand, and to make matters worse, there was a change in fashion away from brown spirits in the U.S.A., Scotch's leading export market since the late 1930s. The competition from white rum and vodka was stiff in both the U.K. and the U.S.A., and there was a large increase in wine consumption in both markets.

During 1981 the world economy slipped rapidly into recession and unemployment rose alarmingly throughout the Western world. At the same time, overseas trade was made more difficult by the strength of sterling, buoyed up by the Conservative government's strong monetary stance, coupled with very high interest rates. Highland Distilleries became a Public Limited Company, so as to be able to trade its shares on the Stock Market.

In the home market, the competition from imported wine was felt keenly. Wine was now much more widely available, and it benefited from preferential tax treatment compared with spirits: in 1984 duty on wine was even reduced by 20% to comply with an EEC ruling on harmonisation, yet five consecutive budgets between 1979 and 1985 raised duty on spirits by nearly one third. While the overall consumption of alcohol remained static, that of wine rose by 40% and Scotch was down 21%.

In 1986 John Macphail commented bitterly in Highland's Annual Report:

The inherent discriminatory nature of the excise duty is still with us, as the duty per degree of alcohol in whisky is taxed at a rate of 83% higher than it is in beer and 93% higher than for imported table wines—a not very encouraging reward for an industry that earns over £1 billion per annum in export earnings.

By 1980 it was clear to the board of Matthew Gloag & Son that the off-trade was becoming increasingly important and would require special attention. That year Robin Butler was appointed Sales Director North in January (later National Accounts Director) and John Hughes, Sales Director South (later Sales Director). At the same time, George Paterson was appointed Market Research Analyst, an indication of how the company was adopting modern business practices.

Despite the poor trading conditions, at the end of 1980 Robin Butler was able to report that sales of The Famous Grouse 'continued to progress at a satisfying level' in the home market, and finished at +3.4% on the previous year (at 1.1 million cases). The top twenty accounts (representing around 70% of the business) were all multiple grocers such as Haddows, the Co-op, Allied, Tesco, Fine Fare and Asda, and generally showed a small decline, and the Management Board were alerted to the fact that 'some large wholesalers were selling to small wholesalers'.

John Hughes was responsible for developing the market in England, working with Deinhard (Gloag's long-standing agents in England), although reporting directly to Alick Sherriff. Before joining Deinhard, he had worked for Watney, Independent Distillers & Vintners, and Gilbey's, so had excellent contacts in the trade. He appointed six regional sales managers,

DIVERSIFICATION

One way for whisky companies to hedge their bets in a declining market was to diversify into other areas. In 1980 Robertson & Baxter acquired Isle of Arran Provisions and, in 1987, Paterson-Bronte, makers of shortbread and oatcakes. This was the first time since 1869 that Matthew Gloag & Son had been involved with groceries. (Picture supplied by Paterson Arran Limited.)

who were also employed by Deinhard until 1985, when the English sales force was directly employed by Matthew Gloag & Son.

Through their wine business, Deinhard had strong relations with many specialist wine and spirits merchants in England, especially small, up-market retailers and specialist wholesalers, and by 1980 they had also obtained listings for The Famous Grouse with several regional brewers, including Allied, Scottish & Newcastle, Tennent's, Whitbread and Courage, so that the licensed premises under their control could stock the brand. But some expected inducements to stock the brand following a meeting with the Managed Houses Director of Drybrough's; Alick Sherriff reported that they expected only to sell 1,000 cases in 110 outlets and required a 'listing allowance'. He did not think this was realistic, and recommended that 'further thought be given to it'.

Alick Sherriff was not alone in the whisky industry in being concerned about the growing power of the supermarkets. The combination of increasing prices with the availability of large stocks of mature whisky resulted in a boom in cheaper, own-label brands. By 1987 it was reckoned that these were accounting for between 25% and 30% of home market sales, at the expense of established brands.

That year the board of management of Matthew Gloag & Son noted that 30% of sales of Scotch whisky in Scotland and 44% in England were controlled by the major supermarket groups: 'almost 50% of their sales are own-label'. This was also impacting upon the on-trade, where: 'inducement for bar owners to stock Grouse is not as high as on the lower-priced products and, with the severe economic situation, the number of bar owners not stocking the brand may continue to increase'. Two months later this was reinforced, especially in the West of Scotland, where 'inexpensive whiskies have made heavy inroads with the middle sector falling out'.

Although Deinhard dealt with the larger multiples—Tesco, Safeway, Sainsbury etc.—these companies' policy of 'stacking high and selling cheap', and demanding discounts, did not fit with Gloag's premium pricing policy, and they were treated with caution. Robin Butler recalled turning down an order from Asda, since they would not accept the premium pricing: 'Certainly, our goal was to go for volume sales, but not simply for volume's sake. We were determined to position Grouse as a cut above its competitors, and this was reflected by its price'.

HIGHLAND PARK

Sales of Highland Distilleries' malt whiskies were also managed by Matthew Gloag & Son. In 1980, Highland Park sold 770 cases, including England, and Tamdhu 464 cases (up 3.6% on 1979). By the end of 1983 the figures were: Highland Park 2,929 cases (up 120% on 1982) and Tamdhu 1,178 cases (up 23% on 1982)—an indication of the growing interest in single malt whisky. In December 1984 the Parliamentarian of the Year Awards were introduced, sponsored by The Spectator *magazine and Highland Park, and thereafter it became customary for the Chancellor to have a glass of the malt on his lectern when he delivered his budget.*

That year 'The Member to Watch' was Mr Malcolm Rifkind; in 1987 it was Mr Gordon Brown …

From: The Rt. Hon. Edward Heath, M.B.E., M.P.

HOUSE OF COMMONS

26 November, 1988.

Dear Mr Sherriff,

    I was delighted to have the opportunity
of talking to you at lunch at the Savoy yesterday.
It was both informative and interesting.

    As you will appreciate, I was particularly
moved at being the recipient of the Parliamentarian
of the Year Award, but this did not prevent
me from enjoying to the full this jovial occasion.

With best wishes.

Yours sincerely,

Edward Heath

Alick Sherriff, Esq.,
Managing Director,
The Famous Grouse.

But the large supermarket chains could not be ignored, and by the mid-1980s, when Robin Butler was put in charge of National Accounts, his remit included the major multiples—Co-op, Asda, William Low, Fine Fare, Safeway, Tesco, Sainsbury and Waitrose. Not surprisingly, the last two—the most up-market stores—were the first to stock The Famous Grouse. Robin Butler's remit also included the national wholesale trade, like Scottish & Newcastle and Forth Wines.

As with the on-trade, personal relationships were nurtured with buyers and managers of supermarkets who were invited as guests to everything the company was sponsoring—through fishing trips, horse racing, clay pigeon shooting, golf, rugby, curling, visits to Orkney etc. After 1982, Matthew was assisted by Iain Halliday, Trade Relations Manager, and (after 1987) John Hughes, Home Trade Sales Director, and Jim Grierson, National Sales Manager.

Matthew himself was by this time a well-known figure in the licensed trade, and was twice elected chairman of the Scottish Licensed Trade Association (1984/85 and 1995/96)—the first time in the Association's history that a chairman had been elected twice. There was a tradition that the incoming chairman each year would take the inner committee as guests on a get-to-know outing. Matthew took them to Paris on the Eurostar for a rugby international, then announced that he wanted to meet every one of the forty-six members of the National Executive at their places of business. This did a huge amount to show the trade that Matthew Gloag & Son was not as aloof as it had once been perceived!

In 1987 the company launched its first national promotion, devised by Patrick Gallagher and Helen Arthur (today a leading whisky writer), and master-minded by Matthew, to whom, as Helen told me 'all credit must go, not least for taking risks!'.

The challenge, delivered on a neck label, was to choose four out of eight illustrations of grouse birds by the painter Stanley Todd suitable for a new advertising poster, then add a slogan of up to ten words which would 'create interest and generate sales, whilst maintaining the quality image of the Brand'. The top prize was £25,000 worth of stocks and shares, supported by one hundred £100 prizes in each of the three months the competition ran.

It was massively successful, attracting 55,000 entries. The winning slogan was 'The Famous Grouse rises to every occasion'. Some of the runners-up

story continued on page 337

THE FAMOUS GROUSE
FINEST SCOTCH WHISKY
PRESENTS

Rugby
CURIOUS FACT No 1.
◆

*N*ew Zealand's 1905 tour of England saw Billy Wallace secure his place in millinery folklore. For the duration of a match against Corn- wall, he sported a particularly handsome sun hat. And in scoring a dazzling try, the cool Kiwi proved the old maxim; "If you want to get ahead..."

OFFICIAL SPONSORS
RUGBY WORLD CUP 1991

THE FAMOUS GROUSE
FINEST SCOTCH WHISKY
PRESENTS

Rugby
CURIOUS FACT No 2.
◆

A 1937 match between France and Romania, witnessed a fascinating battle between two immensely powerful men, Jacques Chaban Delmas and Ion Papa. They squared up to each other again years later, in circumstances considerably less civilised, as Prime Ministers of their respective countries.

OFFICIAL SPONSORS
RUGBY WORLD CUP 1991

THE FAMOUS GROUSE
FINEST SCOTCH WHISKY
PRESENTS

Rugby
CURIOUS FACT No 3.
◆

*I*n the 1965 All England Schools 200 yards low hurdles, a certain A. Pascoe came a breathless second to a fresh-faced, record-breaking Welsh lad. Alan, who went on to gold success in European and Commonwealth competi- tions, must be eternally grateful that the winner, one Gareth Edwards, decided to take his silver-heels into the world of rugby, instead.

OFFICIAL SPONSORS
RUGBY WORLD CUP 1991

THE FAMOUS GROUSE
FINEST SCOTCH WHISKY
PRESENTS

Rugby
CURIOUS FACT No 4.
◆

*S*ome men might be miffed to receive a mere two England caps in their rugby career. Not so Stanley Harris. The ultimate good sport, he played in the South African Davis Cup team, won the All England mixed doubles title, represented South Africa in the 1924 Olympics in the pentathlon and in the boxing ring, played polo for England, and reached the finals of the World Ballroom Dancing championships. But appar- ently, he was rubbish at tiddly-winks!

OFFICIAL SPONSORS
RUGBY WORLD CUP 1991

THE FAMOUS GROUSE
FINEST SCOTCH WHISKY
PRESENTS

Rugby
CURIOUS FACT No 5.
◆

*I*n 1980, New Zealand were reputed to be improving their ball handling skills, using house bricks. This was at the behest of coach Eric Watson, who was unhappy with his threequarters. So successful was this unorthodox ploy, that the New Zealanders went on to beat arch-rivals Australia 26-10, and in the process earn the nick-name, "The All Bricks".

OFFICIAL SPONSORS
RUGBY WORLD CUP 1991

THE FAMOUS GROUSE
FINEST SCOTCH WHISKY
PRESENTS

Rugby
CURIOUS FACT No 6.
◆

*I*n the winter of 1974, a French club match saw Villiers les Nancy a clear 62 points ahead of their opponents, Villeneuve. Villeneuve however, later claimed that they were only beaten because Villiers fielded an extra man — a snowman. Built by the bored Villiers full-back, the little chap, whilst totally stationary, was still quick enough to upend one of Villeneuves' tardy wingers.

OFFICIAL SPONSORS
RUGBY WORLD CUP 1991

THE FAMOUS GROUSE

FINEST SCOTCH WHISKY

Rugby Curiosities

No. 1

The Welsh pack of 1914 was nicknamed, 'The Terrible Eight'. Criticised for excessively brutal play, their ringleader merely rolled his eyes to heaven. His name? The Reverend Alban Davies.

OFFICIAL SPONSORS
RUGBY WORLD CUP SEVENS '93

THE FAMOUS GROUSE

FINEST SCOTCH WHISKY

Rugby Curiosities

No. 2

A good prop is used to taking opponents apart. But Scotland's John Allan had to put them back together again too. Big, butch and burly, this behemoth was also a nurse at his local hospital.

OFFICIAL SPONSORS
RUGBY WORLD CUP SEVENS '93

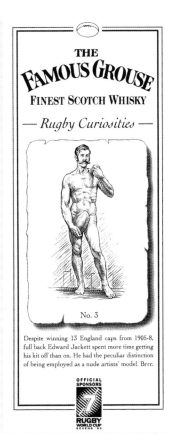

THE FAMOUS GROUSE

FINEST SCOTCH WHISKY

Rugby Curiosities

No. 3

Despite winning 13 England caps from 1905-8, full back Edward Jackett spent more time getting his kit off than on. He had the peculiar distinction of being employed as a nude artists' model. Brrr.

OFFICIAL SPONSORS
RUGBY WORLD CUP SEVENS '93

THE FAMOUS GROUSE

FINEST SCOTCH WHISKY

Rugby Curiosities

No. 4

No line-up in the history of rugby could be more formidable than the one fielded by Western Samoa in 1924. Their opponents, Fiji, were confronted by fifteen bruisers – and a massive tree on the halfway line.

OFFICIAL SPONSORS
RUGBY WORLD CUP SEVENS '93

THE FAMOUS GROUSE

FINEST SCOTCH WHISKY

Rugby Curiosities

No. 5

The 1975 New Zealand v Scotland International was more like water-polo than rugby. Played after a near-monsoon, not one of the thirteen penalties awarded, resulted in a kick at goal.

OFFICIAL SPONSORS
RUGBY WORLD CUP SEVENS '93

THE FAMOUS GROUSE

FINEST SCOTCH WHISKY

Rugby Curiosities

No. 8

In Auckland on the 14th June 1975 Scotland lost 24-0. Playing the full match in near monsoon conditions, the New Zealand skipper was quoted as saying: "This was one of the greatest moments in New Zealand swimming."

THE FAMOUS GROUSE
FINEST SCOTCH WHISKY
The Spirit of Scotland

THE FAMOUS GROUSE

FINEST SCOTCH WHISKY

Rugby Curiosities

No. 9

In 1921, when Scotland met Wales in Swansea, the home fans *really* got behind their team. A group of leek-wielding Welsh supporters tried to block the home try line. They failed and Scotland won a notable 14-8 victory.

THE FAMOUS GROUSE
FINEST SCOTCH WHISKY
The Spirit of Scotland

THE FAMOUS GROUSE

FINEST SCOTCH WHISKY

Rugby Curiosities

No. 10

At Murrayfield, in 1925, England were easy meat for the hard-tackling Scots. With only minutes left to go, England's L. J. Corbett *did* break through the Scottish pack, only to collapse short of the try line suffering from total exhaustion.

THE FAMOUS GROUSE
FINEST SCOTCH WHISKY
The Spirit of Scotland

A variety of adverts used during the Rugby sponsorship of the 1990s.

Witty brand advertising in America.

BRING OUT THE BEST IN YOUR GUEST!

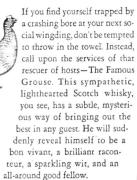

If you find yourself trapped by a crashing bore at your next social wingding, don't be tempted to throw in the towel. Instead, call upon the services of that rescuer of hosts — The Famous Grouse. This sympathetic, lighthearted Scotch whisky, you see, has a subtle, mysterious way of bringing out the best in any guest. He will suddenly reveal himself to be a bon vivant, a brilliant raconteur, a sparkling wit, and an all-around good fellow.

So next time you entertain, prove yourself an understanding and gracious host. It is still possible to talk some dealers out of several bottles if you have a persuasive manner. So serve The Famous Grouse and bring out the best in your guest.

THE FAMOUS GROUSE BRAND

The "Ultimate Experience" in Scotch Whisky

BLENDED SCOTCH WHISKY • 86.8 PROOF.
BALFOUR, GUTHRIE & CO., LIMITED, SAN FRANCISCO,
LOS ANGELES, SEATTLE AND PORTLAND

BLITHE SPIRIT REVEALED AS FAMOUS GROUSE!

Anyone who is unable to distinguish between a professional bird-watcher and an amateur ornithologist will be even more confused to learn that both recognize The Famous Grouse as a blithe spirit. Else, how did it get to the West Coast at a time when indignant Peers are vociferously grousing at The Lord High Constable of Scottish Ports for permitting this rare bird to fly the cooperage?

Ever since the great Gloag family of Perthshire, Scotland, started producing and blending Scotch some 150 years ago, the limited supply has been petitioned by exclusive clubs and people with family crests. Now, for the first time this holiday season, you can impress your friends by serving The Famous Grouse Scotch whisky, and always be remembered as a gentleman and a scholar . . . but don't be a "ten o'clock scholar." The Famous Grouse, like its namesake, is not easy to bag.

THE FAMOUS GROUSE BRAND

The "Ultimate Experience" in Scotch Whisky

BLENDED SCOTCH WHISKY • 86.8 PROOF.
BALFOUR, GUTHRIE & CO., LIMITED, SAN FRANCISCO,
LOS ANGELES, SEATTLE AND PORTLAND

A GROUSE FOR THE SPOUSE
(Exclusive for the Ladies)

Your husband is an old grouser, no doubt — or is that presumptuous? Like cures like, they used to say, so to sweeten him up for the holidays, beguile him with The Grouse — the Famous Grouse Brand scotch whisky. If a bottle brings back that old boyish smile, a case will keep him chuckling for months. Worth it? You know, the grouse is a happy bird, and Perthshire, Scotland, where Matthew Gloag & Son, Limited, have been distilling their precious scotch for a century and a half, is in the heart of the grouse moors where kings once cavorted in tweeds and derby hats in pursuit of the "black cock." You will love to see HIM sedately sipping The Famous Grouse, for the magic in it brings out all the finer qualities in a man...the scholar, the philosopher, the Great Lover. The better dealers have limited supplies, so act! Be impetuous!

THE FAMOUS GROUSE BRAND

The "Ultimate Experience" in Scotch Whisky

BLENDED SCOTCH WHISKY • 86.8 PROOF.
BALFOUR, GUTHRIE & CO., LIMITED, SAN FRANCISCO,
LOS ANGELES, SEATTLE AND PORTLAND

were: 'Scotland without Grouse is like Liverpool without Scouse', 'The whirr of wings—the drink of kings' and 'I'd trade my spouse for a Famous Grouse'!

Export markets continued to be expanded by Roy Bignell and John McDermott: by 1984 they represented 25% of The Famous Grouse case sales (around 50,000 cases), and by 1990, 29%. John McDermott remarked:

Ultimately it was the quality of the whisky which drove its success. Wherever in the world we went we avoided discounting and sold mostly at a premium, or at least at parity with the market leader. Alick Sherriff often repeated to us: 'Grouse must always be seen to be above its competitive set.'
Helping us along the way was the growth of Duty Free. As it became more sophisticated, becoming a boutique you couldn't find on the domestic market, so we built the core brand, then brand extensions around it.

The Management Board received monthly reports on performance in overseas markets, including: the U.S.A., where Seagram was the distributor until 1982, when Heublein replaced them. But the market here was depressed; whisky faced severe competition from vodka, white rum and wine. The American market for Scotch whisky declined by 28.6% during the decade, while vodka rose by 18.8% and rum by 32.3%. Canada was also generally disappointing, largely owing to the stringent purchasing rules imposed by the state-monopolised Provincial Liquor Boards.

France was the leading European market for Grouse during the 1980s and and grew by 6.3% during the decade. The distributors were Gouin until 1988, when a cross-shareholding agreement was reached with Rémy-Cointreau, whereby Highland Distilleries would ultimately have a 25% shareholding. Rémy's massive distribution network in France would later boost the performance of Grouse in this market. Rémy also took over distribution in Germany, replacing Schlumberger.

A listing for **Sweden** was obtained in early 1981, developed by Roddy I'Anson, using Nils Bertil Philipsen, who negotiated with the state monopoly, the Systembolaget. 'We arranged distillery visits, golf tours etc. for members of the Systembolaget, and for key buyers from other markets like Portugal, Spain and Germany'. Swedes have a huge connection with the Great Outdoors, and the brand's clear

story continued on page 340

337

POE-SCRIPT

(USING POE-ETIC LICENSE)

Once upon an hour nocturnal, as I sipped . . . and read the *Journal* and a Scotchly scent of heather seemed to drift about the house, through my window-pane came hurdling, strange to say, a wondrous birdling, and at once my vision told me 'twas the great—the *famous*—Grouse.

Captivated by the meeting, low I bowed in grousely greeting. "Hail, all Hail!", I cried, "I know you—from a hundred years of yore. O Great Spiritus Frumenti, joy of all the cognoscenti, will there ever be a greater? Tell me truly, I implore!"

Quoth The Grouse, "No! Nevermore!!"

(P.S. We're not just Raven, either.)

THE FAMOUS

GROUSE

BRAND

The "Ultimate Experience" in Scotch Whisky

BLENDED SCOTCH WHISKY · 86.8 PROOF.
BALFOUR, GUTHRIE & CO., LIMITED, SAN FRANCISCO,
LOS ANGELES, SEATTLE AND PORTLAND

Famous Detective Observes Adam's Apple

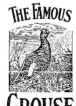

Poincaire LaGarrotte, fashionable French sleuth, reveals in his memoirs how he can name the brand of scotch a man is drinking by the action of his Adam's apple. "The what-you-call Adam's apple," says LaGarrotte, "is a dumb waiter. When a man is sipping The Famous Grouse Scotch, it rises quickly, then rests, comfortably, in the up-position as the precious nectar lingers on the grateful tongue. Then it takes on the sip gradually, lowering it slowly and gently to warm the appreciative stomach. So watch the Adam's apple. Up quickly, then rest, down slowly and gently means The Famous Grouse. The bobbing apple—that means any old brand. Maybe I should call this the not-so-dumb waiter—no?"

All you need to test Poincaire's theory is to pick up a bottle of The Famous Grouse Scotch Whisky at your favorite spirits vendor.

THE FAMOUS

GROUSE

BRAND

The "Ultimate Experience" in Scotch Whisky

BLENDED SCOTCH WHISKY · 86.8 PROOF.
BALFOUR, GUTHRIE & CO., LIMITED, SAN FRANCISCO,
LOS ANGELES, SEATTLE AND PORTLAND

SODA IS FOR THE BIRDS
(not for *the* Bird)

"I was an indifferent Scotch drinker until they gave me *The Bird*," says the eminent cognoscente, Sir Egbert P. Foosh—referring, of course, to The Famous Grouse Brand Scotch whisky. Named for Scotland's national game-bird, Famous Grouse is so distinguished that one hesitates to abuse it with soda. Famous Grouse, as the poet says, tiptoes on the tongue, caresses the throat, warms the heart as gently as a sunbeam. The family of Matthew Gloag, of Perthshire, Scotland, has been making whisky *for taste* during a century and a half, and those who know Famous Grouse taste it, and taste it again, in a ritual of sustained delight.

Not everyone deserves The Famous Grouse. But if you have a few extra special friends on your holiday gift list, the better dealers are prepared to accommodate you. It may take a little persuasion to get a whole case.

THE FAMOUS

GROUSE

BRAND

The "Ultimate Experience" in Scotch Whisky

BLENDED SCOTCH WHISKY · 86.8 PROOF.
BALFOUR, GUTHRIE & CO., LIMITED, SAN FRANCISCO,
LOS ANGELES, SEATTLE AND PORTLAND

BEAUTIFUL FRIENDSHIPS ARE SECURED
(The Transcendental Approach)

You've got to admit shaking hands gets to be a bore, even when preluded by a well-scrawled signature on an important contract. But a transcendental approach is being initiated this holiday season in the inner circles of the inner circles. The ceremonious sipping of Famous Grouse Brand Scotch metamorphoses a business deal into a sacerdotal ritual, complete with enduring vows.

Spirited to the West Coast from the mystic moors of Scotland, The Famous Grouse Brand Scotch Whisky has always been reserved for a few exclusive clubs. This holiday season, we have been favored with a more generous allotment, and some of the better dealers can supply you from their small quotas. The Gaelic blessing of Matthew Gloag & Son Limited, Perth, Scotland, and a century and a half of hallowed tradition makes every drop of . . .

THE FAMOUS

GROUSE

BRAND

The "Ultimate Experience" in Scotch Whisky

BLENDED SCOTCH WHISKY · 86.8 PROOF
BALFOUR, GUTHRIE & CO., LTD., SAN FRANCISCO

Just Right For Silver-Spooners

When your Xmas list includes people who were "born with a silver spoon in their mouths," just think how beastly tired they must be of those old silver spoons. Grouse under— or, rather, *in*— glass would be such a relief. Indeed, The Famous Grouse Scotch, like the famous bird of the Scottish moors, has hobnobbed with silver-spooners and gratified them for a century and a half. To give a bottle of Famous Grouse makes you one with the landed gentry. To give a case makes you nothing less than a Duke. Blind Fortune (possibly a myopic First Mate) accounts for a smallish cargo of The Famous Grouse Scotch being landed on the West Coast, and if your bottled goods man has sufficient prestige, he should have some for you. Be expeditious in checking. The miraculous skill and devout benediction of Matthew Gloag and Son of Perthshire, Scotland, pervades every drop.

THE FAMOUS GROUSE BRAND

The "Ultimate Experience" in Scotch Whisky

BLENDED SCOTCH WHISKY • 86.8 PROOF.
BALFOUR, GUTHRIE & CO., LIMITED, SAN FRANCISCO, LOS ANGELES, SEATTLE AND PORTLAND

NO GROUSE, NO FOX, HUNT CANCELLED !

The mid-winter hunt of the Twiddleton Fox Hunting Society has been suddenly called off due to a tragic shortage of The Grouse, it is announced by Sir Wimply Frothingham, M.P., K.C.B. The grief-stricken Sir Wimply adds that the House of Lords has been asked to investigate (British Intelligence is keeping mum).

It may be pure coincidence that this holiday season marks the initial appearance of The Famous Grouse on the Pacific Coast, except for limited stocks mostly at a few exclusive clubs.

Orders are presently being placed for The Famous Grouse Scotch for holiday giving in lieu of foreign sports cars, uranium stock, opera tickets and political appointments.

If you have horribly important people on your holiday list, send one of your most trusted domestics expeditiously to your bottled goods purveyor for a case or so. Retain an ample supply for yourself, by all means. The price is relative.

THE FAMOUS GROUSE BRAND

The "Ultimate Experience" in Scotch Whisky

BLENDED SCOTCH WHISKY • 86.8 PROOF.
BALFOUR, GUTHRIE & CO., LIMITED, SAN FRANCISCO, LOS ANGELES, SEATTLE AND PORTLAND

OPENING NEW TERRITORY REQUIRES FAMOUS GROUSE

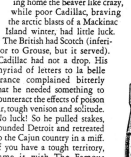

When opening up a new territory or working over an old one, a case of The Famous Grouse Scotch Whisky is quite as important as an initialed brief case and a tailored suit. Look at Antoine de la Mothe Cadillac, sent to the new World by France to cover Canada in the face of stiff British competition.

The wily Britishers were bringing home the beaver like crazy, while poor Cadillac, braving the arctic blasts of a Mackinac Island winter, had little luck. The British had Scotch (inferior to Grouse, but it served). Cadillac had not a drop. His myriad of letters to la belle France complained bitterly that he needed something to counteract the effects of poison air, tough venison and solitude. No luck! So he pulled stakes, founded Detroit and retreated to the Cajun country in a miff. If you have a tough territory, tame it with The Famous Grouse, the affable Scotch.

THE FAMOUS GROUSE BRAND

The Ultimate Experience in Scotch Whisky

BLENDED SCOTCH WHISKY • 86.8 PROOF.
BALFOUR, GUTHRIE & CO., LIMITED, SAN FRANCISCO, LOS ANGELES, SEATTLE AND PORTLAND

How Do You Rate in Grousemanship?

Contrary to what you may have heard on the avenues, Grousemanship is not rated according to size of hat, collar or shoes. Even transportation preferences are irrelevant, except that the side-saddle is considered obsolete. The man who dived into shark-infested waters to rescue a bottle of The Famous Grouse when he had a full case aboard merits study.

However, full status Grousemanship has been granted, only recently, to a dress circle guest at the opera who frankly stated he enjoyed every minute of it because he was dreaming of the bottle of The Famous Grouse Scotch that was waiting for him beside his favorite chair. A Grouseman is candid (*Grouseman's Creed, point 4*). If you can afford The Famous Grouse Scotch Whisky, you, too, can afford to be candid. As one Grouseman to another, today's price is within reach: tomorrow's— who knows?

THE FAMOUS GROUSE BRAND

The "Ultimate Experience" in Scotch Whisky

BLENDED SCOTCH WHISKY • 86.8 PROOF.
BALFOUR, GUTHRIE & CO., LIMITED, SAN FRANCISCO, LOS ANGELES, SEATTLE AND PORTLAND

339

connection with moors and mountains gave it an advantage from the outset, helped by the fact that the state monopoly offered immediate distribution to many outlets and tended to support small, unknown products. By 1995 Sweden was the fourth largest export market for The Famous Grouse.

Spain was the number three market in Europe, growing by 6% since its entry to the EEC in January 1986. Next came **Italy** where Scotch sales grew by 4%. This was unique in being the first major market for malt whisky, which accounted for 26% of the total market for Scotch, and 30% of the global market for single malt whisky. Gloag's had two distributors in this market, Cinzano and Ferraretto.

The Netherlands became an important market for Grouse during the 1980s—the number six Scotch in this market, with slightly over 3% of market share. The distributors were Sovedi.

Australia was predominantly a bulk market, although sales of Grouse and other brands (which were shipped in bulk and bottled in Australia) grew by 5.5%. Elders were the distributors, but, by 1989, doubts were being minuted about their efforts in the on-trade: 'Elders are clearly off-trade order-takers rather than on-trade brand-builders'.

During the 1980s, distributors were appointed in Belgium, Eire, Germany/Austria, Switzerland, Portugal, Malta, the Canary Islands, Cyprus, South Africa, Japan, Hong Kong, New Zealand, Thailand and South America.

A family company, Kaloyannis Bros., owners of the largest-selling brand of ouzo in **Greece**, Ouzo 12, were the distributors, energetically supported by John McDermott. In the 1970s, there were discriminatory levels of duty on Scotch and ouzo, but when Greece joining the EEC in 1981 the levels of tax were adjusted and the market for Scotch exploded: Greece rapidly became the largest per capita consumer of Scotch whisky outside Scotland. Within ten years, sales of The Famous Grouse rose to 100,000 cases, and during the 1990s Greece was the brand's largest export market.

In spite of all this activity in export markets, sales of The Famous Grouse remained at only around 20% of total sales until 1984, when they began to climb slowly but steadily—to 29% by 1990 and 50% in 1995.

The 1980s were difficult years for the Scotch whisky industry. Reduced demand obliged many blenders to cut their orders for new make spirit

THE EXPORT TEAM IN 1987

Left to right: David Noble, Malcolm Watt, John McDermott, Bob Gillies, Roy Bignell, Alick Sherriff, John Goodwin, Rod I'Anson, Phil Taylor, Andrew Kettles, Matthew Gloag.

WHY THE FAMOUS GROUSE ?

In 1984 the company commissioned a promotional film with this title, directed by Bill Forsyth, with a soundtrack by Ossian. A twenty-second segment would also be used for TV advertising abroad, and it was hoped that Ossian's Californian tour in the summer of 1984, combined with Bill Forsyth's friendship with Sam Goldwyn (who was a devotee of Grouse) might support the brand on the West Coast of America.

from distillers, and as a result many distilleries were closed or put on part-time production in order to 'attain the requisite balance between maturing stocks of whisky and anticipated levels of future sales', to quote the Distillers Company management committee. Between 1983 and 1985 thirty malt distilleries closed—sixteen of them terminally.

The operation was a success, however, and by the end of the decade eleven distilleries had resumed production.

Matthew Gloag & Son and Highland Distilleries weathered the storm better than most. In the latter company's centenary year, 1987, John Macphail, the Chairman, was pleased to report:

The Company is a substantial, independent presence in the Industry and supplies not only quality malt to blenders, but quality bottled Scotch whiskies to a wide public.

It is gratifying in this our Centenary year to be able to report record-breaking profits of £12.1 million, an increase of 17% over last year's comparable figure. Turnover, exclusive of home trade excise duty, increased by 11% and operating profits by 14%. All sectors of the business contributed to the increase.

Earnings per share increased by 23% to 6.4p per share. The Famous Grouse is increasingly recognised as a quality blend of Scotch whisky selling at the upper end of the market. It enjoyed increased sales in both home and export markets. The brand continues to be market leader in Scotland, with good growth being seen in England and Wales, particularly in the on-license sector.

Sales of the three single malts Highland Park, Bunna-habhain and Tamdhu increased by 17%, while sales of new fillings were slightly ahead of last year, as were mature sales and the output at the distilleries.

Whilst the markets are now being affected by second-ary brands, there are indications that the surplus stocks of Scotch whisky, that have been the bane of the industry, have been reduced to manageable proportions, and this will result in a more sensible and constructive approach to the marketing of Scotch whisky than has been the case in recent years.

He went on to comment on the lack of governmental support for the whisky industry, a perennial complaint.

The government has continued its seemingly

story continued on page 346

343

THE
ROYAL
WARRANT

On New Year's Day 1984, Matthew Gloag & Son was granted a Royal Warrant of Appointment as Scotch Whisky Blenders and Suppliers of The Famous Grouse to Her Majesty The Queen.

Such warrants are held personally, and Matthew was (and remains) the Grantee, assisted today by Fraser Morrison.

The Royal Warrant is internationally recognised as a mark of excellence and it entitles the holder to display the royal coat of arms, together with the words 'By Appointment'.

To be granted the honour, a company must have direct business transactions with the Royal Household and a history of support for events in association with the Royal Household and the Warrant Holders Association. Any Warrant Holder must also demonstrate their commitment to the highest standards of environmental and social responsibility.

The Royal Warrant is reviewed every five years. Matthew Gloag & Son are proud to have retained the Warrant since 1984. The latest renewal was in December 2013.

BUCKINGHAM PALACE

20th December, 2012

Dear Mr. Gloag,

You will be aware that all Royal Warrants of Appointment are reviewed one year prior to the end of tenure and, in accordance with this practice, your Warrant to The Queen was reviewed by the Royal Household Warrants Committee at their Annual Meeting on Thursday, 6th December 2012.

I am delighted to advise you that the Committee was able to recommend the continuation of your Warrant for a five year period. This means that the end of tenure for your Warrant is 2018 and therefore it will be reviewed again in 2017.

I now send you the revised Counterfoil Copy to reflect this change. The Counterfoil Copy is for **office use only** and not display, and its purpose is exactly to define the limits of the grant made to you. **Please check the details contained in the Counterfoil Copy and advise me, in writing, that all the details are correct and, if appropriate, of any discrepancies.**

Yours sincerely,

Charlotte Martin

Miss Charlotte Martin
Secretary
Royal Household Warrants Committee
Lord Chamberlain's Office

Matthew Gloag Esq.,
Executive Director,
Matthew Gloag & Son Ltd.,
West Kinfauns,
Perth,
PH2 7XZ

Reply to: Lord Chamberlain's Office, Buckingham Palace, London, SW1A 1AA

paradoxical approach to the Scotch Whisky Industry, by being supportive over export market problems and at the same time, highly discriminatory at home. The Industry is among the top half dozen export earners—contributing in excess of a billion pounds per annum in export earnings, together with a similar amount in duty and VAT—and yet suffers ridiculously high excise duties in the home market, in comparison to beer and imported wines.

The alcohol beverage industry in general has been attracting increased attention from the axe-grinding of vociferous minority groups and will be taking increased steps to rebut the considerable amount of erroneous propaganda to which it has been subjected. Needless to say, the Scotch Whisky Industry is against the abuse of alcohol, but believes that, in moderation, it has a part to play in the well being of our society.

Indeed. Such words might have been written today!

By 1990, The Famous Grouse commanded 24% of the Scotch whisky market in Scotland (where it continued to be the category leader) and around 12% of the overall U.K. market. In England and Wales it held only around 10% of the market—'which' as

Alan Gray, the industry's leading analyst, remarked in his annual review for 1991 'gives The Famous Grouse considerable potential'.

However, he went on to say: 'The U.K. was a poor market during the 1980s and although there was a modest recovery between 1984 and 1988, sales have fallen in each of the last three years and will fall again in 1992, probably by around 8.5%'.

A key problem was the inability of established brands to increase prices in the face of growing energy and transport costs, on account of the low-priced own-label brands. Fraser Morrison, Gloag's Company Secretary at the time, remarked:

For about ten years, until the mid-1990s, £9.99 was the average price of a bottle of standard blended Scotch. In 1992 the bottle size was reduced from 75cl to 70cl throughout the European Community, but this had no impact on the price of a bottle, and since it cost the same to produce the bottle and packaging, there was no profit windfall. In effect, we had to increase the number of bottles to sell the same volume of whisky. Between 1990 and 1992, however, duty was increased by 23.8%, and V.A.T. increased from 15% to 17.5%, and retail prices had to reflect this. We always believed

THE
FAMOUS GROUSE
Quality in an age of change.

An advertisement from 1989

1990 ROYAL WARRANT HOLDERS GARDEN PARTY

Back row: Dilly & Matthew Gloag. Front Row: Sylvia McPherson, Vic MacDonald, Gina Harley, June Trail

The Famous Grouse could sustain a higher price than its competitors: in 1991 the R.R.P. was £10.69, against Bell's £9.93; in 1993, £11.99 vs £10.50, and in 1995, when duty was increased yet again, £12.49 vs Bell's £11.49. Although we were still behind Bell's in the U.K. at this time, Grouse was still increasing market share.

When Fraser joined Matthew Gloag & Son in June 1990, the company was still very traditional:

When I arrived I discovered I was not only to look after financial control, but legal, IT, logistics, HR, customer services and the typing pool. Everything was antiquated. We had two computers—a state of the art IBM 400 and an old IBM System 38—and three computer screens. We didn't have an IT team, and we were struggling to move files over to the IBM 400. Monthly sales reports were hand-written then typed—all the girls had typewriters. The cash-book was still kept manually. Even in 1990, although the systems worked, the company was still old-fashioned… It was clearly essential to put together an IT team, and this understandably caused a certain amount of pain over the next five years as modern reporting systems were put in place.

In spite of the old-fashioned nature of the office systems, in 1990 sales of The Famous Grouse in the home market peaked at 1.534 million nine litre cases. This was helped by a significant incentive to supermarkets to sell volume over the Christmas/New Year season, by offering a volume rebate, based on case sales. Fraser Morrison commented:

Sales were astronomical—left Bell's and Teacher's way behind—but they involved more liabilities than we had predicted, so the profit margin was not exceptional. It did however indicate a change in tactics vis-à-vis supermarkets—we had to start playing ball or lose volume. And we had to increase our advertising spend.

Bill Farrar, who had joined Gloag's as Marketing Manager in 1989 from International Distillers & Vintners, having worked on Gilbey's gin, Smirnoff vodka and J&B blended Scotch, remarked:

The Famous Grouse was the best marketed brand I had ever encountered, and much of the inspiration for this came from Alick Sherriff, who paid great attention to detail—what he described as a 'feather by feather' approach. The sales force worked incredibly

349

RAISED IN THE HIGHLANDS.

THE
FAMOUS GROUSE
FINEST SCOTCH WHISKY

QUALITY IN AN AGE OF CHANGE.

hard, without being pressed, and were proud of their jobs and of their brand. They were perceived as being 'different' by the on-trade—more stylish; maybe because they were provided with better cars—the Gloag family had long been keen on motor-cars! Their customers knew them personally, rather than just as 'the guy from Gloag's'.

Our marketing tactics were also very different. Sponsorship, both locally and nationally; support for the licensed trade. Each individual salesman had a budget for local promotions and PR; no free stock was allocated to 'facilitate' the brand being stocked.

Alas, in March 1993 Alick Sherriff, the guiding force behind the premium price policy and so much else in the development of The Famous Grouse, died suddenly. He is universally remembered with respect and affection among those who knew him: 'He was a real gentleman', is the universal comment. Matthew Gloag maintains that 'his death was a watershed for the company'.

He had joined the company in 1956 as a trainee, aged twenty-five, having graduated from the University of Cambridge with a degree in history, served in the Argyll & Sutherland Highlanders and qualified as a chartered accountant in Glasgow. His family had once owned Bowmore and Port Charlotte Distilleries on Islay and Lochhead Distillery in Campbeltown, as well as a rum business in Jamaica.

He was soon given responsibility for sales in Scotland, becoming U.K. Sales & Marketing Director in 1961, joint-Managing Director (with Andrew Kettles) in 1988 and Deputy Chairman in 1992. He was a member of the Royal Company of Archers, the Queen's Bodyguard in Scotland, honorary colonel in the Territorial Army's 32nd Scottish Signals Regiment, a founding member of the Keepers of the Quaich and President of the Wine and Spirits Association of Scotland.

Andrew Kettles, Managing Director of Matthew Gloag & Son since the death of Alick Sherriff, left the company in September 1996 and was immediately replaced by David Maxwell Scott who had been Managing Director of Justerini & Brooks. He brought Richard White, with whom he had worked at J&B, into the company as Export Director, moving the existing Export Director, Simon Sanders, to a new job in Corporate Affairs.

The creation of this job eroded Matthew Gloag's responsibilities, which had already been diminished

The Famous Grouse Wade Highland Decanter was produced between 1994 and 1998, with a limited edition batch of Centenary Decanters produced in 1996, individually numbered 1 to 100.

story continued on page 358

351

These offices in West Kinfauns, on the banks of the Tay, were built by Highland Distillers in 1995.

This is now home to Edrington's sales and marketing departments.

The Brand Ambassador, Iain Stothard, explaining the different whiskies to HRH The Princess Royal
on 20th September 1996 during the official opening of the offices at West Kinfauns.
In the background is Brian Ivory (far left), Edrington Director, talking with
Sir David Montgomery, Lord Lieutenant for Perth & Kinross.

RAISED IN

THE HIGHLANDS

QUALITY IN AN AGE OF CHANGE

as the company transferred budgets from public relations to advertising. In early 1998 he was asked to resign from the board of the family company, but continued to be retained as a consultant and Brand Ambassador. In fact, Matthew had been unhappy with the loss of the 'family atmosphere' in the business, especially since Alick Sherriff's demise, and had bought a house in the Gers Departement in southwest France.

It was very apparent by now that the company had outgrown its long-standing HQ in Bordeaux House—'We were falling over each other', one member of staff told me—and that the Kinnoull Street bond was no longer adequate for even the small amount of bottling that continued to be done there. The bond closed in 1994 and was demolished, and plans were made to move to a greenfield site at West Kinfauns, to the east of Perth, the move being completed in 1996. Initially there were mixed feelings among the staff about the move—many did not like the open-plan office—but parking facilities were much better, and a mini-bus from Bordeaux House ran twice a day for those who didn't drive. And there were excellent cheap lunches!

Increased activity in the off-trade led to an increase in advertising during the late 1980s and throughout the 1990s. Bill Farrar had been appointed Marketing Director in 1993 to supervise this. 'Our media policy was for multiple insertions in broadsheet newspapers, largely small-scale ('ear-tags' on the top corners of newspapers were used extensively), and whole page colour advertising in trade journals and up-market magazines like *Country Life*, *The Field* and *Scottish Field*, always on the right-hand page. Our ads were the "best-liked" of all whisky advertising at the time.'

Saatchi & Saatchi continued as the brand's advertising agency, and retained the tried and tested slogans, 'Quality in an Age of Change' and 'Raised in the Highlands'—market research showed these to be the 'most liked' Scotch whisky adverts at the time. But while they were reassuring, this treatment did not increase brand awareness and in 1996 the board took the bold step of inviting other agencies to pitch for the account.

The highly creative London agency Abbott Mead Vickers adopted a radically different approach, developing the personality of the grouse as a life-like character in a witty, appealing and amusing way. They referred to it as 'The Icon Campaign'. Print ads were launched in 1996, and in 1997 the treatment was computer-animated on film, with a simple but catchy theme tune. The Famous Grouse was one of the earliest whisky brands to be advertised on TV: prior to 1997, whisky companies had held back from TV advertising—by mutual agreement—along with other spirits companies and brands.

Growth in export markets continued during the 1990s, but Gerry O'Donnell—who was appointed Area Director Europe in 1996—admits they were under-exploited. 'When I joined the company, there was one marketing manager and four export sales executives to cover the whole world!'

Richard White was Export Director between 1997 and 1999, when he moved to Maxxium. He recalls:

The most successful markets during my brief tenure as Export Director were Greece, Sweden, Portugal,

A limited edition label and carton for The Famous Grouse commemorating the 1999 Rugby World Cup.

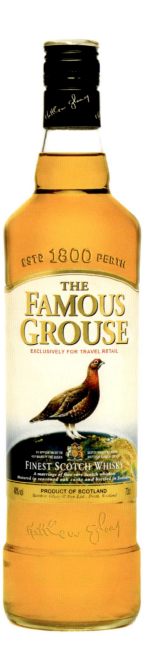

France, Spain and of course European Duty Free. South Africa was also strong after the recent Rugby World Cup. New markets in Angola and Mozambique were also being explored by John McDermott. There were some distribution changes during my time: Gilbeys resigned the brand in South Africa and we went to Brown-Forman. In the U.S.A. we moved from Heublein to Rémy Amérique, which already had The Macallan. In Greece, Kaloyannis down-scaled and became a representative office, working with Karoulias, owned by Berry Bros. & Rudd. In hindsight, this heralded the end of the growth momentum for The Famous Grouse in Greece, but we had no choice in the matter as our distributor was majority-owned by Rémy and they had no interest in that market.

The Famous Grouse Retro bottle produced in 2002 to coincide with the opening of The Famous Grouse Experience at Glenturret Distillery.

Opposite: Some Travel Retail exclusives.

As we have seen, Highland Distilleries had very close relations with the French distiller Rémy-Cointreau, and held a 25% share in the private group which controlled that company. Rémy now took over distribution of The Famous Grouse in Japan and the Far East, as well as in Europe.

Rémy's subsidiary, Eurobrands, also distributed The Macallan in England and Wales, while Scottish distribution of the brand was handled by The Macallan-Lang Partnership, a joint venture formed in 1980 between Macallan-Glenlivet and Robertson & Baxter's subsidiary, Lang Brothers. R&B had also been The Macallan's fillings agents for many years. In 1994 U.K. distribution of the brand was undertaken by Matthew Gloag & Son, and four years later Gloag's international sales team was merged with that of The Macallan, with Richard White, Export Director, taking responsibility for The Macallan in all export markets as well as The Famous Grouse and Highland Park.

The Macallan-Glenlivet had been family owned until 1967, when it became a public company in order to raise money for expansion, the original owners retaining 62% of the shares. By the mid-1990s the family's holding had reduced to around 30%; Rémy Martin held around 26% and the company's Japanese distributor, Suntory, the same. In 1990 Highland Distilleries acquired the Rémy holding, along with Glenturret Distillery.

During the late 1980s and early 1990s The Macallan did phenomenally well, particularly in export markets, and commentators were forecasting a potential takeover. Brian Ivory, Managing Director of Highland, supported by the board of Robertson & Baxter, believed it was essential to acquire the company to protect their interests. In July 1996, having bought out Rémy's holding, he negotiated a shareholder's agreement with Suntory, achieved a narrow majority holding and took over the Macallan-Glenlivet.

Now the spectre of hostile takeover began to haunt the directors of Robertson & Baxter and Highland — which had changed its name to Highland Distillers in May 1998. Both companies were part of Edrington Holdings, which had been incorporated by the Robertson sisters in 1961; each also held shares in the other — Edrington had a 50% interest in The Famous Grouse since 1970 and supplied the grain whisky for the blend through North British Distillery (in which the company also owned 50%); Highland owned 35.4% of R&B (a private company owned by

Edrington), and R&B had a stake in Highland, as well as acting as agent for Highland's fillings and owning 50% of Cutty Sark, which it blended.

The board of Edrington also believed that The City was not giving Highland its proper due, perceiving it as a 'one-brand' business, and felt that it could be developed better as part of a larger group under private ownership, rather than be affected by the whims of the marketplace.

Over the years, Edrington had increased its shareholding in Highland—from 8% in 1980 to 30% by 1999. With the support of William Grant & Sons and a bank loan of £150 million, a take-over bid was mounted and successfully achieved in November 1999. Grant's support came via a new vehicle, The 1887 Company—the name derives from the foundation date of both Highland Distilleries and William Grant & Sons—in which Grants held a 25% stake. The total price paid was £601 million. Highland Distillers PLC was de-listed in 2000 and returned to private ownership.

This was the beginning of a new era for Edrington, and for Matthew Gloag & Son.

A 1999 issue of the company's staff magazine.

THE
ICON
CAMPAIGN

TV advertising made a massive difference to the awareness of The Famous Grouse, and attracted a whole new, younger market to the brand.

The public adored the ads, which won many leading prizes. They were released in dozens of executions in export markets as well.

'At half the cost of running the campaign, we achieved the same level of awareness

as any other whisky campaign' (Bill Farrar).

**BEST LOVED IN SCOTLAND
FOR 30 YEARS.**

FAMOUS FOR A REASON.

ON ICE.

SWIFT ONE.

PERFECT UNION.

SCOTLAND'S FINEST FLY HALF.

CHAPTER IX

THE EDRINGTON GROUP

(2000–2015)

The Naked Grouse was one of the last creations of the company's long-serving Master Blender, John Ramsay (right), who retired in 2009. Having been awarded a Licentiate by the Royal Society of Chemistry, John joined the whisky industry in 1966 as a lab assistant at Strathclyde grain distillery. In 1971 he was appointed Chief Chemist at William Lawson Distillers and ten years later Blender/Chemist with that company. He joined Highland Distilleries as Production Controller in 1990 and became Edrington Group Whisky Quality Manager and Master Blender in 1991. For the previous two and a half years before retiring, John worked with his designated successor, Gordon Motion (left), who also played an important role in creating The Naked Grouse, and bears responsibility for its continuing flavour profile, along with other expressions of the brand.

THE HISTORY OF MATTHEW GLOAG & SON AND THE FAMOUS GROUSE, has unfolded much more rapidly since Edrington's acquisition of the company through its take-over of Highland Distillers PLC. According to the Group's Chairman, Sir Ian Good: 'Controlling our own destiny has played an important part in achieving this success…our ability to make quick decisions, un-beholden to the City'.

As we will see, the dramatic expansion of markets, brand awareness and profitability was owing to international focus, and to the creation of an international distribution network, but immediately following the merger there was a certain amount of restructuring.

Edrington's head office within Robertson & Baxter's long-standing premises at 106, West Nile Street, Glasgow, was relocated to Clyde Bonding's recently refurbished (at a cost of £15 million) bottling complex at Drumchapel—including the famous Sample Room, whose replacement was officially opened by Prince Charles, Duke of Rothesay, in June 2001.

Ian Good, Chairman and Chief Executive and Richard Hunter, Edrington's Finance Director, moved their offices there as well, as did Ian Curle, the newly appointed Group Operations Director, who had overall responsibility for production and bottling, although production was to be based at The Macallan Distillery, Craigellachie, where Graham Hutcheon was appointed Director of Distilling.

Bill Farrar was appointed Managing Director of Highland Distillers, based at West Kinfauns. He had formerly been Marketing, then Commercial Director HD Brands. Sales and marketing were also to be conducted from West Kinfauns, headed by Barrie Jackson, Group Sales & Marketing Director. Gerry O'Donnell, Export Director Highland, now succeeded Bill as Commercial Director and Ken Grier, formerly Global Controller of The Famous Grouse and later responsible for the brand in Europe, was now made Brands Director.

Shortly before the merger, Highland had been in discussion with Rémy-Cointreau and Jim Beam about entering a joint venture for worldwide sales and distribution.

Rémy had been Highland's distributor in many markets since 1988; the two companies were close, with Highland having bought a holding in Orpar S.A., Rémy's holding company, in 1990. By the mid-1990s it was clear to Brian Ivory, now Highland's Chairman and Chief Executive, and Jamie Wilson, the company's

story continued on page 382

2001 The Famous Grouse Vintage Malt — the precursor to the blended malt range.

The Famous Grouse Blended Malt range.

Opposite: Gold Reserve Aged 12 Years still available in some markets, alongside Prestige which was created for Taiwan and discontinued in 2009.

Opposite: The Famous Grouse unveiled its limited edition of 24,000 cartons designed by well-known Scottish designers Timorous Beasties, and announced an exclusive listing with Waitrose over the 2009 Christmas period. The nostalgic illustration takes the style of the iconic Timorous Beastie toile designs, and depicts a visual history of the brand and its origins in Perth, Scotland at Bordeaux House, along with the famous bird itself. The name Timorous Beasties comes from the Robert Burns poem 'To a Mouse'. Timorous Beasties was founded in Glasgow in 1990 by Alistair McAuley and Paul Simmons, who met while studying textile design at Glasgow School of Art. Timorous Beasties is a design led manufacturing company specialising in fabrics and wallpapers.

Right: Bordeaux House sold in 1996 now houses The Bothy Restaurant (with private dining room called The Matthew Gloag Room) and The Famous Grouse Bar where one wall features a specially designed paper by Timorous Beasties.

Finance Director, that in order to take advantage of the growing importance of export markets, a broader international distribution was required. They opened negotiations with a number of compatible partners, and in 1999 a formal arrangement was made between Highland, Rémy and Beam Global Wines & Spirits.

The new company was named Maxxium, and each of the founding shareholders injected elements of their own management into it at the start-up. Richard White left his role as Highland Export Director to become MD Continental Europe, Canada and Global Duty Free, and Paul Grimwood, hitherto Highland U.K. Sales Director, took on the role of MD Maxxium U.K.; Rémy provided the CEO of Maxxium, Roland van Bommel, and the Asia MD, Guillaume Penot. Beam provided the MD Emerging markets, Philip Craig, and the HR Director, David Borthwick.

On 31st May 2001 the three founders were joined by Vin & Sprit (V&S), the state-owned Swedish spirits company (and owners of Absolut Vodka), until it was privatised and sold to Pernod Ricard in March 2008.

The original company was based on Rémy's distribution network; Maxxium owned around 80% of its distributors and appointed third party distributors in forty other markets. Each of the four participating companies held a 25% stake and enjoyed 'gatekeeper' rights to block the distribution of competing brands in certain markets; all benefited from the commercial expertise offered by Maxxium, while Rémy and Beam benefited from the popularity of Absolut and The Famous Grouse, backed by highly successful advertising. Indeed, 'the appeal of the bird' in global markets was crucial.

The Famous Grouse and the company's malt whiskies now had an international footprint in around sixty markets, and this was vital to their growth. In regard to the home market, the greater scale and professionalism of Maxxium U.K. halted the decline in sales which was becoming evident in the late 1990s and drove it to clear leadership in the U.K. market, overtaking Bell's.

The Famous Grouse also played a part in the huge success of The Macallan in Taiwan where it had previously been distributed by Rémy, now Maxxium Taiwan.

Like Mainland China (where an office was opened in 2003) and other countries in the Chinese diaspora, Taiwan had long been an important market for Cognac, but major inroads had been made from the mid-1990s by Chivas Regal and Johnnie Walker, and

In 2008 a partnership was formed with the RSPB to help preserve the increasingly rare black grouse.
In 2009 The Famous Grouse Team had an exhausting but worthwhile day of tree-planting at the RSPB Inversnaid reserve
at Loch Lomond. To date £500,000 has been donated to the charity, and the partnership
was renewed for a further three years in 2014.

The Macallan was fast winning favour. Maxxium's sales force in Taiwan suggested that, as a way of supporting The Macallan and reflecting the premium values associated with the Grouse brand, Edrington might introduce a vatted malt into this market.

This found favour with the board, which was already turning its attention to extending the brand's portfolio. Before 1999 was out The Famous Grouse Blended Malt—a blend of The Macallan and Highland Park, and originally named The Famous Grouse Vintage Malt 1987 in other markets—was launched. This was the precursor to a range of The Famous Grouse Blended Malts with different ages—10, 12, 15, 18, 21 and 30 year olds, which became very big in Taiwan. (The 12, 18, 21 and 30 year olds continue there to this day.)

Price-positioned between blends and malts, and acting as a bridge between the two, Blended Malt soon became very popular, but the sales pitch, that 'malts were superior to blends', worked against The Famous Grouse itself, so promotion was abandoned after about five years. But it did a lot to develop the interest in single malts in Taiwan—from 2004 this became a major market for The Macallan (and remains so). It established Edrington as a serious

Port Wood was launched as a premium line extension to The Famous Grouse family.

It has to date achieved an annual volume of 8,894 cases at a price premium of 25% to The Famous Grouse.

The majority of sales are in Portugal, Sweden, European Travel Retail and Denmark.

This product uses specially selected Port Wood casks to deliver a rich, sweet flavour.

The first day of April 2012 saw the launch of a brand new product, The Famous Goose, described as
'a product which has caused excitement for all of us at The Famous Grouse, as we welcome a new breed into our Famous Family.
The Famous Goose gets its name from the celebrated Canada Goose, a migrant that ousts the Red Grouse as
Scotland's favourite game bird, once a year in early April.' Of course, an April Fools' Day joke, but it did not stop a few eager consumers
trying to buy a bottle from the shop at The Famous Grouse Experience.

Stuart MacPherson (above)
joined the Clyde Cooperage in Glasgow in 1979,
beginning his four year apprenticeship as a cooper
and rising through the ranks to become manager
in 2001, and then Edrington's
Master of Wood in 2012.

Today, Stuart oversees a team of
sixteen production coopers, three apprentices
and seven service coopers, based at two cooperages.
He and his team ensure the supply and repair of
the oak casks that are such an essential element of
Edrington's whiskies. As well as the cooperage,
he is responsible for production planning and
ensuring that the distilleries receive casks
that meet the company's
exacting standards.

player and increased the company's confidence in what might be done with the Grouse brand.

Further expressions began to be introduced, in the interests of using the brand equity in The Famous Grouse to attract new consumers and offer existing consumers the opportunity to 'trade up'. Since these were invariably priced above the original, they offered a greater profit margin to retailers and enlivened the brand's presence on the shelf.

In 2003 Ian Good commented: 'We are adopting a targeted, focused approach to develop our key

In 2007 a campaign was launched where consumers could purchase a personalised bottle of The Famous Grouse with their own Famous Name, together with a personal message on the back label. This campaign continues to this day not only in the U.K. but in many markets worldwide, now with the option to include a photograph.

brands on the international stage. We see great growth opportunities for The Famous Grouse and the new variations of the brand are showing signs of benefiting from what is known as the "halo" effect'.

Even before this, the company had launched The Famous Grouse Prestige and Gold Reserve in Asia (1996); then, in 2003, The Famous Grouse Islay Wood Finish and Port Wood Finish were introduced. The former died quickly but Port Wood remains popular in Sweden and Portugal.

Islay Wood was resurrected in 2006 as The Black Grouse, a peated expression proposed by the Swedish marketing team: smoky flavours are very popular in Sweden. Later it was supplemented by The Black Grouse Alpha Edition (a duty free exclusive).

To satisfy the other end of the flavour spectrum The Snow Grouse arrived in 2008—a blended grain whisky; younger and lighter, designed to be served direct from the freezer.

The recommended signature serve for The Famous Grouse was with ginger beer and a wedge of lime, named Ginger Grouse, and this was later developed as a bottled brand of lightly alcoholic ginger beer.

The Naked Grouse (2010)—was and is a premium offering. It is presented with minimal labelling and an embossed glass bottle, which allows the liquid to be the 'hero' rather than the packaging and expresses 'environmental friendliness'.

Gerry O'Donnell:

Although some of these innovations were not 'break-through' in terms of scale, this was a decade in which The Famous Grouse grew its top line volume and revenue every year. There is no doubt in my mind that, as well as being innovative (and therefore newsworthy), they were incremental to brand awareness, helping sales people to open doors and grow the Scotch whisky category. Their introduction also encourage the trade to stock and support the brand.

At the same time as developing brand extensions of The Famous Grouse, the board of Edrington was increasingly aware that Maxxium was being asked to distribute potentially conflicting products in certain markets: Black Bottle, Lang's Supreme and Cutty Sark blends as well as Grouse, and Bunnahabhain, Tamdhu and Glengoyne malts as well as The Macallan. It was resolved to focus on 'core brands'.

Accordingly, in 2003, Bunnahabhain Distillery

and Black Bottle were sold to Burn Stewart Distillers (for £10 million) and Glengoyne Distillery with Lang's blends to Ian Macleod Distillers (for £7.2 million). Tamdhu Distillery also went to Ian Macleod in 2011.

In March 2008, V&S was privatised and Absolut was sold to Pernod Ricard. The company accordingly prepared to leave Maxxium. For some time Rémy-Cointreau had believed it could make greater headway independently, especially in China, and wanted to concentrate on a smaller number of markets. As a result they also gave notice that they would leave the joint venture, and after the required notice period, an agreement to terminate Maxxium was signed by all parties the following year.

Edrington and Beam Global received compensation from Rémy in order to restructure the company, and some of the individual distributors owned by Maxxium were sold.

Now a new sales and distribution alliance with Beam Global Wines & Spirits was drawn up in twenty-four key international markets. Edrington took direct control of six international distribution companies in Norway, Sweden, Denmark, Finland, Taiwan and South Korea (joined by China and Hong Kong in 2011). Spain, the u.k., Europe and Russia

were important to both, so the original Maxxium infrastructure was adapted and retained. This still exists.

For the first time in the company's history there were more employees based overseas than in Scotland: in 2010, the company employed 2,200 people worldwide, with 60% overseas.

The United States was never part of Maxxium—both Rémy and Beam had their own distribution companies there, although for a time Rémy acted as distributors for The Famous Grouse. In 2014 Edrington incorporated its own distribution company here, Edrington America, in order to have direct control of the route to market.

The long-standing partnership with a family business, Berry Bros. & Rudd of St James's Street, London, resulted in Cutty Sark becoming wholly owned by Edrington in 2010. Cutty had been blended (and 50% owned) by Robertson & Baxter since 1997, although the brand had been made by R&B since the 1930s. Maxxium's international distribution network was a perfect vehicle for Cutty; at the same time the board of Berry Bros. & Rudd were unhappy with the way their license to market Glenrothes single malt was operating—the distillery being owned by

A scene for the 2015 television advertisement for The Famous Grouse.

Highland/Edrington. Accordingly full ownership of Cutty Sark went to Edrington, and full ownership of the Glenrothes brand to Berry Bros. & Rudd.

In 2011 The Edrington Group celebrated the 150th birthday of Highland Distilleries with a record-breaking set of results, secure in its position as a leading international drinks company. That year was also the fiftieth anniversary of the foundation of The Robertson Trust, which benefited massively from the Group's success: the Trust's income rose from just over £4 million in 2000 to over £10 million in 2011 to £18 million in 2014.

This stems directly from Edrington being a group of private limited companies, rather than in public ownership. As Sir Ian Good says: 'There is no leakage when a dividend is paid: it either goes to our employees or to charity. Private ownership also secures the companies' independence, fulfilling the dreams of the Robertson sisters.'

Over the past decade, The Robertson Trust has been able to distribute £119 million to a very wide range of deserving charities.

Today it is Scotland's largest charitable trust.

In 2015 The Famous Grouse is in a strong position—apart from one other premium standard blended Scotch (Ballantine's), it is the only brand to have grown volume over the three years 2012–2014, a difficult period for the industry during which standard blended Scotch has been flat globally (in terms of volume growth) and has been declining in many mature markets, such as Spain, the United States and the U.K. The latter continues to be the largest market for The Famous Grouse, representing 30% of total volume, and here the brand has continued to cement its position as the number one blend—not just in Scotland but in the rest of the U.K. as well.

2015 is an important year for the brand, as it embarks on the next stage in its history. The management strategy has three elements: 1) Premiumisation of the portfolio by launching more products between £20 and £30 a bottle; 2) Strengthening the brand's key associations—'Quality', 'Premium' and 'Authentic'—introduced so long ago, but as relevant today as ever before; 3) Growing share in emerging markets and seeking new market opportunities. Much of the marketing investment will be channeled to such markets, especially Russia, Turkey, Angola, Hungary and Nigeria.

A number of initiatives have been put in place

to create this growth. First, new packaging. The brief to the design agency, Soho Square in London, was to make the packaging more up-market and to create distinctive design features which would make it stand out. The revised packaging includes a new bottle shape, taller and prouder, with a longer neck closure; the new metallic label makes subtle use of the colour purple, to represent the heather hills that grouse thrive in, with a scarlet line along its arched upper edge — a subtle reference to the cock grouse's red 'eyebrows'. The label also gives more prominence to the word 'Famous': in many markets (Sweden, for example), consumers say 'Give me a Famous', not 'I'll have a Grouse' — the latter call is peculiar to the U.K.

Second: new brand extensions. The Black Grouse is being re-launched as The Famous Grouse — Smoky Black. The whisky tastes the same as the popular Black Grouse, although the blend has been adjusted by using Glenturret peated malt. This is communicated in the new packaging and is part of a broader strategy to magnify the link between the brand and Glenturret Distillery. As an example, in Taiwan Edrington offers single cask Glenturret single malt under The Famous Grouse trademark. The Famous Grouse is the only blend that uses Glenturret.

For some years now consumers in many markets across the world have been able to order a personalised label online after buying a bottle of The Famous Grouse. Since 2014 consumers have also been able to upload photos and personalise the label with a picture. The 'personalisation' project has been very successful — over the Christmas period 2013 in excess of 40,000 labels were ordered — and it is planned to develop it.

Third, a new advertising campaign. After many years of running the animated 'icon' television commercials, a new advertising campaign has been created by Abbott Mead Vickers, one of the U.K.'s most creative agencies, which has held The Famous Grouse account since 1996.

The new campaign uses the strap-line 'Famous for a Reason'. It tells the story of Matthew Gloag I and his early commitment to the quality of his blends and to sherry wood maturation, then reflects on how his descendants followed his example and how the company takes the very same approach to making whisky today.

With this, Matthew Gloag & Son and their famous brand have come full circle.

Mellow Gold was launched in July 2015, to provide a contrast to Smoky Black by taking the blend in a sweet rather than smoky direction.

The 2015 packaging was designed to drive the premium credentials and ambitious long-term development plans. The new label echoes the brand's roots, but with a contemporary twist. The new bottle shape with its premium closure and metallised paper will make sure it stands out from its rivals.

Glen Gribbon, Director of The Famous Grouse said: 'The new packaging has been developed in response to consumer demand for higher quality packaging and will further differentiate the brand from our competitors, setting a new benchmark for others to follow. In our view this design is a modern expression of our key assets: the grouse, and our "famous" name.'

The Famous Grouse is the number five standard blended whisky in the world (IWSR 2013). However, Edrington has ambitions of reaching the number three spot after this bold new move and substantial investment. From 2009 to 2013, the blended Scotch whisky category grew at 1.3%, while The Famous Grouse grew at more than double this rate at 2.7% (IWSR 2013). The brand is already number three in Travel Retail and holds the number one spot in the home of Scotch, the U.K. and many other markets.

Sir Ian Good CBE

Chairman of The Edrington Group 1994–2013

Ian Good joined Edrington in 1969, becoming a member of the board ten years later and Chairman in 1994. The same year he was appointed to the Council of the Scotch Whisky Association, vice-Chairman in 1995 and Chairman in 2000, retiring in 2006. He was appointed a director of the North British Distillery Company in 1991 and Chairman in 1995, retiring from the Board in 2002. He has been on the Board of Simpson's Malt since 2004.

Ian's main hobby is horse racing. He was the driving force behind the creation of Scottish Racing in 2004 and is currently its Chairman. He was elected to the Jockey Club in 2005. In 2006 he was appointed director of the Tote by the Department for Culture, Media & Sport, senior director the following year, Interim Chairman (January to June 2008). He is currently trustee of The Racing Foundation.

He became a trustee of The Robertson Trust in 1978, has been Chairman since 2000 and was made Honorary Life President in 2014. He was created CBE in 1992 for his services to the Scotch whisky industry, and was knighted on 1st July 2008.

IAN B. CURLE

Edrington's Chief Executive

Ian Curle graduated from Glasgow University where he gained a B.Acc (Hons). He undertook his CA training with Arthur Andersen & Co, qualifying in 1985. Ian then joined The Edrington Group in 1986, working in finance before moving into operations management. He was appointed group operations director in 1997 before taking on the role of chief executive in 2004.

He is also chairman of The North British Distillery Company Limited and former chairman of the Scotch Whisky Association.

SPECIAL EDITIONS

(1999-2015)

In 2013, The Famous Grouse released a rare 40 Year Old blended malt (ABV 47.3%) in an elegantly crafted decanter created in partnership with Scottish designers, Timorous Beasties.

Just 270 decanters were produced, each hand-engraved with a bespoke design of the red grouse nestled amongst beautifully detailed foliage, completed with a Scottish silver stopper and cased in a luxury wooden gift box.

As part of the celebrations as official spirits supplier to Rugby World Cup 1999 and sponsor of the Scotland team, The Famous Grouse challenged Bill McLaren ('the Voice of Rugby') to select his all-time World Cup XV from players who participated in the World Cup 1987, 1991 or 1995. His Famous XV are listed in the booklet accompanying this specially produced 15 Year Old Scotch.

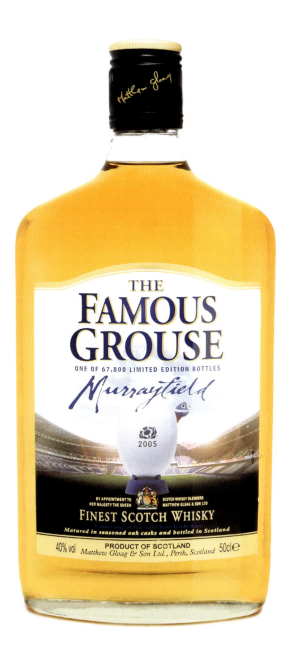

In 2005 The Famous Grouse celebrated its long-standing sponsorship of the Scottish rugby team

with a one-off design label depicting Murrayfield, the home of Scottish rugby.

Only 67,800 bottles were filled—one for every seat in the stadium.

2009 WAS THE TWO HUNDRED AND FIFTIETH ANNIVERSARY OF THE BIRTH OF OUR NATIONAL BARD.

The Scottish Government pronounced it The Year of the Homecoming, to encourage overseas Scots and others to visit.

To mark both occasions, The Famous Grouse Robert Burns, a limited edition 37-year-old blended malt, was created by John Ramsay, the company's Master Blender, from casks laid down in 1971, with a label commissioned from John Byrne, the well-known Scottish artist and playwright.

The bottles were offered to Burns Clubs around the world, to be auctioned for charity, with a recommended reserve price of £400 — one bottle went for £1,945! In all, the promotion raised £75,853 for various charities worldwide.

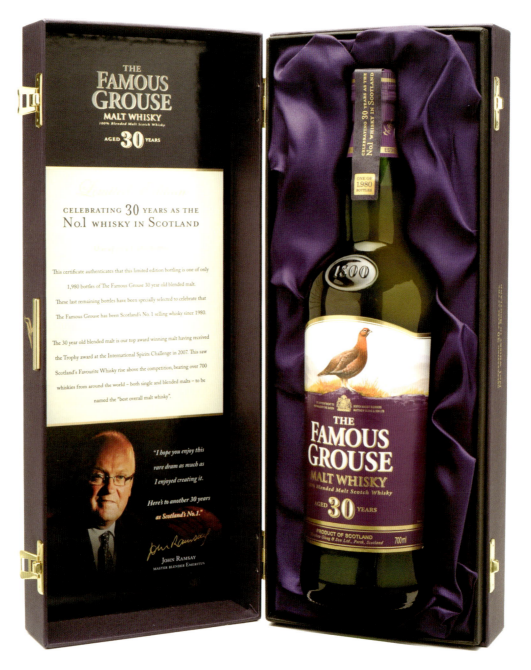

This exclusive pack was created in 2010 to mark The Famous Grouse's 30 year reign as Scotland's favourite whisky since 1980.

The Famous Grouse 30 year old blended malt was first released in 2004, forming the jewel in the crown of The Famous Grouse's blended malt range—a project undertaken by The Edrington Group's former Master Blender, John Ramsay.

Destined to become a collector's item, the precious final bottles each bear a seal confirming that they are one of the last 1,980 bottles of The Famous Grouse 30 year old blended malts ever to be produced, along with a certificate signed by John Ramsay.

Launched in 2011, The Famous Grouse Celebration Wade Decanter contains blended whisky from the year in which
The Famous Grouse became Scotland's No.1 selling whisky (Nielsen, Scottish Off Trade, Jan/Feb 1981).
A limited edition of 10,000 decanters were available worldwide, each featuring three unique illustrations of
the iconic grouse taking flight, painted by the famous British wildlife artist, Rodger McPhail.

The Famous Perth was created in 2012 to celebrate Perth being awarded city status. The special gift carton displays well-known sights from in and around the city including St John's Kirk, Perth Concert Hall, Bordeaux House (home of The Famous Grouse until 1996), the Perth Bridge over the Tay, Balhousie Castle (home of The Black Watch), St Matthew's Church, the tower on Kinnoull Hill, 51st Highland Division war memorial on the North Inch, Scone Palace, Glenturret Distillery (home of The Famous Grouse Experience) and the Grouse statue on the Broxden roundabout.

Cartons were also created for other cities around the world. The Famous Crieff, where The Famous Grouse Experience is located, was created in 2012. The cartons above depict Drummond Castle, Crieff (South) Bridge, Loch Turret, the bandstand in Macrosty Park, the Murray Fountain in James Square, the Crieff Hydro Hotel and, of course, The Famous Grouse Experience.

The Famous Jubilee, Special Edition Reserve —aged in oak casks —an exclusive to Waitrose. The 2012 bottle carries a commemorative label and is displayed in a gift carton inspired by Her Majesty The Queen's 60 year reign.

In 2013, the artist Vic Lee was commissioned to create packaging for

The Famous Grouse 16 Year Old Double Matured Blended Scotch Whisky.

He created a wraparound of the grouse in flight for the carton with typographic embellishments.

For the bottle label he illustrated a stylised grouse with his penwork.

1986 GLENTURRET

Using only the best ingredients, the purest highland water and two centuries of distilling excellence at Scotland's oldest distillery, there's good reason why Glenturret single malt has always been at the heart of The Famous Grouse blend.

Back in 1986, when athletes last battled for glory at a Scottish Commonwealth Games, Glenturret's own athletes, our stillmen, mashmen and coopers, were running a team relay of their own. The result of their efforts? A cask strength single malt, distilled by hand and laid down in 1986, rich with notes of fresh mango, passion fruit and honeycomb.

THE 1986 GAMES HOSTED 161 EVENTS ACROSS TEN SPORTING GENRES WITH 29 NATIONS TAKING PART

THE FAMOUS GROUSE
SINGLE MALT SCOTCH WHISKY

GLASGOW 2014
LIMITED EDITION

GLASGOW 2014
XX COMMONWEALTH GAMES

CASK STRENGTH

1986 GLENTURRET

DISTILLED IN 1986, BOTTLED IN 2014

DISTILLED AT GLENTURRET DISTILLERY CRIEFF, SCOTLAND PRODUCT OF SCOTLAND

OFFICIAL WHISKY OF THE GLASGOW 2014 COMMONWEALTH GAMES

OFFICIAL WHISKY OF THE
GLASGOW 2014 COMMONWEALTH GAMES

OFFICIAL WHISKY OF THE GLASGOW 2014 COMMONWEALTH GAMES

GLASGOW 2014
LIMITED EDITION

As Scotland's favourite whisky, it's only right that The Famous Grouse is the official whisky of the 2014 Glasgow Commonwealth Games. The Famous Grouse believes there's a joy in participating in something bigger than ourselves – of being part of something famous – and that the same spirit is present at the very core of the 'friendly games', Glasgow 2014.

To celebrate a summer of awe-inspiring sporting feats and incredible dedication to their craft, our master blender has turned his attention to a much sought after single malt from 1986, the very year the Commonwealth Games last visited the land of Scotch Whisky. So pour a dram, raise a toast to Glasgow 2014 and Be Part of Something Famous...

As official whisky provider to the Glasgow 2014 Commonwealth Games, The Famous Grouse released a limited edition single malt to mark its sponsorship of this momentous sporting event with 1,800 bottles only of Glenturret 1986 Cask Strength.

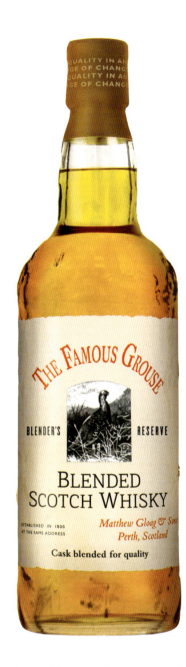

In 2015 Gordon Motion created a fantastic sherried heritage liquid inspired by Matthew Gloag's original cask blending

in his shop cellar at 24 Atholl Street, Perth.

GLENTURRET DISTILLERY

GLENTURRET DISTILLERY IS SITUATED IN A WOODED GLEN KNOWN AS 'THE HOSH', THROUGH WHICH FLOWS THE RIVER TURRET. It claims to be the oldest distillery in the Highlands, based on the fact that there was a farm distillery in the Hosh in the 1770s. Indeed, parish records reveal that there were many stills in the district, going back to at least 1717.

The first licence to distil here was granted in 1818. The first legal distiller continued until going bankrupt in 1842; his successor also went bust, as did the next tenant (who immediately changed the name from 'Hosh' to the more attractive 'Glenturret') in 1903, when Glenturret was taken over by a company which went into liquidation in 1929.

Not an auspicious history so far! Enter James Fairlie, who bought the site in 1957, reinstated the equipment (often acquiring second-hand plant) and integrated new buildings with the old. His intention was to 'preserve the craft traditions of malt distilling and develop their appreciation', to which end he opened Glenturret to the public—which was almost unheard of at the time: only Glenfiddich had installed visitor facilities by the end of the 1960s.

James Fairlie sold the distillery to the French distiller, Rémy-Cointreau, in 1981.

The Glenturret stillmen of 2015.

Left to right: Ian Smith, Brian Garriock, Neil Cameron (Distillery Manager), Kenny Smith, Ian Renwick.

THE FAMOUS GROUSE EXPERIENCE

In 1981 Rémy-Cointreau had bought Glenturret Distillery on the edge of Crieff, at the foot of the heather-clad Perthshire hills—the natural habitat of the red grouse. Highland Distilleries had a long-standing trading relationship with Rémy, and in 1993 the distillery was taken over by the Scottish company. The idea of creating a 'brand home' there for The Famous Grouse had been raised and rejected in 1998, but in 2002 it was taken up in earnest. Edrington invested £2.2 million in upgrading the visitor facilities—massively and innovatively.

The idea came from Ken Grier, Brands Director, and Derek Brown, Brands Heritage Director.

The latter told me: 'Our intention was to celebrate the skill and mastery of blending—a different approach to that of other distilleries, which focus on single malt Scotch whisky—but also to create a unique day out—to provide both fun and education through a range of 'sensory' interactive displays which immersed them in the alchemy and

wonder of The Famous Grouse'. To this end, a cutting-edge German company, Art+Com, was employed to design advanced 'motion sensor' technology which used pioneering audio-visual effects to cheerfully interact with the visitors' movements.

The Famous Grouse Experience won a coveted BAFTA award in 2002, in the Interactive Entertainment category, beating the Chelsea Flower Show and World Cup Interactive. It has become a leading Scottish visitor attraction 'for all the family',

On the 29th May 2014, The Earl and Countess of Strathearn, (Prince) William and Kate, visited The Experience and officially reopened the centre. They were welcomed by Matthew and Dilly Gloag, and guided by Stuart Cassells, General Manager (right), with Sarah Duncan, Marketing Executive (far right).

attracting up to 100,000 visitors a year and a clutch of prestigious tourism awards.

THE FAMOUS GROUSE EXPERIENCE:

Top left:
the Conference Suite

Bottom left:
Dramming Bar

Top right:
The Famous Grouse clock

Bottom right:
In 2011 Jack Daniel's entered the Guinness Book of World Records with 'the largest bottle in the world' at 184 litres. This was a challenge, eagerly taken up by The Famous Grouse, for which a 228 litre replica bottle was created, to be filled with more than 8,200 drams on Sunday 12th August 2012, the anniversary of the re-naming of The Grouse Brand as The Famous Grouse on 12th August 1905. Members of the public were invited to bid for an opportunity to help fill the gigantic bottle, with all proceeds going to ABF The Soldiers Charity. The bottle entered the Guinness Book of World Records in 2014. Seated is Lucy Whitehall, Global Brand Ambassador.

IN SCOTLAND, ON AVERAGE, THREE DRAMS OF
THE FAMOUS GROUSE ARE DRUNK EVERY SECOND

THERE GOES ANOTHER THREE....

THE
BROXDEN
BIRD

PERTH WAS CREATED A ROYAL BURGH BY KING WILLIAM THE LION IN 1210. Edrington supported a number of celebrations during 2010—the 800th anniversary year—including the creation of the 'Perth 800' cocktail, which was served at a number of keynote events. The company also commissioned a large sculpture of a red grouse taking flight, as an enduring gift to the people of Perth (see opposite). 14.5 metres tall—including its plinth—the galvanized steel erection was designed by Ruaraig Maciver, from the Beltane Studios in Peebles. It rises up from the traffic island at the Broxden roundabout, as if the low flyer were taking off from the heather of one of Perthshire's famous grouse moors. When St Johnstone—Perth's football team—won the Scottish Cup in 2014, Perth & Kinross Council adorned the sculpture in a Saints' hat and scarf.

THE FAMOUS COLLABORATION

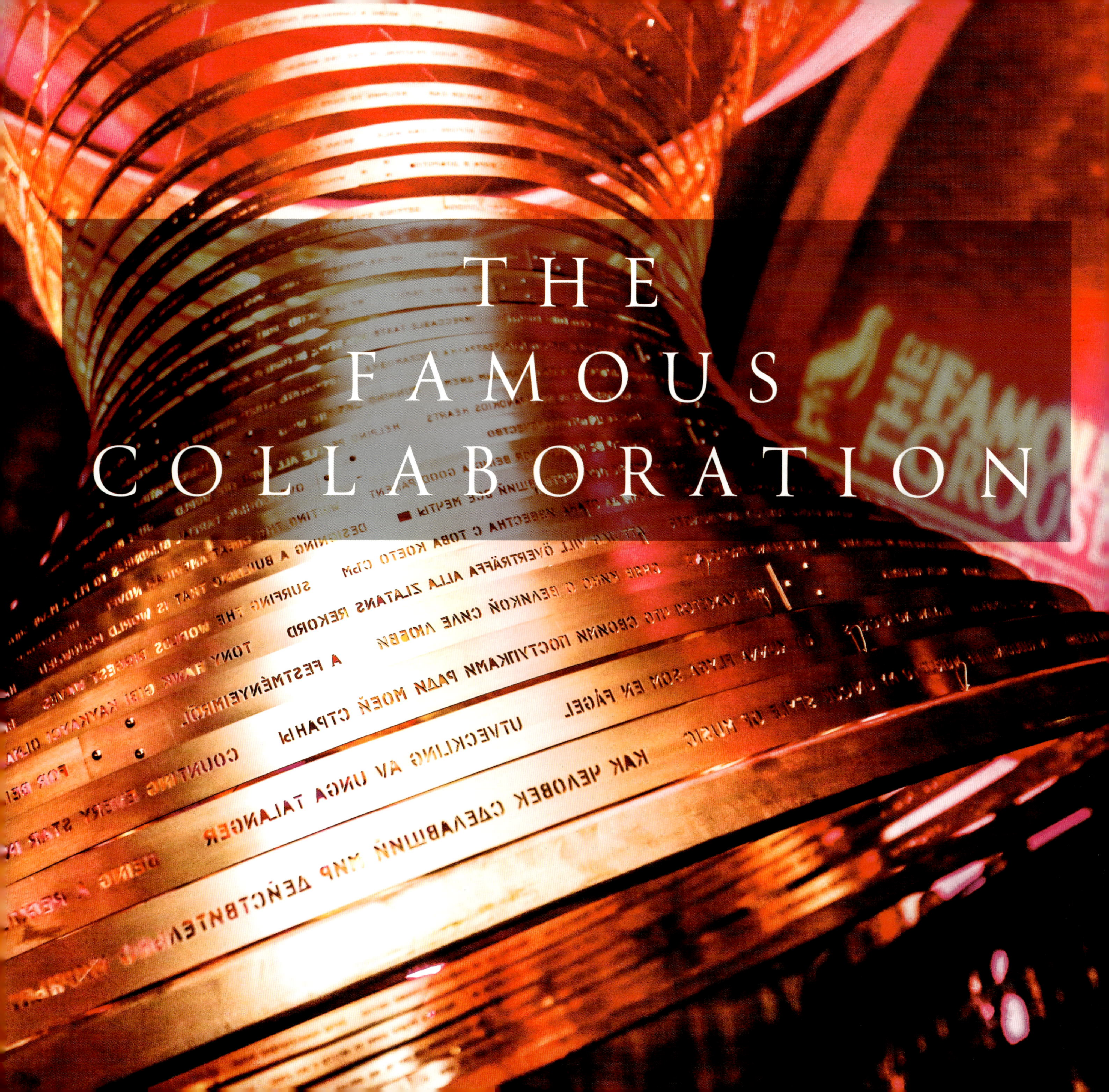

The Famous Grouse asked 'What would you like to be famous for?'. Thousands from twenty countries provided comments that ranged from the evocative to the humorous, the courageous to the caring. The mix of statements may suggest that fame should come from everyday success, personal achievements and discovering global solutions. It was a rejection of the celebrity culture. One thousand five hundred gnomic hopes were used to create a vast sculpture.

Dreams of fame included: 'I wish to help abandoned children', 'For the charity events I am organising', 'For my beauty in imperfection', 'For being the person who stopped poverty and misery' and 'Creating an unlimited energy source', 'Stopping a robbery', 'Crossing the Himalayas from Beijing to Delhi', 'Crossing the Atlantic Ocean in a sailing boat', 'Building a hospital in every city in Africa', 'Being the first double amputee to climb Everest', 'Cleaning up the oceans we surf in', 'What was the Mona Lisa really smiling about', 'Carrying the biggest smile in the world all the time', 'Uniting people and cancelling borders'. By far the greatest number of witty responses came from the U.K., including: 'Solving the great mystery of who let the

dogs out' and 'Fitting Wally with a tracking device'.

The creation of the sculpture was led by Marshmallow Laser Feast in conjunction with Studio Roso. The kinetic and lighting elements were created by Ruairi Glynn. The team consisted of thirty-four engineers and digital specialists.

The project finished in August 2013. In 2014 the sculpture went on display in the Perth Concert Hall.

C. Stanley Todd
1983

INDEX